THE LIVING FOREST

THE EARTH, ITS WONDERS, ITS SECRETS

THE LIVING FOREST

Reader's Digest

PUBLISHED BY

THE READER'S DIGEST ASSOCIATION LIMITED

LONDON NEW YORK MONTREAL SYDNEY CAPE TOWN

THE LIVING FOREST
Edited and designed by Toucan Books Limited
with Bradbury and Williams
Written by David Burnie
Edited by Jane MacAndrew and Helen Douglas-Cooper
Picture Research by Adrian Bentley

FOR THE READER'S DIGEST
Series Editor Cortina Butler
Editorial Assistant Alison Candlin

READER'S DIGEST GENERAL BOOKS
Editorial Director Robin Hosie
Art Director Bob Hook

Printing and binding: Printer Industria Gráfica S.A., Barcelona
Separations: David Bruce Graphics Limited, London
Paper: Perigord-Condat, France

ISBN 0 276 42219 8

FRONT COVER *Autumn colours tinge larches growing in a plantation in
New Zealand. Inset: A mule deer looks out from the deep shade of a forest
in Oregon.*

BACK COVER *Some of the last remaining Asiatic lions laze in the heat of
India's Gur National Park.*

PAGE 3 *Displaying all the agility of a gymnast, a common langur jumps
to reach food on a low branch.*

CONTENTS

KINGDOM OF THE TREES

From the fringes of the polar regions to the warm, humid tropics, forests are the most complex assemblages of life on land. Our knowledge of their plant and animal inhabitants, and the way they influence each other, is still not complete.

In August 1994, an Australian biologist lowered himself to the bottom of a gorge in the Blue Mountains northwest of Sydney. What he found there stunned the world of science. Scattered among the rocks were the botanical equivalent of living dinosaurs – extraordinary evergreen trees up to 400 years old, whose lineage dates back millions of years. Although the trees were only 125 miles (200 km) from the centre of Australia's biggest city, nobody had any inkling that they were there.

Within a few months of this astonishing revelation, details were being pieced together about these living survivors from the past. Named Wollemi pines, after the National Park in which they were found, the trees turned out to be cousins of unusual conifers that live only in the Southern Hemisphere. One of their relatives is the bunya pine (*Araucaria bidwillii*), also from Australia, and another the monkey puzzle or Chile pine (*Araucaria araucana*) from the mountains of South America. But while bunya pines and monkey puzzles are still fairly common, Wollemi pines seem to be fantastically rare. To date, only about 50 trees have been found.

SECRET SURVIVORS *Despite growing to 130 ft (40 m) tall, Wollemi pines escaped detection until the closing years of the 20th century.*

As botanists investigate these new arrivals in the plant world, many questions await an answer. How did these trees evolve? How long have they existed, and why are there so few of them? Are today's trees a thriving group, or are they – as seems more likely – the final remnants of a dying species, clinging to life long after most of their kin have perished? In a tiny spot in the vastness of Australia, the search is underway to find the answers.

To many people, forests are islands of tranquillity in an increasingly busy world. Ancient trees, gnarled by centuries of growth, epitomise everything that is serene and steadfast, while forest animals seem refreshingly free of the cares and complications that face us in everyday life. Paradoxically, forests have a darker side, as places of mystery that conceal hidden dangers. Although few of these dangers still exist, they have been kept alive by countless nursery stories, and have also been fanned by myths designed for adult consumption. A classic example of the latter occurred during the 1780s, when a Dutch surgeon visiting the East Indies reported on the legendary upas tree (*Antiaris toxicaria*), which was reputed to emit a vapour so toxic that it killed everything around it, including not only the forest, but even birds that flew overhead. 'Not a tree, nor blade of grass is to be found in the valley or surrounding mountains,' the surgeon wrote. 'Not a beast or bird, reptile or living thing, lives in the vicinity.' He went on to recount how hundreds of refugees, imprudently camping within a few miles of the tree, had also fallen foul of its deadly emanations. As visiting Europeans later discovered, the upas tree's powers had been grossly exaggerated. It did contain poisonous sap, but its lethal vapours were a human

invention. The tree's fearful reputation – once accepted as fact – highlights the mysterious aura that forests have always held and their capacity to surprise.

Nearer our own times, these surprises have been based on fact rather than fiction. One of the most outstanding is the okapi (*Okapia johnstoni*), a striped forest-dwelling relative of the giraffe, which stands up to 6 ft (1.8 m) at the shoulder. Long hunted by forest pygmies in its native habitat in Central Africa, it became known to outsiders only in 1901, and caused a sensation when the first living specimen arrived in Europe in 1918.

Less than two decades later, the same part of the world produced almost equal excitement in the ornithological world with the discovery of the Congo peafowl (*Afropavo congensis*). This stocky, ground-feeding bird is one of nearly 50 species that make up the pheasant family, but it is the only one known to live outside the forests of Asia.

Even at the close of the 20th century, relatively large forest animals are still being encountered for the first time by scientists. They include a new species of lemur, discovered in Madagascar in the 1980s, and another primate, this time a monkey-like tamarin, which was discovered in the forests of eastern Brazil a few years later. Both share the sombre distinction of being extremely rare and threatened by the disappearance of their natural habitat.

As exploration techniques and scientific surveys become ever more refined, it seems unlikely that many large or conspicuous forms of life still await discovery in the world's forests. However, the Wollemi pine shows that nothing can be entirely dismissed. Persistent reports of mysterious human-like primates, such as the North American sasquatch or 'bigfoot', and similar animals

LIFE AT THE EDGE Quiver trees or kokerbooms have fleshy trunks and leaves that store water – a vital adaptation in their Namibian home.

LIVING SWAMP In this tropical peat forest in Borneo, the trees are anchored in a layer of waterlogged peat up to 60 ft (18 m) deep.

in western China, suggest that there may yet be surprises in store. It is a brave biologist who would rule them out.

THE RIGHT ENVIRONMENT

Life on Earth is phenomenally durable and widespread. Bacteria have been discovered in rock far beneath the seabed, and they can also survive on the highest mountains and in polar ice. Some insects ride on winds 5 miles (8 km) above the ground, and spores – tiny packages of cells that act like seeds – are often carried to even greater heights. Together, living things populate a region known as the biosphere, which has been aptly likened to a thin green smear around the planet.

Unlike many bacteria and other simple forms of life, trees are quite demanding about the conditions they need to survive. All of them need light, but each species also needs the right mix of several other environmental factors, including moisture, warmth, and supplies of essential chemical elements. If that mix is available they thrive, but if not they fail to grow, and often die.

Despite ancient legends to the contrary, no tree can live permanently under water, and only a limited number – the mangroves – can cope with having their roots washed by the sea. Fresh water is another matter: throughout the world, from the cypress swamps of the American deep south to forests of the tropics, some trees live quite successfully in a wet or waterlogged habitat.

While too much water is rarely a problem, too little often is. Most trees cannot survive in places that are extremely dry, and the few that do have special adaptations for coping with their arid habitat. They either store precious rainwater in trunks that act like reservoirs, or grow immensely long roots that seek out water underground. The record root depth recorded for any tree was achieved by a species of wild fig growing in southern Africa. Its roots were spotted

FOREST THRESHOLD *Flanked by the open ice of frozen lakes, hardy conifers mark the northernmost limits of the great boreal forest.*

breaking through the ceiling of a cave, a full 400 ft (122 m) beneath the surface.

Warmth, or lack of it, affects trees in different ways. If the overnight temperature falls a few degrees below freezing, a fir or spruce tree will be none the worse for the experience. Nor will many desert palms, which often have to cope with extremes of heat by day, but severe cold at night. But some trees, such as the olive from southern Europe, are far more tender. For them, just a few hours of frost can be fatal.

Among the most fundamental requirements are the chemicals that trees need to survive and grow. Just over 90 chemical elements exist naturally on Earth, but of these, trees use less than 20. They obtain three of the most important – carbon, oxygen and hydrogen – from air and water, and the remainder they usually gather from the soil.

Some of these earth-borne elements make up a significant fraction of a tree's weight; others are present in the tiniest amounts. Zinc, for example, forms only about 20 millionths of an oak tree's weight (if the tree's water content is excluded), while molybdenum makes up just 6 millionths. Even for a mature tree, this is not much more than a spoonful. But while the amounts may seem insignificant, all these elements play a crucial role in a tree's chemistry. If just one is in short supply, the tree will be unhealthy and even if it reaches maturity it is unlikely to reproduce successfully.

THE FOREST FRONTIER

How do all these needs affect trees and the forests that they form? One way to determine this is to survey each type of forest, as biologists frequently do, to find out what

BROAD-LEAVED BEAUTY *Leaves are tinged by autumn in the Great Smoky Mountains, home of some of the richest temperate forest in the world.*

plants and animals it contains and how they interact. But this work is often long, complex and arduous. If time is more pressing, another way is to take an imaginary aerial journey – one that stretches from Pole to Equator and encompasses almost every major forest type found in the world.

That journey begins in the bright sunshine of the northern summer, high over the crumpled pack ice of the Arctic Ocean. Below, there are few signs of any kind of life, despite the fact that this frozen ocean teems with living things. There are microscopic plants here, but they float in a hidden world, soaking up the light that shines through the ice, which, even in summer, can be several feet thick.

As the southward flight continues, the ice thins and begins to break up and the first signs of land appear on the horizon. These are the islands of the Canadian High Arctic. Fashioned from some of the oldest rocks on Earth, they are bleak places, locked in winter for nine months of the year. Lichens and other simple forms of life exist here, as do Arctic foxes and polar bears, but the climate is far too hostile for trees.

Soon, the complex jigsaw of ocean, ice and islands falls behind, to be replaced by the northernmost reaches of the North American mainland. Initially, little seems to change, but once the Arctic Circle has been crossed, conditions on the ground below become marginally less adverse. Low-lying plants stand out against unmelted snow, as do herds of caribou, looking like flecks of grey as they move over an almost infinite landscape. Although no trees are visible from high up, shrubby dwarf willows – often not much more than ankle-high – are very much at home in these surroundings. These small but robust plants, with their creeping woody stems, indicate that true trees are not so far away.

After the great expanse of open tundra, the treeline seems to pass quickly. There is no single line as such, but a ragged front of stunted conifers that shelter where they can. These pioneers are soon joined by others, and both the height and the density of the trees continues to increase, until open ground is the exception rather than the rule. The journey ahead lies across North America's share of the great boreal forest. It is the home of wolves, bears, moose and giant owls, and – taken as a whole – is the largest forest on Earth.

THE TEMPERATE WORLD

Several hours later, great changes have taken place. The boreal forest, with its dark and tightly packed conifers, is fragmenting into splayed fingers extended across the highest ground. Between these fingers, wedges of brighter green mark the transition to temperate broad-leaved woodland, where a milder climate and more fertile soil nurtures trees of a very different kind.

Every hour that ticks away is mirrored by a surge in natural diversity on the ground. Near the beginning of the voyage, the number of tree species could be counted on the fingers of one hand, and the number of mammals on the fingers of two. But even at the northernmost fringes of the broad-leaved forest, the number of trees runs into several dozen, and from now on climbs rapidly. The variety of forest wildlife soars even more quickly, particularly when small animals such as insects are included.

In the temperate world, trees have almost ideal growing conditions in summer, but they also have to be equipped to withstand severe winters. However, this is a major problem only in the north of the region. As the broad-leaved forest of North America's eastern flank continues to roll past, summers become even warmer and the winter chill less severe. Forest inhabitants include a wealth of warmth-loving birds, lizards and butterflies, as well as exotic-looking magnolias with leaves up to 30 in (76 cm) long.

Where the high ground gives way to the low-lying plain of the deep south, the forest changes once again. Pines and oaks become the dominant trees, and the first hint of the tropics arrives in the form of dwarf palms with fan-shaped leaves. But now the Gulf Coast is approaching, and soon the forest drops behind. The journey progresses over the open sea, towards the distant backbone of Central America.

INTO THE TROPICS

The northern summer is Central America's wettest time of year, and much of the land is smothered by banks of cloud. In northern Yucatan – the part of Mexico that juts

PINES AND PALMS *In Florida, lofty slash pines dominate an area of forest, while dwarf palms thrive beneath the open canopy.*

northwards into the Caribbean – the rain brings life to scrubby forest that is otherwise dusty and dry. But beyond this flat peninsula, along Central America's volcanic spine, the clouds part to reveal a blanket of much lusher forest, dissected by rivers that swirl down volcanic hillsides on their journey to the sea.

Even from the air, this kind of forest looks very different to the ones farther north. The trees seem to clutch at the clouds, and their leaves are a deep and glossy green. In many places, the forest cover is so complete that it is impossible to judge its height, despite the fact that trees on the lowest ground may be ten times taller than those on the highest ridges. Brilliantly coloured birds occasionally speed over the backcloth of foliage, before vanishing into trees to feed, or being swallowed up by the immensity of their surroundings.

This marks the start of a zone of evergreen forest that stretches south to the Equator and far beyond it. In some places, the forest is flanked by newly cleared fields, but past the swamp-filled Darién Gap, where Central and South America are welded together, it widens out into one of the last great wildernesses left on Earth. Here trees can grow all year round, and the forest is home to sloths, tapirs, giant cockroaches and poisonous frogs, countless snakes and lizards, and of birds both beautiful and bizarre.

Over this vast ocean of

ON THE MOVE *With rapid flicks of their powerful wings, two macaws speed across a South American rain forest.*

CLOUD FOREST *In the mountains of the tropics, mist and cloud nurture luxuriant forests clad with ferns and mosses.*

green, which seems to creep past with mesmerising slowness, the Equator invisibly approaches, and the airborne survey nears its close. In a distance of about 6000 miles (9600 km), it has embraced the most distant frontiers of the world's forests, and also their very heart.

As a species, most of us live on the margins of this forest world, or in places with much wider horizons. In this, we contrast strikingly with the ways of our closest living relatives, which include monkeys and apes. They are very much at home in forested surroundings, and are well equipped to make use of them. Grasping hands make them good at gripping and climbing, while forward-pointing eyes help them to judge distances as they move from branch to branch. Over 4 million years ago, our ancestors left the forest world and moved out into open savannahs, and they eventually turned their forest-dwelling adaptations to very different ends. However, forests helped to shape our species, and their legacy is with us still.

THE FOREST WORLD

1

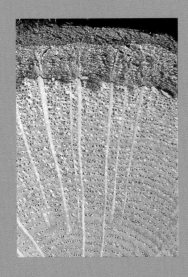

BUILDING MATERIAL *Wood's complex structure produces strength with flexibility.*

FROM THE MOMENT THAT PLANTS TOOK UP LIFE ON DRY LAND, OVER 400 MILLION YEARS AGO, THEY BECAME ENGAGED IN A RACE TO ADAPT TO A NEW AND CHALLENGING WORLD. TODAY'S TREES AND FORESTS, TOGETHER WITH THE IMMENSELY RICH ANIMAL LIFE THAT THEY SUPPORT, ARE THE MOST SPECTACULAR AND MAJESTIC PRODUCTS OF THIS LONG PROCESS OF CHANGE AND DEVELOPMENT. SHAPED BY LOCAL CONDITIONS AND CLIMATE CHANGES OVER MILLIONS OF YEARS, FORESTS VARY ENORMOUSLY FROM ONE PART OF THE WORLD TO ANOTHER, BUT THE TREES FOUND IN THEM SHARE ONE FEATURE THAT SETS THEM APART FROM ALL OTHER PLANTS: AN ABILITY TO REACH HIGH ABOVE THE GROUND IN THE ENDLESS QUEST FOR LIGHT.

SOWING THE SEED *Most trees spread by forming seeds.*

THE LIVING TREE

In trees, the architecture of living things is stretched to its furthest limits. Using special building materials and growth patterns, trees have gradually increased in size to become the largest life forms that have ever existed on our planet.

Hurrying through a single drop of water, a minute speck of green tumbles into view. Although it is travelling at only a few inches an hour, its progress – when seen through a microscope – seems infinitely faster, and it vanishes as quickly as it appears. Suddenly, it returns, but its movement is so fast and unpredictable that little of its structure can be made out. To see it clearly, a chemical thickener must be added to the water. When the microscope is brought into focus once again, the swimmer is more subdued and its hidden structure is revealed.

This tiny, single-celled organism, which lives in fresh water throughout the world, is called *Chlamydomonas*. Its pear-shaped exterior surrounds a green chloroplast, an organ that harnesses the energy in sunlight. Two tiny hairs, mounted at the narrow end of the pear, thrash like miniature oars, pulling the cell through the water, while a small red spot, which senses the difference between brightness and shade, guides it towards the light. With this

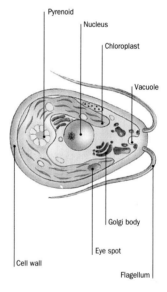

Pyrenoid
Nucleus
Chloroplast
Vacuole
Golgi body
Eye spot
Cell wall
Flagellum

SINGLE-CELLED LIFE *Like a microscopic solar panel, Chlamydomonas collects light to power vital chemical reactions. Left: In China's Jiuzhaigou nature reserve, water plunges down a pine-clad hillside. Here, as in many parts of the world, forest is the natural vegetation cover.*

equipment, *Chlamydomonas* can position itself to soak up sunshine, and it uses its energy to carry out photosynthesis – the fundamental process that builds up plants and allows them to live.

Despite its ability to move, *Chlamydomonas* is not an animal, but an alga – a form of life that has much in common with Earth's earliest plants. From such humble beginnings, based on single, independent cells, all of today's plants have evolved. At one end of this spectrum of life are the simplest plants, which have no true leaves or roots and which are often just a fraction of an inch high. At the other – far removed both in shape and lifestyle – are trees, land-based giants that include the tallest and most massive things that have ever lived.

REACHING FOR THE LIGHT

When plants first took up life on land, about 400 million years ago, they faced a world that was alien in many ways. Instead of being bathed by a benign and life-giving liquid, they found themselves surrounded by a medium that was much less kind. Air dries out living cells and – unlike water – its temperature can soar and plunge in the course of a day. While water buoys up and cradles the most delicate structures, air weighs next to nothing and provides practically no support. To make matters worse, it is capricious. On some days it is calm, but on others it races over the ground, battering anything in its path.

Despite these problems, plants did manage to adapt to this new habitat. At first, there would have been little competition for light, because the early pioneers would have struggled as much against their surroundings as against each other. But as more and more plants became able to survive out of water, the contest for light began. In the most

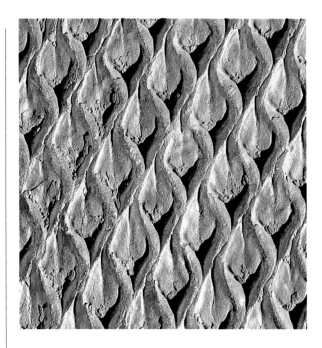

FOSSIL TRUNK *Diamond-shaped scars on the trunk of an extinct* Lepidodendron *tree show where its leaves were once attached.*

favoured spots, where light and water were abundant, those that could grow tallest gained the upper hand, monopolising the light and throwing their neighbours into shade. The result was the natural equivalent of a building boom, as plants tested new ways of outstripping each other in the race upwards.

As this struggle accelerated, evolution produced many designs that met the need to capture light while withstanding the pull of gravity. But as time went by, one design in particular proved superior to all others. It was based around an engineering breakthrough – a single giant stem, reinforced by

a substance called lignin. When plants with these stems – or trunks – appeared, trees as we know them were born.

THE FIRST TREES

In nature, there is no such thing as industrial espionage, but neither are there any patents. As different groups of plants struggled for their share of the light, they independently hit upon the same solution in the struggle to gain height. Instead of appearing once, trees evolved several times, and the results of this mixed ancestry are still very evident today.

One of the earliest trees was *Lepidodendron*, which dominated warm and swampy parts of the Earth in the late Carboniferous period, from about 320 million years ago. *Lepidodendron* no longer exists, but its fossils, which are often found in coal, give a clear picture of what it looked like. When mature, it had a scaly trunk topped by a cluster of disproportionately short, stubby branches bearing narrow leaves, and it was held upright by stout roots. The tree

GROWING UP Unlike most of today's trees, Lepidodendron *branched only as it neared its final height.*

Immature tree

Initial branching

Secondary branching

Mature tree

reached a height of up to 130 ft (40 m); the race for light had already produced impressive results.

This early tree had a curious way of growing. For much of its life, it consisted of an unbranched trunk topped by a single tuft of leaves, making it look like a gigantic bottlebrush. Each leaf started life at the apex of the brush, and gradually worked its way down the sides as the trunk grew taller. When the leaves reached the base of the brush they fell away, leaving small diamond-shaped scars arranged like interlocking tiles. These scars gave the tree its scaly appearance, and also its name – *Lepidodendron* means 'scale tree'.

As the tree approached maturity, a gradual change took place. The upward growth slowed and the trunk divided into two or three branches; many more divisions followed until the tree's crown was complete. Once the tree had reached this stage, it was ready to reproduce. Like most plants of its time, *Lepidodendron* did this by making

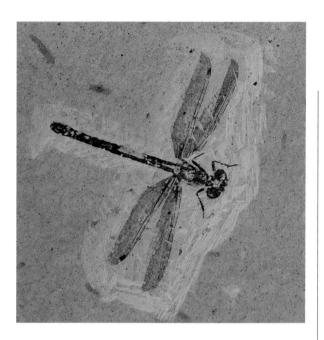

ANCIENT INSECT *Despite being over 200 million years old, this fossilised dragonfly differs very little from its modern relatives.*

microscopic packages of cells called spores, which it formed in vast numbers. When the spores were ripe, they were scattered into the air like clouds of dust.

For several million years *Lepidodendron* was a phenomenal success, and the group of plants that it belonged to, known as the club mosses, were among the most important on Earth. But in the natural world, as in the human one, today's winners are often tomorrow's losers. Beset by changes in climate and by competition from other plants, *Lepidodendron* eventually lost the fight for survival. Some of its relatives still exist, but today's club mosses are creeping plants living in damp places, and few grow more than 12 in (30 cm) high.

What was life like in a *Lepidodendron* forest over 300 million years ago? One way to imagine the scene is to think of all the forms of animal life present in a forest today, and remove those that have evolved since *Lepidodendron* vanished. No mammals climbed along the giant club moss branches or hunted over the forest floor, and no birds broke the silence with their songs or darted through the clearings. There were no flowers, and so no animals that fed on pollen or nectar; without flowers there were no fruits, so animals that ate fruit were also missing.

ANCIENT SURVIVORS *Dark green club mosses sprout from a woodland floor. The yellow structures produce the plants' spores.*

However, although they lacked many of the animals we take for granted, these primeval forests were far from lifeless. When plants made the move from water to land, animals soon followed to exploit them as food. With the plant-eaters came their predators, so that by the time forests were widespread, they teemed both with hunters and the hunted.

Of these animals, by far the most successful were the arthropods – a vast and varied group that includes insects, spiders, centipedes and their relatives. Giant but harmless millipedes, measuring up to 6 ft (1.8 m) long, crept over the leaf-litter in search of edible plant remains; large cockroaches – among the oldest forms of insect life – scavenged food among the fallen leaves, scuttling away at the first sign of danger. Giant scorpions were common, and so were predatory centipedes, which killed their prey with poison-injecting claws.

To modern eyes, among the most alarming of these early forest-dwellers would have been primitive dragonflies, whose wingspan could reach up to 2 ft 6 in (76 cm). Darting among the trees on softly rustling wings, these sharks of the air swooped on other primitive flying insects, grasping them with their legs before carrying them to a convenient perch where they could feed.

SURVIVORS FROM THE PAST

Although giant club mosses disappeared long ago, some of their contemporaries have fared better in the fight for survival. In damp and shaded habitats, particularly in the tropics and the Southern Hemisphere, trees with an equally ancient pedigree are still alive today. With their beautiful fronds, ferns are among the most graceful members of the plant kingdom. Originally, all ferns were low-growing plants, and most modern species still are. But, even while *Lepidodendron* was still thriving, some ferns had abandoned the ground-hugging way of life and risen up towards the light.

Topped by a rosette of finely divided fronds, a tree-fern's trunk is similar to a self-extending pillar. It grows only at its tip, and is formed partly by the stumps of leaves that have died and fallen away. In the damp climate that tree ferns need to thrive, these leaf stumps make perfect perches for mosses and other simple plants, and their entire trunks are often clothed by a thin but spongy carpet of greenery.

Like the extinct giant club mosses, tree ferns reproduce by forming spores, which blow great distances on the wind. When a tree-fern spore lands on a suitable patch of damp ground it germinates, but the plant it produces could not be more different from its parent. Instead of developing a trunk topped by leaves, it forms a flat, ribbon-like structure that is often smaller than a fingernail and just a single cell thick.

This strange object, called a gametophyte, nestles on the forest floor and initially seems to do very little. But although it is small enough to be crushed out of existence by a single footstep, it is a crucial stage in the tree-fern's life cycle and the main reason for its addiction to moisture.

The next development takes place on the underside of the gametophyte, and can only occur when it is thoroughly wet.

Clusters of tiny blisters grow and then burst, releasing male cells onto the underside of the plant. Working their way through a thin film of water, these cells swim towards pockets containing female cells, where fertilisation takes place. Once this has occurred – and as long as it stays damp – one of the fertilised cells develops into a new tree fern and slowly grows up through the gametophyte, which shrivels away. When that tree fern is old enough to make spores of its own, the entire cycle starts again.

This extraordinary process, with its swimming cells, is a legacy of the days when

TREE FERNS *The elegant fronds of tree ferns flank a stream in New South Wales. The fronds of some species reach 15 ft (4.6 m) in length.*

IN HOSTILE GROUND *A pinyon pine clings to the edge of a canyon. In spring, bright yellow male cones (top) release clouds of pollen into the air.*

plants lived in water. To spread beyond swampy ground to places that were much drier, trees had to reproduce in a quite different way, and break many other links with their distant past.

THE WORLD OF CONIFERS

In the arid mountains of Arizona and New Mexico, the low-growing pinyon pine (*Pinus edulis*) shows how thorough this transformation has been. Here the annual rainfall is often not much more than 12 in (300 mm) a year, and most of the high ground consists of bare rock, scoured by the mountain wind. In these conditions, the delicate fronds of tree ferns would quickly be scorched to death, and even if the adult plants could survive, they would be quite unable to reproduce. However, the pinyon pines flourish, and are quite at home beneath the burning sun.

The pinyon pine is a conifer, a member of a highly successful group of trees that first appeared about 290 million years ago. Throughout the world, there are about 550 species of conifers and, like the pinyon pine, many of them specialise in living in places where water is in short supply. Instead of having soft fronds, they have much smaller wax-covered leaves that are better at coping with harsh conditions. Most conifers keep their leaves all year round, but a few – including the larches (*Larix*) and swamp cypress (*Taxodium distichum*) – are deciduous, shedding all their leaves in autumn, and growing a new set in the spring.

Instead of making spores, conifers reproduce by growing seeds. Seeds are not only bigger than spores, they are also vastly more complex. Each one contains a complete embryonic plant, together with a store of food, and is surrounded by a tough outer case that stops it drying out. Many seeds can survive without water for months or even years. When they do germinate, their supply of food works like an on-board battery pack, helping them through the difficult first days of life.

The cones that give conifers their name have a two-fold function. Male cones, which are usually small and soft, release microscopic grains of pollen that blow through the air. If these pollen grains land on the right part of a female cone, they fertilise female cells and seeds are formed. In most conifers, including the pinyon pine, the male cones wither once their pollen has been shed, but the female cones often stay on the tree for several years and become hard and woody. When their seeds are ripe, the female cones release them – either by opening up or by slowly disintegrating on the tree.

Compared with many other conifers, the pinyon pine's seeds are above average in size, but its cones, which are about 2 in (5 cm) long, are fairly modest. Farther west, in the mountains of California, the sugar pine (*Pinus lambertiana*) has cones that are ten times longer. But even these are not the heaviest cones in the conifer world. That distinction probably goes to the Australian bunya pine (*Araucaria bidwillii*) which, despite its name, is not a true pine at all, but one of an unusual group of conifers found only in the Southern Hemisphere. Its enormous oval cones can be up to 12 in (30 cm) long and 8 in (20 cm) in diameter, and can weigh a colossal 11 lb (5 kg).

THE BROAD-LEAVED CONQUEST

In some parts of the world today – particularly in the far north and on high mountains – conifers dominate. Their straight trunks and dark green leaves make them easy to recognise, although the identification of individual species is sometimes more tricky. Elsewhere in the world, conifers have been forced into a retreat. Over the last 150 million years their supremacy has been challenged, and they have gradually lost ground to new and far more diverse competitors – the broad-leaved trees.

AUTUMN HARVEST *The giant cones of sugar pines drop soon after they ripen. In other pines, the cones may stay on the tree for a decade or more.*

Conifer leaves consist of variations on a fairly limited range of themes. Compared to them, the leaves of broad-leaved trees are spectacular and almost bewildering in their variety. In the raffia palm (*Raphia farinifera*), for example, the leafstalk alone can be 12 ft (3.7 m) long, while the leaf blade measures a staggering 60 ft (18 m), making this leaf the largest in the entire plant world. Many other tropical trees have leaves that are big enough to act as umbrellas, and some forest animals take advantage of this by nesting or roosting underneath them. They include small birds called spiderhunters (*Arachnothera*), which sew their nests into position using spiders' silk, and tent-making bats (*Uroderma*), which bite through leaf ribs, making the edges of leaves flop down to form a private shelter for themselves.

At the other extreme, the leaves of trees from dry places are often anything but broad. She-oaks or casuarinas (*Casuarina* and *Allocasuarina*), which grow in South-east Asia and Australia, are broad-leaved trees, but their leaves look more like tiny teeth. They are arranged in rings that circle the twigs, and each one is just a fraction of an inch long.

As well as varying in shape, these leaves also develop in different ways. In parts of the world with cold winters or a long dry season, most broad-leaved trees are deciduous, so their branches are bare for some of the year. But this feature is not a reliable way of telling broad-leaved trees from conifers. Originally, all broad-leaved trees were evergreen, and in the humid tropics, most are still.

FLOWERS AND FRUIT

The one feature that does distinguish broad-leaved trees from conifers is the way they make their seeds. Instead of having cones, broad-leaved trees grow flowers. Some of their flowers are so small and inconspicuous that they are easy to overlook, but others turn trees into beacons of

colour. These massed blooms are sometimes so magnificent that the most flamboyant species – such as magnolias (*Magnolia*), cherries (*Prunus*) and horse chestnuts (*Aesculus*) – have been cultivated for centuries, and plant-breeders have managed to make some even more spectacular than they are in the wild.

DOUBLE DIET *The streaked spiderhunter from Malaysia feeds on spiders and nectar, and helps to pollinate the flowers of broad-leaved trees.*

But exquisite though they are, flowers have not evolved for our benefit. Instead, they are living advertisements that attract a tree's animal partners. Lured by their colour or scent, animals flock to the flowers to collect food, which is usually in the form of a sugary fluid called nectar. While they feed, they become covered with pollen, and they transfer the pollen to the next tree they visit.

In temperate regions, animal pollinators are usually insects, but in the tropics they include a much wider range of animal life, from hummingbirds and parrots to bats and even monkeys. In many of these partnerships, wherever they occur, the lives of trees and their pollinators have become so intertwined that each can no longer survive without the other.

Given the tremendous success of animal pollination, it might seem odd that some

THE SECRET LIFE OF GALLS

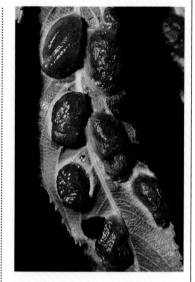

A close look at trees sometimes reveals strange objects that grow from leaves or twigs. Some of them look like fruit, while others are like tiny buttons or warts. They may be few and far between, but often hundreds are packed closely together.

These swellings are called galls. They develop when small animals lay their eggs on a tree, and trigger off a brief burst of growth that the tree is unable to suppress. The result is a swelling that provides the animal's young with food, and also with a secure home.

SPANGLE GALLS *Crowded together on the underside of an oak leaf (right), these spangle galls will fall to the ground in autumn. The grubs inside the galls (below) hatch in spring into adult insects that will form a new crop of currant galls.*

Galls are caused by a variety of animals, such as mites and microscopic worms, but the most common gall-makers are insects. They include a sawfly called *Pontania proxima*, which produces bean-like galls on the leaves of willows (*Salix*), and an aphid called *Adelges*, which lives on spruces and other conifers, making galls that look like miniature cones. But in the insect world, two groups of animals – the gall wasps and gall midges – are the supreme specialists in this way of life. Although they are often tiny and inconspicuous, their handiwork, particularly in oak trees, clearly shows where they have been at large.

Many gall wasps and gall midges have complex life cycles involving different kinds of galls at different times of the year. For example, a gall wasp called *Neuroterus quercus-baccarum*, which lives on European oak trees, produces two generations of adults each year. The first generation produces round 'currant galls' that develop on leaves or catkins in spring, while the next produces small, button-like spangle galls on the undersides of leaves in summer. The first generation contains only females, which lay eggs without mating. The second generation contains both sexes, which mate before the eggs are laid.

Most galls house a single grub, but some are divided into several compartments, each containing a single occupant. But with their tempting combination of food and security, galls attract other residents. These animals, known as inquilines, turn galls to their own advantage without helping to create them.

LIVING TOGETHER *Most plant galls house a single grub each, but this gall on a wild rose has several dozen. Each grub lives in a separate chamber.*

broad-leaved trees – such as oaks (*Quercus*) and poplars (*Populus*) – have abandoned their animal pollinators and gone back to using the wind. These trees often shed their pollen from long catkins, and because they do not need to attract animals, they have none of the bright colours of their animal-pollinated relatives. At one time, biologists thought that these trees were more primitive than animal-pollinated ones. However, careful detective work has revealed tiny remnants of coloured petals and traces of scent that suggest that with these trees evolution simply doubled back on itself.

Once a flower has been pollinated, it sets about making seeds. Here, broad-leaved trees deploy one of their most potent weapons in the struggle for survival. Instead of growing seeds in cones and letting them fall, they grow them inside closed chambers called ovaries. Ovaries developed to protect seeds from hungry insects, but over millions of years they have acquired another, even more important function – they help seeds to travel far from the parent tree.

The variety of these structures vividly shows how evolution can take one object and mould it in very different ways. Some ovaries develop long flaps that act like wings, making them spin away like heli-

THE FINAL FLOWERING

Once they reach maturity, most trees flower every year. However, for the talipot palm (*Corypha umbraculifera*), flowering is a cataclysmic event that happens only once in the tree's lifetime. This statuesque tree from South-east Asia produces a branched flower cluster, or inflorescence, that can measure up to 20 ft (6 m) high and more than 35 ft (10.5 m) across, and which may contain over 250 000 flowers. Having exhausted all its energies in flowering and forming fruit, the tree then dies.

copters. Others have fluffy hairs that work as parachutes, or curved sides that slowly dry out and then suddenly burst apart, showering seeds into the air. A few have hooks that catch onto fur or feathers, or

wooden lids that fly off when they hit the ground, scattering the seeds in all directions. Many become soft and juicy, forming an edible fruit that attracts animals. The animals eat the fruit for its tasty flesh, but the seeds pass through their bodies unharmed, and germinate away from the parent tree.

Armed with so many ways of spreading, broad-leaved trees have been able to adapt to a huge variety of habitats. There are now more than 10 000 species, and they have managed to reach some of the remotest places on Earth.

WOOD AND BARK

In their conquest of dry land, conifers and broad-leaved trees have both reached heights that would have humbled their ancient relatives. In some parts of the world, trees commonly grow to over 200 ft (61 m), and in the recent past a few have probably touched 500 ft (152 m). Modern trees are able to do this because they have perfected the art of growing a trunk. Instead of simply growing taller, they also grow thicker.

Like all other forms of life, trees grow mainly by cell division, which creates new

COLOURFUL LURE *The rusty pittosporum produces brightly coloured fruits that attract birds. The seeds survive being eaten and are distributed widely.*

cells from existing ones. In a tree fern, cell division takes place only at the top of the trunk, so once a length of trunk has been formed, it can grow no more. But in conifers and most broad-leaved trees, cell division takes place across the whole surface of the tree, in a thin layer called the cambium, which lies just beneath the bark. The cells in the cambium keep dividing throughout the tree's life, and so the trunk – together with every branch and twig – constantly expands as the tree reaches up towards the light.

When the cells in the cambium divide, they produce living tissue of two very different kinds. On the side facing out from the tree, they form phloem, which carries sugary food away from the leaves and delivers it to other parts of the tree. On the side facing towards the centre of the trunk, they form xylem. The cells in the xylem are

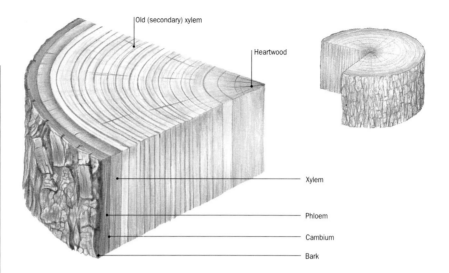

Old (secondary) xylem

Heartwood

Xylem

Phloem

Cambium

Bark

tougher than those in the phloem, and they make up a system of microscopic pipelines running up the tree. These pipelines carry water and dissolved minerals in a one-way flow from the roots to the leaves, where the water evaporates.

To begin with, xylem cells are very much alive. But as they get older, something remarkable starts to happen. The cambium continues its work and produces new layers of xylem cells farther and farther from the centre of the trunk. While this happens, the cells deeper in begin to change. They gradually stop carrying water and become impregnated with a battery of chemicals, including resins and oils, that helps to make them even stronger and better at fending off decay. Finally, the oldest cells die off, but by now they are so heavily reinforced that they retain their shape. The result of this build-up of more and more xylem cells is wood – an immensely hard material that gives the trunk its strength.

On the outside of the tree, a similar process is at work, but it happens the other way around. Here, the delicate cells of the phloem are protected by a jacket of bark. Bark grows like xylem, but its innermost cells are alive, while its outermost cells are dead. The layer of dead cells forms a barrier that stops moisture escaping from the tree, and prevents many of the tree's enemies gaining access to the living wood within. Because the outer part of the bark is dead, it cannot grow as the trunk expands, and instead it cracks and splits as new bark is built up underneath.

The only major exception to this way of growing is shown by the palms, which form a very distinctive group of broad-leaved trees. Their trunks are fibrous, and they grow very much like tree ferns, getting taller without becoming any thicker. Palms have no bark, and they cannot repair any damage done to their trunks. This is the reason why steps cut into a coconut tree (*Cocos nucifera*) are permanent, while steps cut into most other trees heal up as living wood engulfs them.

WOODS AND FORESTS

For every foot that it grows upwards, a tree creates new opportunities for other living things. Its trunk may stand on just a few square feet of ground, but its bark and leaves form a surface that is hundreds or even thousands of times larger. To simple organisms such as algae and lichens, which need little more than a space, light and moisture to survive, this alone is immensely useful. By setting up home on a tree's trunk and branches, they can become far more

TREE RINGS *In trees that grow outside the tropics, each spring sees a burst of growth. The result is a growth ring — one of many formed during a tree's life. Right: For native North Americans, the bark of the paper birch had many uses, including roofing and tinder for lighting fires.*

WOOD STRUCTURE *The cambium is a thin layer just beneath the bark. It produces two kinds of cells – the inner xylem and the outer phloem. Old (secondary) xylem forms wood.*

abundant than if the tree had not existed.

What is true of an individual tree is even more the case with entire forests. By living together, trees form a multilayered environment of enormous scope and complexity. The forest's physical structures, from bark and branches to leaves and flowers, make

up just one set of factors that vary from one part to another. Added to this are less-tangible features – endless grades of light and shade, subtle differences in temperature and humidity, and different degrees of exposure to the wind. Like cards dealt from an immense pack, they help to create a tremendous range of habitats influencing what can live where and when.

But despite this riot of small-scale detail, the way that trees grow gives forests a recognisable framework. The most obvious part of this can be seen overhead, where the crowns of the tallest trees meet to form a layer called the canopy. In some forests, the canopy contains large gaps, but in others – particularly in the far north and in the tropics – the canopy is dense and continuous, so very little light breaks through and reaches the ground. In these forests, sometimes only the sudden swaying of a branch or the call of a bird gives any hint of animal life in the sunlit world overhead.

Beneath the canopy, other plants compete for their share of the light. This layer of life, between the forest's roof and the ground, is the understorey – a place where some trees await their place in the sun, while others make do with the light that they can gather beneath their taller neighbours. In dense tropical forests, the understorey often has several layers, and is the home of a multitude of animals from birds to tree frogs. In the temperate world, where forests are usually simpler in structure, the understorey is often much

lower. Its life is less diverse, but it is the chief nesting zone for birds, which need to keep clear of predators on the ground and those in the treetops overhead.

Finally, sometimes as much as 200 ft (61 m) below the canopy, is the world of the forest floor. With its saplings, dead leaves and spring flowers, this is the part of the forest with which human visitors are most familiar, and it is also the home of animals

that cannot venture aloft. But although it rarely intrudes into our experience, forest life does not end at soil level. Beneath the surface, teeming micro-organisms reap a hidden harvest from dead leaves and wood, silently undoing structures that have been refined through millions of years of evolution. Only through their work can nutrients be recycled, allowing the forest to renew itself continually from below.

IN THE SHADE *European beech woods have an unusually simple composition because the trees' dense foliage shades out most other plants.*

DEATH AND REBIRTH

Tree life spans vary from a few decades to thousands of years. At the end of its life, a tree's fabric is gradually broken down, releasing nutrients that find their way back into the soil. These nutrients help to sustain new tree life.

If lightning strikes a tree, the effect can be cataclysmic. In less than a second, boiling sap explodes into superheated steam, and bark is flung aside as the irresistible pressure rips apart living wood. If the bolt is large enough, the tree may die.

Few trees actually end their lives in such a dramatic fashion. Some are rocked and then toppled by storms, while others are brought down by heavy snow, or by the ground slipping away beneath them. But for most, death comes much more slowly. It is heralded by events of such small proportions that they seem completely without significance: a tiny floating spore – no bigger than a speck of dust – settles on the exposed wood left by a broken branch, or a slender and almost transparent thread, working its way through the ground, makes contact with a root, and clasps it in the darkness.

Trivial though both may sound, either of these encounters can initiate a deadly struggle that pits a tree against an implacable and unrelenting adversary. Once the struggle has started, the ensuing battle may last for decades, or even for centuries.

THE UNSEEN ENEMY

For humans, fungi have always evoked a mixture of curiosity and confusion. Immobile, soft and sometimes lethally poisonous, they seem to be like plants, but have no leaves, flowers or seeds. Until the late 16th century, they were not thought of as being alive at all, but even after they had been recognised as living things, their exact place in the natural world remained unclear.

Today, biologists view fungi as forms of life that are quite distinct from all others. Instead of making their own food by using light, as most plants do, they plunder the produce of other living things. With the help of minute feeding threads called hyphae, they penetrate organic matter, and slowly break it down before absorbing the nutrients that it contains. Some species of fungi live exclusively on living things, forcing their way into their cells and then robbing them of their resources, while

THREADS OF DEATH *The threads of a fungus spread over a dead tree-trunk, releasing chemicals that break down food substances in the wood.*

others tackle dead remains. A few carry out the double role of murderer and scavenger, feeding on tissue while it is still alive, and continuing to do so once it is dead.

Throughout all the woodlands and forests of the world, fungi kill more trees

ENERGY FROM ABOVE
The energy in lightning converts the air's nitrogen – an essential plant nutrient – into a form that trees can use.

than any other agents of death. But, paradoxically, not all fungi are a tree's enemies. Many kinds form beneficial partnerships with trees, and live either inside their roots or, more often, in thin layers around the tips of the roots. These fungal growths, called mycorrhizae, help trees to take up nutrients from the ground. The process is not entirely understood, but it could be that fungi, which are usually present in the soil before the tree seed germinates, are better than plants at seeking out essential minerals in the soil. The fungi are particularly useful to trees that grow from seeds that landed on infertile soil. One example of such a fungus is the fly agaric (*Amanita muscaria*), which produces beautiful but poisonous red-and-white toadstools up to 6 in (15 cm) across. It forms mycorrhizae on the roots of birch trees (*Betula*), and is rarely seen except where these trees grow.

But whether trees have mycorrhizae or not – and the overwhelming majority do – they are still at risk from fungi of a much more dangerous kind. Once a tree-killing species has established itself in the soil, its feeding threads can span an extraordinary distance in their search for victims. In 1992, a single network of threads in a forest in Washington State was found to cover over 1500 acres (600 ha), making it the largest known single organism on Earth. Within this vast territory, the threads would have sought out every tree, persistently testing their defences and their suitability as a source of nourishment.

Even if a tree does manage to escape the attention of these relentlessly probing threads,

BRIEF BEAUTY *Poisonous fly agaric toadstools cluster around the trunk of a silver birch. Below: Touched by a passing foot, a puffball releases a cloud of microscopic spores.*

another source of infection lies in store. Once a fungus is sufficiently well nourished, it sets about producing offspring by making immense numbers of minute spores, which are like microscopic stripped-down seeds. The spores are released from special fruiting bodies, ranging from mushrooms to objects that look like fleshy fingers or exploding pinheads, and once airborne, they can be blown hundreds of miles by the wind. If just one of them lands on a susceptible tree, the slightest graze or break in the bark allows it to germinate and work its way inside.

BATTLE FOR SURVIVAL

In the contest against such ubiquitous enemies, trees are not entirely defenceless. Their roots contain physical and chemical barriers that stop unwelcome fungi breaking in, and their bark acts as a protective jacket against airborne invasion. But if these protective shields are breached, and the fungus gains access to the wood within, all is still not lost. Like someone applying a tourniquet to a snakebite, the tree partitions off the infected area in an attempt to prevent the invader's further spread. It does this by laying down chemicals that block the path of fungi, or slow their growth.

BRACKET FUNGUS *The sulphur polypore, one of the most widespread of the bracket-forming fungi, will eventually kill its host tree.*

These substances are often thick and resinous, and they create dark bands that show up very clearly when infected wood is sawn.

The effectiveness of a tree's defences depends partly on its foe. Many fungi attack particular trees, and can make little progress in infecting different species. Others are less selective and much more aggressive. The honey fungus (*Armillaria mellea*), for example, which lives throughout the world, is one of the most voracious of these unseen killers. It produces unusually thick bundles of feeding threads, called rhizomorphs, that look like black shoelaces. These spread through the ground where they infect roots, slowly killing almost anything woody that lies in their path.

For a tree, the most essential tissues – apart from those in its roots – are in its sapwood, just beneath the bark. The older wood towards the centre of the trunk is less crucial

DEADLY EMBRACE *Honey fungus rhizomorphs, revealed here by pulling away bark, clasp a tree that they have helped to kill. Below: A cluster of honey fungus toadstools sprout near the base of a tree.*

to survival, and is often the first to be sacrificed to the invader. If this heartwood is attacked, it sometimes rots away completely, leaving a hollow trunk. But as long as the outer wood is still healthy, the tree is safe, and may remain so for many years.

But as the battle wears on, the sapwood itself may eventually become infected. Once this happens, the first hints of serious trouble begin to appear. Starved of water and mineral nutrients, the tree's leaves often discolour and fall prematurely, and entire branches may die. Then, as new intruders follow in the path of the original attacker, deadly confirmation comes of the tree's desperate condition. Squeezing their way slowly out of the bark, shelf-like fruiting bodies of bracket fungi expand to shed their spores into the air. They are a sign that a fungus has spread far up the tree's trunk, and that the tree is being drained of everything it needs for survival. The contest, played out for so long, is drawing to its inevitable conclusion.

HOMES IN DEAD WOOD

In natural conditions, the interval between a tree's death and its final fall can be a long one. Without life-giving sap, the wood gradually loses its flexibility, and the outer branches snap off in the wind. The trunk, however, is far more sturdy. If its roots hold, it may stay standing for a decade or more.

To human eyes, the mutilated remains of a once-majestic tree can seem like an intrusion against the luxuriant backcloth of a woodland or forest. But for some animals, these standing trunks are a resource far more precious than any living tree. Like high-rise homes, they offer somewhere to bring up a family, and a place to shelter from enemies. As the years pass, a trunk often becomes pockmarked with entrance holes, as more and more animals discover it and move in.

The inhabitants of these dead trunks vary from one part of the world to another, but the earliest residents are almost always woodpeckers (family Picidae). With their sharp, chisel-like beaks, these are among the few animals that can actually start large holes in hard, dry wood. Once well into the trunk, they excavate downwards, digging out bottle-shaped chambers in which they lay their eggs. Their only nesting material is a layer of wood chips, but at least their young grow up in a secure, rainproof environment, where they are protected by their noisy and often aggressive parents.

FEEDING TIME *An adult green woodpecker is greeted by a hungry nestling clamouring for a meal. Below: A young nuthatch peers out from the security of its nest. The entrance has been plastered with mud to prevent larger birds getting inside.*

For other birds that nest in dead trees, such as nuthatches (*Sitta*) and redstarts (*Phoenicurus phoenicurus*), abandoned woodpecker holes make perfect homes. However, woodpeckers themselves are not the best of neighbours. As well as eating insect grubs, many of them also have a liking for young birds, and they frequently try to peck their way into nests that hold out the promise of a meal. Sometimes, the contest is very

uneven, with a large woodpecker pushing aside the panic-stricken parents, but in tropical forests particularly, the parents are sometimes more than a match for the would-be raider. The screeching of infuriated parakeets, fluttering around their nest high in a dead palm tree, is often a sign that a woodpecker has been repelled and sent on its way.

The disadvantage of tree-holes is that

URGENT DELIVERY *With its tail fanned out against a tree-trunk, a male rhinoceros hornbill passes food to his mate, who is sealed up inside the tree.*

they are easy to spot, particularly if their occupants keep arriving with fresh supplies of food. In the forests of Africa and Asia, one group of birds – the hornbills – have evolved a remarkable way of improving their domestic security. Once the female is about to lay her eggs, she retires to the nest and the male walls her in, using mud to seal the entrance. He leaves just a small gap, and while the eggs are hatching and the young developing – a period that can last for up to three months – he passes food through the hole to his imprisoned mate. Eventually the female pecks her way out, but the young are reluctant to follow. They often repair the wall, breaking it down again only when they are ready to leave the nest.

Dead upright trunks – especially ones that are hollow – also provide housing for a very different group of flying animals. Gripping the wood with the sharp claws of their back feet, bats use trees as daytime roosts, and as nurseries for their young. Most insect-eating bats that set up home in dead trees tuck themselves away out of sight, but in tropical forests, a few species roost in the open. They cling unobtrusively to the bark, looking more like brown diamond-shaped blemishes than living animals.

In choosing their homes, bats are just as

selective as birds, and the species that roost in dead trees, such as the noctule (*Nyctalus noctula*) of Europe and Asia, are often among the first animals to suffer when old continued on page 29

A PRIVATE ROOST *Tucked away inside a hollow tree, noctule bats are safe from most of their enemies.*

THE WORLD'S OLDEST TREES

Instead of living in a benign habitat, where temperatures are mild and water is abundant, the world's most ancient trees live in one that seems almost impossibly harsh. Clinging to bare mountain slopes at altitudes of up to 12 000 ft (3650 m), North American bristlecone pines endure sub-zero temperatures, icy winds, and drought that can last for most of the year.

Bristlecone pines are found in the mountains of the American west, from the southern Rockies to the Great Basin region. At one time, there was thought to be a single species, *Pinus aristata*, but most botanists now consider that there are two – the Rocky Mountain bristlecone pine (*Pinus aristata*) and the Great Basin bristlecone pine (*Pinus longaeva*). The Rocky Mountain pine can grow to be about 2000 years old, but the Great Basin species more than doubles this span. The oldest tree that survives today is estimated to have started life more than 4300 years ago.

In sheltered gullies, bristlecone pines have a single, straight trunk and can reach up to 50 ft (15 m) high. But on the highest slopes, where trees are exposed to the full force of the wind, they look very different. Here,

STALWART SURVIVOR *An ancient bristlecone pine in the White Mountains, close to the border between California and Nevada. When ripe, the male cones (below) will shed their pollen into the mountain air.*

many of the pines look like the survivors of some natural catastrophe. Their trunks are often gnarled, with some three or four dead limbs for each one that is still alive.

Paradoxically, the harsh climate actually helps to prolong life, as well as making it difficult. Because it is so cold, bristlecone pines grow extremely slowly, and their resin-filled wood is immensely tough. Insects find it almost impossible to attack, and even fungi have difficulty gaining a foothold. Although there is so much dead wood, the extreme conditions mean that the trees are widely spaced. If fire does break out –

for example, from a lightning strike – it has very little chance of spreading from one tree to its neighbours.

Because bristlecone pine wood resists rotting, its growth rings provide a unique record of yearly changes in climate. The width of a growth ring shows how well a tree grew in any year, and from this one can make deductions about the weather during the growing season. A run of warm years produces wide rings, while cold years produce narrow ones. By examining living wood, and wood from trees that died long ago, scientists have been able to 'stretch' the record so that it now extends back over 8000 years.

RESILIENT FOLIAGE *Needles 1 in (2.5 cm) long are built to withstand intense cold and strong winds.*

FOREST FLOOR *A fallen tree-trunk in the subtropical forests of Australia provides food for a range of insects.*

tree-trunks are 'tidied away' by well-meaning humans. In the spring, when pregnant noctules form maternity colonies, up to 400 of them can be crammed together inside one standing trunk. By keeping so close together, these tiny mammals – which weigh no more than $1^1/_2$ oz (45 g) – conserve their body warmth, essential in a habitat where both weather and food supplies are unpredictable. Immediately after being born, the hairless young huddle together, but they grow quickly, and are as big as their parents within just six weeks.

Like many bats in the temperate world, noctules have different summer and winter quarters. When autumn arrives, and the supply of flying insects dwindles, the colony flies off to a winter roost – often another dead tree – where they hibernate. The noctule's summer and winter roosts can be nearly 1500 miles (2400 km) apart.

DECLINE AND FALL

After a period of several years, the inevitable happens. Propped up by roots that are slowly rotting, the trunk gradually becomes too heavy for its weakening foundations, and topples over. In the ensuing fall, birds and bats are evicted, and another group of animals takes over. Instead of using the tree-trunk for shelter, these animals use it as a source of food.

Wood is a difficult substance for animals to eat, and an even harder one for them to digest. It contains large amounts of cellulose – the tough building material used by all plants – together with other substances that give wood its strength, and its resistance to attack. To make matters worse, it is a poor source of the nutrients that animals need to grow. However, on the positive side of the balance sheet, wood does have one outstanding advantage. It is produced in such vast quantities, and over such huge areas of the world, that it is an almost unlimited source of food.

The animals that feed on living or dead

wood are drawn from a fairly limited section of the natural world. One of the most unusual is not a land animal at all, but a sea-dwelling mollusc. Known as the shipworm (*Teredo navalis*), this fleshy burrower uses its sharp-edged shell like a drill bit to bore through submerged timber, from the pilings of piers to the hulls of boats. Because it grows as thick as a finger, the damage it can do is considerable. However, on land, the shipworm's distant relatives – which include slugs and snails – seem reluctant to tackle the same challenging source of food. Here, the specialist wood-eaters are the insects.

When a log has lain on a damp woodland floor for several years, it is often quite easy to pull apart. Jacketed by the last remnants of the bark, the outer wood often crumbles to the touch, while beneath this, the interior is usually more solid. It is often dissected into loose blocks, which fit together like pieces of a three-dimensional jigsaw. These blocks are created by fungi, which feed on dead

WOODLAND SKIRMISH *With antlers locked, a pair of stag beetles demonstrate their strength. The antlers do not close fully, so do little harm.*

EXPOSED *A stag-beetle larva is revealed beneath the surface of a rotting log. Most of its body is soft and pliable, but its dark brown jaws are much harder.*

wood and break down the bonds that hold it together. In this mass of moist decay there may be few signs of life, but hidden in logs such as this, some of the world's largest wood-eating insects go about their work.

Glistening white and up to 4 in (10 cm) long, the C-shaped grubs of stag beetles (*Lucanus*) are among the most impressive of these wood-eating animals. Each grub has six legs just behind its head, but these are so small that they can barely shift its heavy body. However, deep inside a decaying log, there is little call for active movement, and instead the grub slowly chews its

way through its surroundings. At the end of this stage of its life, which can last five years, it makes its way to the surface for its dramatic transformation into an adult.

Adult stag beetles feed on weeping sap rather than wood, and are strong fliers, taking to the air after dark to find places to feed and to lay their eggs. With their glossy brownish-black bodies, the females are impressive enough, but it is the males, with their spreading 'antlers', that really catch the eye. A male stag beetle's antlers are actually enlarged mouth-parts, which hinge together like a pair of tongs. They look formidable, but are actually quite weak, and are used mainly for grappling with rival males in ritual combats during the breeding season. In the course of these fights, the stronger beetle often lifts his opponent right off his feet, before dropping him back to the ground. After suffering such a humiliation, the loser makes a hasty retreat.

THE FUNGUS GARDENERS

Almost all wood-eating animals face a common problem: they cannot digest wood. They are good at rasping or chewing their way through it, but their digestive systems lack the enzymes, or chemical catalysts, that split cellulose into its simpler components.

How then do they survive? The answer is that they enlist the help of living things

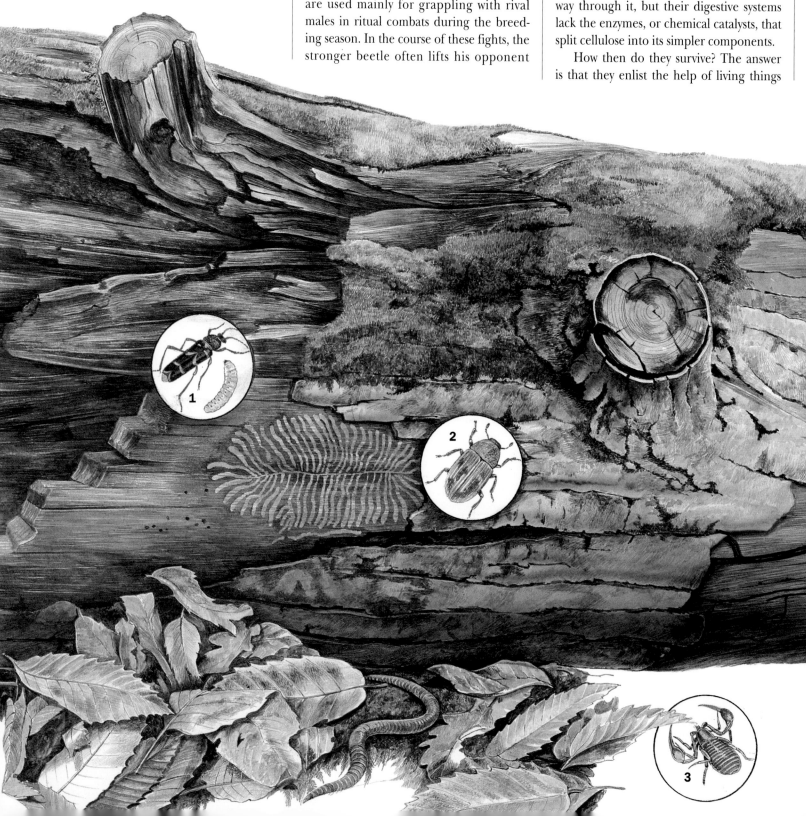

that can produce these crucial enzymes. These cellulose-splitters include fungi, and also two other groups of microscopic organisms – bacteria, and more complex microbes called protists. By providing these micro-organisms with a steady supply of wood, in a form that suits them best, animals can then exploit them or their nutritious by-products.

At its simplest, this partnership involves an animal and its accomplices living side by side. For example, ambrosia beetles bore deep holes in living or newly dead wood, and infect the lining with a species of fungus. The fungus forms a fluffy coating on the exposed wood, and the beetles treat this like the equivalent of a vegetable plot, cropping selected parts but otherwise leaving it intact. While it may not be quite as appetising as the mythical ambrosia of Greek legends, the fungus provides the beetles with a reliable source of food, and the

LIFE IN ROTTING LOGS
The inhabitants of rotting wood have a variety of interlocking lifestyles. Bacteria (7) and fungi break the wood down, and then absorb the nutrients. Vegetarian animals either feed on the wood itself, in the case of longhorn beetles (1), bark beetles (2), and the formidable-looking but harmless stag beetles (5), or on a wider range of plant remains, as in the case of woodlice (4), and millipedes (8). Two common hunters are very different in scale: tiny pseudoscorpions (3) are just visible to the naked eye, but the much larger centipedes (6) scuttle away as soon as they are exposed to light.

beetles can therefore riddle logs with their tunnels in order to produce it. Ambrosia beetles are most common in the tropics, but in northern forests, wood wasps (family Siricidae) feed in a similar way.

Ambrosia beetles and wood wasp grubs live on their own, so their fungus gardening is necessarily small-scale. But in the world of social insects, some termites have turned fungus cultivation into the animal equivalent of a major industry. Instead of living in the wood itself, these insects often live underground, in nests that can contain over a

---

LIGHTS IN THE DARKNESS

Light usually plays little part in the lives of fungi. Unlike plants, they do not use light as a source of energy, and they often spend the whole of their lives hidden away from daylight, either in soil or in their food. But strangely, a few species of fungi – particularly in tropical forests – are able to make light of their own. The light creates an eerie glow that emanates either from their feeding threads, or from the fruiting bodies that make their spores. As yet, biologists have no real idea what function this light may serve. Glowing fruiting bodies may attract insects, which could help to spread spores. However, the function of glowing feeding threads, hidden inside wood, is much harder to fathom.

---

million individuals. When night falls, they march into the forest, travelling through specially constructed tubes to nearby sources of wood, which can include anything from dead tree-trunks to fence posts. The termites chew away the wood from inside, taking care to leave the surface layer intact. They then return to the nest, where the chewed wood passes through their bodies. The result of this collection and processing operation is a spongy compost, fashioned into ball-shaped gardens up to 2 ft (61 cm) across, buried beneath the forest floor. The fungus spreads rapidly through this rich medium, and the termites crop it as it grows. Each species of termite cultivates its own type of fungus, producing the right environment for the fungus to flourish.

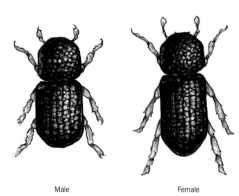

Male   Female

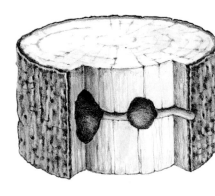

For these fungus gardeners, moving home poses something of a problem. Without their fungus they cannot survive, so some of it has to come with them. Ambrosia beetles and wood wasps carry pockets of fungus on the outsides of their bodies, and they infect the wood with the fungus when they lay their eggs. King and queen termites are thought to do the same, so the fungus is ready to grow when their nuptial flight comes to an end, and a new colony is founded.

PARTNERS WITHIN

For many wood-eaters, including stag beetle grubs, the relationship with their microscopic allies is an even more intimate one. Instead of cultivating fungi, these animals harbour micro-organisms inside their bodies. Wherever they are, their captive partners are always at hand, ready to produce nourishment from food that the host animal cannot tackle unaided.

Many non-gardening termites live in this way, and so do a host of woodboring insects, including the infamous furniture beetle or 'woodworm' (*Anobium punctatum*), and its larger relative the deathwatch beetle (*Xestobium rufovillosum*). In the wild, these

AMBROSIA BEETLES *Unlike bark beetles, these insects often bore their way deep into living wood. They feed mainly on fungi, but also on the sap that oozes into their tunnels.*

two insects often tunnel into dead branches on living trees, and their neat round exit holes, just a fraction of an inch across, show where adult beetles have emerged from the wood. In their natural home, these insects play a useful role in breaking down dead wood, but inside houses, their handiwork is much less welcome. A heavy infestation, over many years, can make the largest timbers crumble.

The furniture beetle is always mute, but during the mating season, the deathwatch announces its presence with sound. It strikes its head against the wood, sending out bursts of staccato tapping just a few seconds long. If another beetle is in the vicinity, it taps back, and the original signaller taps more and more frequently, as it feverishly tries to locate its prospective partner. In houses, this tapping is most noticeable late at night, when everything else is quiet.

It is easy to imagine how this beetle originally got its name, as its eerie tapping interrupted the silence of the small hours, when anxious relatives sat up to watch over the sick.

The partnership that enables

BEETLE BREAKOUT *The adult furniture beetle creates round exit holes in pieces of wood by rotating its body as it bites its way to the surface.*

NATURE'S ENGRAVERS

When trees are dead or dying, patches of bark often fall away, revealing elaborately sculpted tunnels that run over the surface of the wood. These are the work of bark or engraver beetles, a group of insects that are among the most deadly of trees' animal enemies.

Bark beetles are rarely more than $2/5$ in (5 mm) long. They feed mainly on soft sapwood, and have cylindrical bodies and small heads. In most species, the hardened hindwings or elytra have scooped-out tips, which

work like miniature snowploughs. To clear debris from its tunnel, a bark beetle simply reverses into it, using its elytra to push the woody waste backwards and out of the tree.

Adult bark beetles are easy to overlook, but their excavations are eye-catching and highly distinctive. Each species produces a characteristic pattern of main tunnels and blind-ended galleries that identify it as readily as a fingerprint. Even when a tree is dead and the diggers themselves long gone, evidence of their identity still remains.

Instead of being dug by a single beetle, each set of tunnels is the work of two generations. The tunnelling begins when an adult female, accompanied by her mate, digs straight into the bark perpendicular to the surface, until she encounters the wood below. She then turns through a right angle, and starts to dig parallel to the surface. The male excavates a small chamber, where the two beetles mate, and the female starts

BARK BEETLE LARVAE Hidden under the bark of a dying tree, beetle grubs excavate their way through the wood. Each gallery widens out as its excavator grows bigger. Right: The forlorn outlines of dead elms mark the edge of a field. Dutch elm disease kills trees by blocking the tiny vessels they use to carry water.

burrowing once again, laying eggs at precise intervals as she chews her way through the wood.

When the eggs hatch, the beetle grubs bore tunnels of their own. In many species, they dig perpendicularly to the original tunnel, creating straight or meandering galleries that fan out on both sides. Each gallery widens out and, after a distance of 1-2 in (2.5-5 cm), comes to an abrupt end. This marks the point where the excavator turned into a pupa, before finally boring its way up through the bark as an adult beetle.

Bark beetles usually attack mature trees. They often select ones that have already been weakened by disease or drought, and they hasten their death by destroying their sapwood, and sometimes by spreading fungi. In Europe and North America, the elm bark beetle (*Scolytus scolytus*) carries a particularly virulent fungus called *Ceratocystis ulmi* which causes Dutch elm disease. This infection has destroyed millions of elms on both sides of the Atlantic.

these wood-eaters to survive is a special form of symbiosis, or working alliance between different species. This particular kind of partnership, with micro-organisms living inside much larger hosts, is very common in the natural world, and is found not only in wood-eaters, but also in a wide range of leaf-eating mammals, from deer to koalas. Although the host and its partners benefit by working together, animals sometimes seem to break the spirit of the arrangement. They often digest some of their captive partners along with their food, cropping them rather like termites crop fungi in their underground gardens. However, micro-organisms reproduce very quickly, so they soon make up for this loss.

In the bone-dry air of high mountains, or in the cold and acidic clutches of a peat bog, dead wood can remain intact for thousands of years. But on the floor of a woodland or forest, where microscopic life abounds, even the largest tree-trunks eventually disappear. The time this takes depends partly on the climate, and partly on the wood itself. Some kinds of wood, for example beech (*Fagus*) and lime (*Tilia*), decay quite quickly – a branch from a lime tree in an English wood, for example, would take about five years to decay – but others, such as oak (*Quercus*) and western red cedar (*Thuja plicata*), are far more durable. Their timber can survive for many decades in natural conditions, and for much longer when used in buildings, where they have some protection from damp.

When a fallen tree is gradually dismantled by living things, the organisms that feed on it – collectively known as decomposers – throw the process that originally built it into reverse. Instead of taking in energy to build up carbon-containing chemicals, they release energy by breaking them down. Because this process takes place inside individual cells it is called cellular respiration, and is the biological equivalent of a slow-burning fire. Just like a fire, cellular respiration uses up oxygen and produces carbon dioxide – precisely countering photosynthesis, the process by which trees grow.

When a real fire flashes through a forest, the carbon fuel locked up in trees is burned in a matter of minutes, and an immense amount of heat is suddenly liberated. However, when trees are decomposed by living things, their energy is released in a much more controlled way. It has to be, because for all forms of life, too much energy is just as dangerous as too little. Through complex cascades of chemical reactions, the decomposers release the energy in small and measured amounts, and they use it both to build themselves up, and to power the processes that keep them alive.

Like workers on a disassembly line, decomposers reduce all the parts of a tree – from fallen leaves to dead wood – to small and smaller fragments. The visible result of their work is a rich substance called humus, which contains the last traces of the tree's organic matter, together with the minerals that it originally drew up from the soil. It is into this fertile mix, which is constantly replenished from above, that the seeds of the next generation fall.

SEEDS AND SAPLINGS

When an acorn drops through the leaves of its parent tree and lands on a woodland floor, humus provides the perfect seedbed on which to start a new life. However, with its generous built-in food reserves, a seed of this size attracts many kinds of animal. If it falls onto open ground, it is likely to be spotted by birds or squirrels, but if it falls

WELCOME FOOD *A North American deer mouse finds a pair of recently fallen acorns. Neither is likely to germinate.*

into the dense cover, small rodents such as mice are likely to catch its tempting scent. In either instance, the acorn's chances of survival are slim.

STARTING LIFE *After germination, a growing acorn quickly gets into step with the seasons. By the end of its first summer, it forms tough buds that protect next year's shoots.*

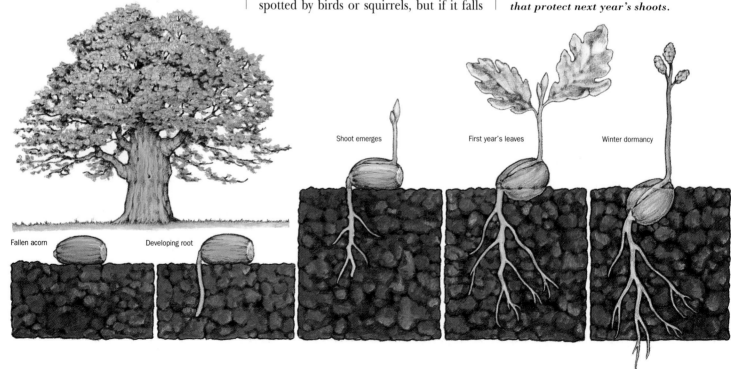

Fallen acorn   Developing root   Shoot emerges   First year's leaves   Winter dormancy

To deal with this problem, oaks and many other nut-producing trees rely on sheer force of numbers to overwhelm their seed predators. For a few weeks each year, they swamp the market, ensuring that a small proportion of seeds get overlooked, and have a chance of survival. In some years, they produce vastly more seeds than animals could ever consume. These 'mast' years, which get their name from the nuts or mast of woodland trees, are like a deliberate tipping of the normal balance. By being unpredictable, the trees ensure that small animals never have the chance to adjust to a stable supply of food.

For a few weeks, the bloodless carnage is intense. But while the unlucky majority are being nibbled, chewed, or swallowed whole, some of the surviving acorns are embarking on a critical stage of their lives. Stimulated by moisture and warmth, they begin to germinate.

In temperate woodlands, many tree seeds do not begin to grow until winter has passed, but acorns often seize their chance while they can, and soon develop a root that forces its way downwards into the soil. The root starts to soak up moisture and the acorn swells, splitting the seed-case to reveal a tiny shoot, tipped by the almost invisible rudiments of leaves. Guided on its journey by light-sensitive chemicals that control its growth, the shoot steers its way steadily upwards and away from the shade of the forest floor.

The acorn's food store is packed in two special leaves that remain inside the seed. As the seedling grows, their reserves begin to run low, and they start to shrivel. However, if all is going well, the first true leaves are now opening on the developing shoot. Once they are in place, photosynthesis can begin, and the seedling becomes truly self-sufficient.

Of the original acorns that fell from the tree, perhaps fewer than one in a thousand survive to reach this stage. But even now, future success is far from assured. The young oak's leaves are thin and delicate, and are often stripped away by caterpillars and other insect grubs, forcing the seedling to grow another set. Worse still, the entire shoot may be bitten off by a passing deer, inflicting damage that usually proves fatal.

But if the seedling manages to survive its animal enemies, it now has others to contend with. Its need for light is absolute, and it cannot survive forever if it is overshadowed by other plants. Herbaceous plants, which die back every year, are no competition, because the oak has the potential to outgrow them. But other trees – particularly other oaks – are a different matter.

In rain forests, the saplings of some trees are specially adapted to cope with life in the shadows, and their slender trunks – often half the thickness of a wrist – reach upwards many feet in their search for light. However, the oaks of temperate woodlands are not like this. Deprived of their share of

TREES OF THE FUTURE *English oak saplings in their spring foliage. They are between two and three years old, and only a few of them will survive.*

IMPORTED ENEMIES

Over millions of years, trees have evolved a degree of resistance to many of their natural enemies. Although some trees die, mass mortality is rare. However, when humans introduce alien organisms from distant parts of the world, this natural balance is sometimes upset, and the results can be catastrophic. In 1869, the gypsy moth (*Lymantria dispar*) was accidentally introduced from Europe into North America. Its caterpillars were able to feed on the leaves of many North American trees, and the moth quickly spread. The gypsy moth is now one of the most prevalent insect pests of North American trees. During the 1970s, when the moth population surged, millions of broad-leaved trees were killed.

---

daylight, their saplings remain thin and stunted, and are vulnerable to many enemies before they eventually perish on the woodland floor.

Among the acorns that do germinate in the shadows, a fortunate few have unexpected allies in their struggle for survival. As spring merges into summer, the leafy canopy above, normally so dense and opaque at this time of year, starts to thin, so that its shade is slightly less heavy than before. The following year, the same pattern repeats itself, but with greater effect, and in the year after that, many buds fail to produce leaves at all.

In a tree overhead, the feeding threads of fungi are at their work, and are cutting off the flow of water and nutrients that are essential for survival. Life is slowly coming to an end for one tree, but for those in its shade, it is only just beginning.

PATTERNS FROM THE PAST

The forests that exist today sometimes seem as old as time itself. But forests constantly change as the world around them alters. Some have a long history, but others are recent additions to the map of the forest world.

Pushed by an unstoppable force, a boulder lurches into life. Its 1000 ton bulk crashes down a slope into a ledge of rocky debris, where it halts for a moment, balanced unsteadily at the brink of a further fall. Gravity reasserts its grip, and the boulder careers onward with ever-increasing speed. Reaching the bottom of the incline, it is hurled forwards by its own momentum, and ploughs through a stand of stunted trees, which snap like cocktail sticks beneath it. Finally it stops, surrounded by the shattered wreckage of splintered timber, and by living trees that are doomed to die.

The place is the state of New York, and the time is about 20 000 years ago, when the last Ice Age is nearing its height. A massive sheet of ice, which will eventually become $1/2$ mile (800 m) deep, is inexorably sliding southwards under its own weight, and is engulfing everything that stands in its way. The trees in its path have already been tortured by the cold winds blowing down from its crevasse-ridden surface, and many of them have perished. But even for the survivors, little time is left. An immense wall of rocky rubble, gathered up by the ice and pushed south for hundreds of miles, is spilling towards them like crumbling lava. Travelling at the rate of over 12 in (30 cm) a day, it will soon crush them out of existence.

FORESTS ON THE MARCH

Standing on the same spot today, it is almost impossible to believe that any of this actually happened. The ground is obscured by trees, and a tremendous variety of animals, from beetles and butterflies to birds and deer, use the forest as their home. The same is true of other regions of the Northern Hemisphere that were bulldozed by the advancing ice. The woodlands and forests of Scandinavia, northern Germany and parts of the British Isles all seem to have existed almost since time began.

The reality, however, is very different. For reasons that are still imperfectly understood, the polar ice caps have expanded and contracted many times in the past few million years, and each time forests have been erased like writing on a blackboard. The last of these catastrophic rubbings-out reached its climax about 18 000 years ago, when one ice sheet completely covered the North American Great Lakes region, another reached as far south as Central Europe, and several more capped high ground in

ADVANCE GUARD *Dwarf willows – seen here on a mountainside in Iceland – can survive in a climate that is too cold for tall-trunked trees.*

other parts of the world. But about 10 000 years ago, the ice sheets began to retreat, and the most recent glaciation came to an abrupt end.

As the ice sheets withdrew, they left behind a sterile landscape that had been scoured clean of every trace of life. Initially, few things could survive in this wasteland, but as the climate became warmer, life began to creep back. The first arrivals were lichens, which were able to survive on bare rock in temperatures that hovered near freezing. They had spread from areas that were not affected by the ice sheet by means of tiny packages of cells that were blown by the wind. After the lichens came mosses and other low-growing plants, and then dwarf willows (*Salix*), which grew into

THE FOREST FRINGE *Caribou on summer pastures in Alaska. In winter they feed on lichen. Right: A musk ox tugs at an Arctic willow. Despite its appearance, it is more closely related to goats than to cattle.*

dense mats on the water-logged ground. In their wake came the animals that fed on them, including reindeer or caribou (*Rangifer*), and musk ox (*Ovibos*), and migratory birds that arrived for a few weeks each summer. But even as these pioneers were establishing themselves, the climate was growing milder still, and even greater change was to come.

At first, the only signs would have been scattered splashes of dark green, huddled on slopes where the shelter and drainage were slightly better than in the surrounding ground. As the centuries passed, the number of these splashes increased, as did their size. Growing from winged seeds that fluttered northwards on strong winds, these were conifers – the vanguard of an evergreen forest that was slowly marching north.

Most people are familiar with the idea that animals migrate from one place to another. However, trees do something very similar when the conditions around them change. Although individual trees are rooted to one spot, their seeds are not, and with the help of wind or animals they can spread far and wide. By studying tree pollen that has been preserved in boggy ground, botanists have been able to piece together the northward march of forests after the most recent ice retreat. In eastern North America, the evergreen forest was often made up of ranks of spruces (*Picea*) and firs (*Abies*), which at one time dominated the landscape. But as the climate grew milder and moister, these were exiled farther north, and their place was taken by broad-leaved trees, such as oaks (*Quercus*) and maples (*Acer*). The most recent arrivals were warmth-loving species, including tulip trees (*Liriodendron*) and hickories (*Carya*), which had been banished to the far south by the ice.

PRISONERS OF TIME

On the opposite side of the Atlantic, in southern Spain, another piece of living history shows how ice has influenced the forests we see today. Close to the sun-baked plain of the River Guadalquivir in Andalucia, a range of limestone hills forms a cool upland oasis in a part of the world that is often hot and dry. The hills are the haunt of the huge griffon vulture (*Gyps fulvus*), which nests in scattered colonies in the most inaccessible crags, and also of the much rarer European black vulture (*Aegypius monachus*), a species that is

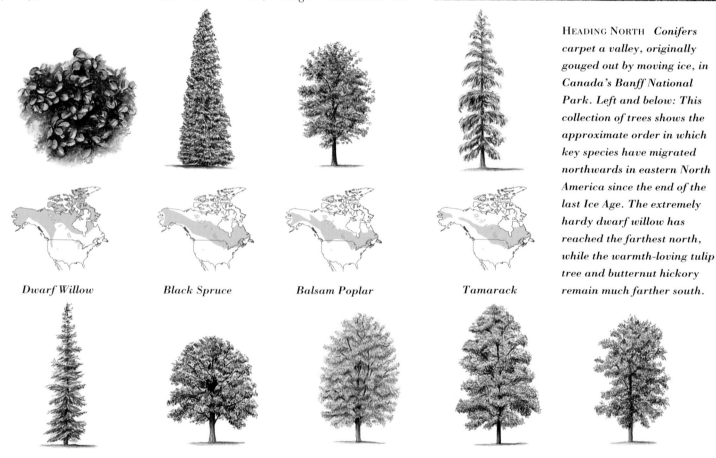

Dwarf Willow

Black Spruce

Balsam Poplar

Tamarack

HEADING NORTH *Conifers carpet a valley, originally gouged out by moving ice, in Canada's Banff National Park. Left and below: This collection of trees shows the approximate order in which key species have migrated northwards in eastern North America since the end of the last Ice Age. The extremely hardy dwarf willow has reached the farthest north, while the warmth-loving tulip tree and butternut hickory remain much farther south.*

Balsam Fir

Northern Red Oak

Sugar Maple

Tulip Tree

Bitternut Hickory

READY FOR TAKEOFF *For these griffon vultures the clear sky promises good conditions for searching out food.*

practically extinct in the rest of the continent. Most of the area is treeless, but on one north-facing slope, a blanket of green clings to the scree-strewn hillside. Covering just a few hundred acres, this is the largest surviving expanse of a forest trapped by time.

Thousands of years ago, Spanish firs (*Abies pinsapo*) used to be found over much of Europe, but as the ice pushed southwards, the firs fell back. In southern Spain, they thrived in the mild but damp conditions in the hills, and here they remained, waiting for their chance to spread north once more. But when the northern ice sheet melted and that chance arrived, the firs faced an insuperable problem. On the low ground, the climate had become too dry for them to survive, so they were trapped on a number of separate hillsides with no way of breaking out.

These 'relict' forests are a common feature of regions where the climate has changed in the distant past. The most famous relict tree of all – the giant sequoia (*Sequoiadendron giganteum*) of California – once covered huge areas of North America, at a time when the climate was much wetter than it is today. But like the Spanish fir, the sequoia could not cope when the climate became progressively drier. As a result, these giant trees became confined in the wild to about 75 isolated mountain groves, where the temperature and rainfall allows their survival.

BRIDGES BENEATH THE SEA

Imagine being able to reach Alaska from Siberia, or Ireland from France, without leaving dry land. It sounds absurd, and – today at least – it is. But at the height of the last Ice Age, trees, animals and people were able to do just that, and in some cases the aftereffects are still evident today.

In the rain forests of South-east Asia, a curious mammal can sometimes be spotted on moonlit nights, as it threads its way cautiously between the trees. From the back, it looks like a very large pig, with bristly fur and a short, pig-like tail. The rest of its body is more ambiguous. Its stocky feet, which are often caked with mud, end in toes rather than hooves, and its colours – a bold splash of white surrounded by black – mimic the play of the moonlight on the ground. However, there is nothing pig-like about its head. Instead of a snout it has a short

SOUTHERN SANCTUARY *A pocket of Spanish fir forest survives in an area of southern Spain not reached by the last Ice Age.*

trunk, which it uses to feel and smell its way over the ground, searching for plants and fruit. Just one glance shows that this is clearly not a pig, but a very different animal indeed.

The nocturnal wanderer is the Malayan tapir (*Tapirus indicus*). With a body that weighs up to 600 lb (270 kg), it is one of the largest mammals of the Asian rain forests, and ranges from Myanmar (Burma) in the north to the islands of Indonesia in the south. It has no other living relatives in these forests, so it might be called unique. However, the Malayan tapir is not the only one of its kind. Thousands of miles away, in Central and South America, three other species of tapir roam the forests. Their trunks are shorter than those of their Asian counterparts, and their fur is a different colour, but they are clearly tapirs.

The strange distribution of the tapir family has its origins in another effect of the advancing ice. When ice sheets grow bigger, a vast amount of extra water becomes locked up in a frozen form. As a result, the sea level can fall by up to 250 ft (76 m), and the shallow undersea shelf that skirts many coastlines emerges as dry land. During successive glaciations, the floor of the Bering Strait, which separates Alaska from Siberia, has emerged from the sea, and similar land bridges have existed in

other places, for example between the British Isles and mainland Europe.

When these land bridges appeared, many living things, from tapirs to trees, were able to travel between North America

THE LAND-BRIDGE TRAVELLER

THE LAND-BRIDGE TRAVELLER

The European strawberry tree (*Arbutus unedo*) is a common sight in the Mediterranean region, and is one of the plants that makes up *maquis* – an impenetrable tangle of shrubs and small trees. But the same tree can also be found in very different surroundings, among the beautiful hills and lakes of south-west Ireland. The strawberry tree is a classic example of a land-bridge traveller. Several thousand years ago, it spread northwards along the coast of western Europe, and eventually reached Ireland by crossing a land bridge from the mainland. When the land bridge disappeared beneath the waves, the Irish strawberry trees became cut off from their relatives farther south.

and Asia, and between other places that are now separated by seawater. When the ice melted and the land bridges were swamped by the rising sea, the connections were broken, and the tapir family was split apart.

In the tapir's rain forest habitat, ice sheets and Ice Ages seem a world away. Here, beneath the tangled roots of trees,

there are no signs that ice has ever scraped its way over the ground, and the forest looks as though it has existed unchanged for millions of years. At one time, this is exactly what scientists believed. But even here, in the heart of the tropics, the Ice Ages brought great changes. The evidence for them has come not from the land itself, but from living things.

In the 1960s, a German geologist and birdwatcher called Jurgen Haffer noticed that South American birds called toucanets (*Selenidera*) seem to be spread out in a curious way. Like pieces in a patchwork quilt, each species lives in a different region of the Amazon forest, with one in the northeast, another further west, another to the south, and so on. The species do not seem to be separated by any physical barriers, yet each one keeps to its own region, and neighbouring species never interbreed. As the species are so similar, they must have had a common ancestor, but the origin of their separation seemed a mystery.

To investigate this problem, Jurgen Haffer turned back an imaginary clock to the time of the Ice Ages. With each glaciation, or ice advance, the tropical climate would have cooled slightly. More importantly, it would have become drier. In some places

FAR-FLUNG RELATIVES *Despite living so far apart, both the Brazilian tapir (left) and the Malayan tapir (right) have a trunk-like snout.*

TELLTALE TOUCANETS
The distribution of toucanets has been used to chart changes in the extent of South America's rain forest.

there would still have been enough rain to allow the forest to flourish, but in others there would have been too little, turning the forest into tree-studded grassland. By looking at today's rainfall patterns in Central America, Haffer identified areas where the forest would have remained. Like islands surrounded by a sea of grass, these expanses of rain forest would have been the only places where toucanets could have survived.

Initially, these islands would have hosted the same original species of toucanet. But as time went by, the birds in each island would have evolved in slightly different ways, so they came to look and behave differently. When each glaciation ended, and the climate grew more damp, the islands expanded, taking their toucanets with them. Eventually, after this process had been repeated several times, the toucanets bore the imprint of their prolonged separation. Unable to interbreed, they remain distinct species to this day.

MYSTERIES FROM THE SOUTH

Long before the most recent glaciation, and indeed before the first trees appeared on our planet, an even more powerful force for change was already at work. One

STUDYING POLLEN

To produce seeds, conifers and broad leaved trees make immense quantities of pollen. Each pollen grain is a microscopic package of male cells, protected by a tough outer wall. This wall often has an intricate shape that varies between species, so pollen can be used to identify almost any kind of tree.

The study of pollen – called palynology – provides a detailed insight into the forests of the past.

Trees that are wind-pollinated often shed pollen onto the surface of nearby bogs and lakes, where the pollen grains become covered by peat or sediment. The pollen from insect-pollinated trees can also be preserved in the same way. Hundreds or thousands of years after the pollen has been shed, palynologists only need to retrieve a small amount of peat or sediment to see exactly which trees once lived in the area.

To establish when any particular tree existed, the pollen must be dated. To estimate the absolute age of pollen, a technique called radio-carbon dating is used. This compares the ratios of two forms of carbon that are found in living things – carbon-12 and carbon-14.

Carbon-12 is stable, but carbon-14 changes into nitrogen at a slow but very precise rate, with exactly half its atoms being transformed every 5730 years. Living things are constantly exchanging carbon with their surroundings, taking it in by photosynthesis (in plants) or food (in animals) and giving it out – in the form of carbon dioxide – when they break down substances to release energy. This exchange keeps their carbon ratio stable. When pollen is buried, this exchange process stops. The pollen's carbon-12 remains unaltered, but the carbon-14 changes without being replaced. By measuring the ratio of the two forms of carbon, the age of the pollen can be gauged.

UNDER THE MICROSCOPE
A mixed group of pollen grains (left) has an immense variety of shapes. Magnified about 12 500 times, a single grain (below) reveals a precise structure.

of its effects – the close fit between the coastlines of South America and Africa — was spotted as far back as 1620, but more than 300 years were to pass before this strange correspondence was finally explained. In the intervening time, naturalists began to explore some of the world's most remote places, and made detailed records of what they found. Amid wave after wave of biological discovery, some puzzling and awkward observations slowly came to light.

When the first European settlers arrived in New Zealand, they found forests that contained several species of southern beech (*Nothofagus*). There is nothing particularly unusual about these attractive broad-leaved trees, except for one remarkable fact. Similar trees, although of different species, also grow in Australia and New Guinea, and further species – with the same unmistakable characteristics – are found in far-off Chile, on the other side of the Pacific Ocean.

Southern beeches are not the only plants to be spread out in such a strange way. Shrubs called proteas are found only in the continents of the Southern Hemisphere, while rush-like plants called *Leptocarpus* are found only in Australasia, Malaysia and South America. None of these plants produces seeds that survive well at sea, and there are no fossil remains suggesting that they spread via continents farther north. How, then, did they become so strangely scattered?

In *The Origin of Species*, published in 1859, the English biologist Charles Darwin tackled this problem, and came tantalisingly close to the answer. Drawing on the theory of Ice Ages, then still in its infancy, he wrote: 'I am inclined to look . . . to a former and warmer period before the last glacial period, when the Antarctic lands, now covered

FLOWERS FROM THE SOUTH
*The scarlet banksia, a
striking member of the
protea family, is found in
western Australia.*

with ice, supported a peculiar and isolated flora.' He went on to speculate that some of the Antarctic's plant life may have spread north to the shores of the southern continents and the islands between them.

Darwin had no idea how the plants might have travelled, although he suggested 'occasional means of transport', meaning – for example – seeds floating on logs, or being carried on birds' feet. However, since his time, a very different explanation has become accepted.

RAFTS OF LIFE

Using lasers carried aboard satellites, geologists can now see daily evidence of the process that was once dismissed as impossible and preposterous. As the stream of data arrives on the ground for analysis, it confirms a startling and profoundly important fact – the Earth's continents are on the move. The movement is tiny, amounting to no more than $15/1000$ in (0.4 mm) each day. But this movement has carried on for so long that it has completely rearranged the Earth's surface. Continental drift is a continuous process, without a definite beginning or predictable end. Five hundred million years ago, there were four large continents, but by the time the first trees appeared these had coalesced into one. Since then, the single supercontinent has broken up, spawning new continents that have scattered and then collided, carrying their living passengers with them.

For plants and animals, the far Northern Hemisphere has been least affected by this majestic dance. Although an entirely new ocean – the Atlantic – has opened up in the past 200 million years, much of the far north has been connected by land bridges, allowing plants and animals to cross before spreading south. But in the Southern Hemisphere, the continents have burst apart, and the effects of this intercontinental explosion are still evident today.

DRIFTING WITH THE CONTINENTS

Primitive forest-floor animals called onychophorans look like worms with stubby feet, and have soft velvety skin. These unique forms of life have probably existed for over 500 million years, and may represent a 'missing link' between worms and the arthropods – more advanced animals that include spiders and insects. The present-day distribution of onychophorans shows how continental drift can scatter living things across the surface of the Earth. One group of onychophorans is found throughout the tropics, while another is found in the Southern Hemisphere, in places as far apart as Chile, South Africa, Australia and New Zealand. Onychophorans cannot travel over the sea, and the only plausible explanation for their distribution is that they spread when today's continents were joined in a single landmass.

Southern beeches and proteas developed in the south of the great supercontinent until that gradually tore itself apart. Some of them were rafted away aboard South America and Africa, while others travelled on a southern landmass that consisted of India, Antarctica and Australasia. When this in turn started to break up, Australasia and India slid northwards, carrying their plants and animals to warmer and drier climes. Antarctica, however, drifted south, following a course that brought a momentous change of climate. For a continent that had lush forests and teeming land animals, the journey had deadly results.

FAR-FLUNG RELATIVES *King
proteas, which grow on Table
Mountain in South Africa,
have many similarities with
the banksias in Australia.*

TEMPERATE 2 FORESTS

ON DISPLAY *A male Temmick's tragopan displays his lappet – a flap of skin – to attract females.*

TOUCHED NEITHER BY THE INSISTENT HEAT OF THE TROPICS, NOR BY THE PUNISHING COLD OF MUCH HIGHER LATITUDES, THE WORLD'S TEMPERATE REGIONS ARE HOME TO THE TALLEST AND MOST MASSIVE TREES ON OUR PLANET. TEMPERATE FORESTS ARE MOULDED BY THE YEARLY CYCLE OF THE SEASONS, AND THEIR ANIMAL INHABITANTS — FROM DEER AND BEARS TO CUCKOOS AND BUTTERFLIES — SYNCHRONISE THEIR LIVES WITH THE CHANGES AROUND THEM. MORE THAN ANY OTHER FORESTS, THOSE OF THE TEMPERATE WORLD HAVE BEEN PROFOUNDLY INFLUENCED BY HUMANS, BUT DESPITE THESE CHANGES THEY REMAIN NATURAL HAVENS FOR A WEALTH OF LIVING THINGS.

WINTER WARMTH *Japanese macaques huddle together.*

CRADLE OF GIANTS

In North America's far west, evergreen conifers flourish in the moist climate near the coast and in the sunshine on high mountains. This is the realm of the world's most spectacular trees and the animals that rely on them for food.

When seafarers from Portugal and Spain first set foot on the coast of northern California, in the middle of the 16th century, they encountered forests that staggered the imagination. Here were trees of almost unbelievable dimensions, with towering arrow-straight trunks, that were sometimes crammed together so closely that a man could not pass between them. On the ground, a deep carpet of dead leaves muffled the sound of moving feet, and the eerie silence was interrupted only by the occasional chirp of unseen birds, or by the sigh of the wind blowing in fog from the Pacific Ocean. To people accustomed to the bright sunlight of southern Europe or Mexico, it would have seemed an awe-inspiring and forbidding prospect.

Four centuries later, giant trees still grow along the coast of northern California. Many of the oldest have long since been lost to the saw, but in protected areas of forest, particularly where broad creeks provide deep soil and shelter from the wind, the largest survivors remain untouched. Known as coast redwoods (*Sequoia sempervirens*), these towering conifers often reach heights of over 300 ft (90 m) – the equivalent of a 20-floor building. What makes them even more striking is their slender profile and the fact that they are so impeccably perpendicular. Few are more than 12 ft (3.7 m) thick at the base, and whereas most conifer trunks display at least some irregularities, these seem to have followed some invisible plumb line in their growth towards the light.

The accolade of world's tallest tree has changed hands several times during the past two centuries, as new trees have been discovered, and as existing record-holders have either toppled over, or have shed crucial feet through the effects of wind, snow or old age. Most have been conifers, although a handful have been broad-leaved trees, and nearly all have been measured – with various degrees of precision – while still standing. However, to complicate matters, there have also been posthumous claims to the title. The height of some dead giants has been calculated by assessing old reports, or by measuring their shattered trunks after they have fallen to the ground.

Despite the scope for confusion, there is little doubt that coast redwoods currently hold the crown. The largest specimen in existence, in the Tall Trees Grove of the Redwood National Park, has reached 367 ft (112 m) after about 600 years of growth, and is still thriving. Coast redwoods have an average life span of about 800 years, but they can live for over two millennia. Given clement conditions in the years ahead – which are by no means guaranteed – today's record-breakers stand a real chance of breaching the 400 ft (122 m) mark.

FORESTS IN THE FOG

For many people, California is synonymous with sunshine. But while many conifers prosper in the brilliant sunlight of California's valleys and mountains, the coast redwood needs altogether gentler conditions. It is a lover of moisture and fertile soil, and through a unique combination of geography and geology, the coast of northern California provides both. The

HIGH-RISE FOREST *The spire-like crowns of coastal redwoods pierce the morning mist. Right: Tightly packed redwood trunks soar upwards towards the light. Unusually for conifers, they sometimes sprout ground-level shoots.*

redwood grows in a narrow band that stretches 500 miles (800 km) from north to south, and is rarely found more than about 30 miles (48 km) from the sea. This long and often rugged strip of North America lies at roughly the same latitude as the Mediterranean, and is backed by a hinterland where summer temperatures can soar to over 38°C (100°F). But along the coast, the climate could hardly be more different. Winter often brings heavy rain, and in summer, when the rest of California basks in the heat, the sun is often nowhere to be seen.

The progenitor of these sun-starved conditions lies out in the ocean, in the form of a current that drags cold water down from the North Pacific. In summer, the ocean chills the air that blows onshore, condensing its moisture into dense banks of fog that steal inland under the cover of darkness. On some days the sun burns away the fog by early afternoon, but on others the fog remains all day, cloaking the coast in a damp embrace.

Everything that the fog touches – from leaves and bark to birds' nests and spiders' webs – becomes spangled with beads of moisture, and throughout the coastal forest, redwood trunks are streaked by fog-borne water starting its short journey back to the sea. For the redwoods, and for the mosses and ferns that grow beneath them, this summer fog is the key to survival and growth. Without it, they would be exposed to the full strength of the sun, and their growth would soon be checked by drought.

A TALE OF TWO LIVES

Trees and understorey plants are not the only forest inhabitants that flourish in this damp regime. For the forest's amphibians, which include tree frogs and salamanders, constant moisture is essential. Many adult amphibians breathe partly or wholly through their skin, which is paper-thin, and through the lining of their mouths. This unusual kind of breathing works well in damp conditions, but if an amphibian becomes exposed to bright sunshine and starts to dry out, its life is soon in danger.

CALIFORNIA'S REDWOODS The coast redwood forms a band of forest near the Pacific Ocean, while the giant sequoia grows only on the slopes of the Sierra Nevada, in scattered groves.

SLOW MOVER The California slender salamander hauls itself along on tiny limbs. To move more quickly, it folds its legs and flicks its body and tail.

With a body up to 12 in (30 cm) in length, the Pacific giant salamander (*Dicamptodon ensatus*) is a relative heavyweight among these creatures of the redwood forests. Like other salamanders, it has a roughly cylindrical body slung between spindly legs, and slender toes that give it a good grip on bark and wood. It spends most of the day hidden under rotting logs and bark, where its dark colour helps to keep it concealed.

When night falls, or when the daytime fog is particularly thick, the salamander emerges from its damp lair in search of food, moving slowly and deliberately over the forest floor. Although it is principally a ground-dweller, it can climb up shrubs or over fallen tree-trunks, and can sometimes be spotted at head height, where a partly fallen tree gives it an easy path upwards. Its food includes slugs, snails and insects, but it also relishes many of its own smaller relatives. One species that sometimes crosses its path is the California slender salamander (*Batrachoseps attenuatus*), a pencil-thin animal that wriggles like a snake when it needs to move at speed. Even with the help of this unusual trick, it is no match for its giant relative, which can catch and swallow it in a matter of seconds.

Like frogs and toads, the majority of

Map

OREGON

IDAHO

NEVADA

COAST RANGES

SIERRA NEVADA

San Francisco

CALIFORNIA

Los Angeles

■ Coast Redwood

■ Giant Sequoia

MEXICO

salamanders spend the first part of their lives in pools or streams, where they breathe through feathery gills. Towards the end of its watery childhood, which can last for two or three years, a young salamander sheds its gills and loses the flattened webbing along its tail that helps it to swim. Suitably modified, it is ready for life on land.

This change of shape, like the transformation of a tadpole into a frog, is an example of metamorphosis – a remarkable sequence of events during which the body slowly reshapes itself to suit it to an entirely different way of life. However, not every salamander divides its life between water and land in this way. Like some forest frogs and toads, there are salamanders that have evolved quite different cycles of life.

At one extreme, the California slender salamander misses out the aquatic stage altogether, and lays its eggs under rocks and logs, where damp air keeps them moist. Its young do not have gills, and they spend the whole of their lives on land. At the other extreme, some salamanders sidestep the terrestrial stage and spend all their lives in water. They keep their immature bodies, complete with gills, and become able to reproduce without ever leaving the water.

The Pacific giant salamander is one of these 'Peter Pan' amphibians. In some parts of its range, practically all individuals become adults in the normal way. However, in others, a substantial proportion never truly grow up, and instead remain in water for the whole of their lives.

This form of arrested development, called neoteny, is found in several branches of the animal world, but amphibians specialise in it to an unusual extent. Like gamblers that leave the table instead of doubling their stake, the Peter Pan adults avoid both the rewards and the dangers of life beyond their freshwater home.

EXPLOSIVE SONGSTERS

During the middle of the day, a redwood forest can seem a place of unsettling stillness. Although there is life on the forest floor, particularly in open glades where wild flowers attract visiting insects, little seems to be on the move. In the depth of the forest, where dense trunks screen out most of the light, it is easy to feel that nature has concentrated all its energy into giant trees, leaving little for anything else.

Such an impression is often shattered by the explosive song of one of North America's smallest and noisiest birds. Fluttering to the top of a small sapling or dead

---

SOUTHERN TEMPERATE RAIN FORESTS

In rain forests, rainfall is so heavy and evenly spread that the growth of trees is never checked by drought. These conditions extend far inland in the tropics, but in temperate regions they occur only on coasts that are drenched by moisture-laden winds. True temperate rain forests exist only in three places – the American north-west, southern Chile and New Zealand's South Island – but forests that are almost as wet can be found in other regions, including the east coast of the Black Sea and parts of Japan.

The Magellanic rain forest, in southern Chile, grows among some of the wildest and most dramatic scenery in South America. The mountainous coast is flanked by a jigsaw of jagged islands, separated by deep and tortuous fiords. It was through these fiords that the survey ship HMS *Beagle*, carrying the young Charles Darwin – who was later to develop the theory of evolution – threaded its way in 1834.

Darwin was deeply impressed by the region's forests, and wrote that they closely rivalled anything he had seen in the tropics. Today, the cloud-draped hillsides are clothed by a mantle of uniquely southern trees, including southern beeches (*Nothofagus*), the prickly leaved Chile pine or monkey puzzle (*Araucaria araucana*) and the Patagonian cypress (*Fitzroya cupressoides*), which can live to be over 2000 years old. The wildlife of the forest includes the widespread mountain lion (*Felis concolor*) and its much rarer relative the kodkod (*Felis guigna*), a little-known nocturnal cat that measures about 2 ft (61 cm) from head to tail.

Across the other side of the Pacific Ocean, but at exactly the same latitude, the precipitous coast of New Zealand's Fiordland drops almost vertically into the sea. Rainfall often totals 240 in (6100 mm) a year, making this one of the wettest places on Earth. As in Chile, southern beeches are common, but here they grow alongside New Zealand specialities such as the southern rata (*Metrosideros umbellata*), one of a group of trees with brilliant red, brush-like flowers.

With its rugged terrain, Fiordland has escaped the deforestation and replanting that has affected much of the rest of New Zealand. It is one of the last strongholds of several native birds, including one species of kiwi (*Apteryx*), which has recently been named the tokoeka, and the South Island weka (*Gallirallus australis*). All three are flightless, and are threatened by mammalian predators that have been introduced from other parts of the world.

FIGHTING BACK *With its strong beak, the chicken-sized weka can kill predatory mammals.*

branch on small whirring wings, the 4 in (10 cm) winter wren (*Troglodytes troglodytes*) delivers a burst of high-pitched sound that would not disgrace a bird many times its size. This diminutive insect-eater, with its streaked brown plumage and jauntily cocked tail, is scattered throughout damp coniferous forests in North America, but is particularly abundant among the redwoods. It is also found in Europe and Asia, and has the distinction of being the only wren – out of a total of 69 species – that has managed to reach beyond the Americas.

The winter wren is a bird of the forest understorey. It scuttles through the thickets of Pacific rhododendron (*Rhododendron macrophyllum*) and western azalea (*Rhododendron occidentale*) with great agility, often looking more like a mouse than a bird. But to broadcast his territorial claims to other wrens, the male leaves the protection of the dense understorey and flies upwards, resting on a perch where his song can be heard far and wide. At all other times, he is practically invisible.

In colonising different habitats across the Northern Hemisphere, the winter wren has had to evolve ways of coping with a range of different climates. In the redwood forests of California, the climate is mild enough for it to be a year-round resident, while in eastern forests it migrates southwards to escape the bitter winter weather. In most parts of Europe, it is also a year-round resident, but here the strategy of staying put is not always so successful. Prolonged cold can be fatal to a bird whose body weighs less than $1/2$ oz (15 g), because its heat soon drains away to the air outside. Despite crowding together to roost in tree-holes or nest-boxes, many wrens fail to see the spring after a succession of hard frosts. However, for the species as a whole, the tragedy is short-lived. Wrens can raise up to four broods of young in a single breeding season, so within two years of a severe winter, its population can be back to normal.

LIFE IN THE HIGH TREETOPS

Like fish swimming in the surface waters of the sea, the animals of the redwood canopy often have little contact with those on the forest floor. Theirs is a very different world, bounded by the lowest living branches, often up to 100 ft (30 m) above the ground, and by the sky above. Such is the height of the redwoods that even the climate differs between the upper canopy and the ground. The fog often slides inland from low ground upwards, so the treetops can be in clear sunlight, while the regions below are shrouded in a damp gloom.

In this three-dimensional maze of gently sloping branches, the redwood's leaves and seeds provide food for a host of insects – particularly moth caterpillars – and also for many birds and some remarkable 'flying' mammals which glide between the trees. But for a tree that attracts superlatives, the redwood's flattened needles are of surprisingly modest dimensions, rarely exceeding 1 in (2.5 cm) in length. Its winged seeds, which grow in small barrel-shaped cones, are far smaller still, and contain only a small store of food to sustain life once they have been shed. But what the tree's leaves and seeds lack in size, they make up for in abundance.

Flitting among the redwood's branches, the chestnut-backed chickadee (*Parus rufescens*) benefits from the redwood's bounty at second or third hand. This ceaselessly active member of the tit family searches out leaf-eating caterpillars, and also small spiders that trap airborne insects. With the agility of an acrobat, it hangs from the thinnest twigs, and rapidly checks the undersides of its leaves before moving on. Like the winter wren , the chickadee's small body burns up food at a rapid rate, and it

TREETOP COMPANIONS
A nuthatch, two warblers and a chickadee search for food high in the branches of a coast redwood.

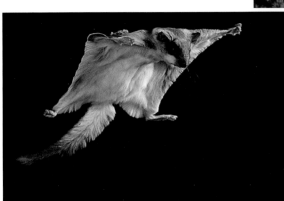

NIGHT FLIGHT *The northern flying squirrel is nocturnal, and 'flies' only after sunset. Right: giant sequoias provide food for the squirrel and its non-gliding relatives.*

has to feed almost nonstop during daylight hours to avoid starvation.

On its journey through the canopy, the chickadee is often joined by other small insect-eaters, including kinglets (*Regulus* sp.), warblers (*Dendroica* sp.) and nuthatches (*Sitta* sp.), which also follow a free-ranging life in the treetops. In autumn and winter months, these birds often form mixed flocks containing several dozen individuals, drawn from five or six species. As the birds move about, they make sharp chirps, known as contact calls, which enable them to move on as a group. On the floor of the forest, these sounds, filtered into faintness by the overlapping branches, are often the only sign that the birds are feeding high above.

Such mixed flocks of small insect-eaters are a common feature of temperate woodlands, and ornithologists have long wondered why they form. The most likely explanation is that group foraging helps the birds to feed more efficiently when food is in short supply, because it increases their chances of finding food and escaping their enemies.

To test out this idea, two almost identical areas of North American forest were once selected for observation during the winter months, with one being artificially stocked with extra food, and the other left

untouched. Mixed flocks formed only in the area with less food, suggesting that the birds banded together only when they were unable to feed well enough on their own.

FURRED FLIERS

It comes as no surprise that a bird like the chickadee should display such confidence when feeding several hundred feet above the ground. But in the redwood forests, a small number of mammals also climb the trees to feed at these dizzying heights, apparently risking all if they miss their footing. One of them, the Douglas squirrel (*Tamiasciurus douglasii*), relies entirely on its sure-footedness to reach its food and escape enemies, scampering up and down the redwood trunks with great alacrity, and using its rear claws as anchors as it descends. Its distant relative, the northern flying squirrel (*Glaucomys sabrinus*), also lives among the redwoods, but its method of moving about is startlingly different.

'Flying' squirrels are found in forests in many parts of the world, but despite their name, none actually fly. Instead, they glide, using flaps of loose skin that stretch between each front and back leg. When opened out, these flaps – together with the flattened tail – act as a sail, allowing the squirrel to slide through the air

Female cones

Male cones

from one tree to another, sometimes travelling over 150 ft (45 m) in a single 'flight'.

If flying squirrels did not exist, their method of locomotion would probably be dismissed as impossible. Because the squirrel has only limited powers of steering, using its legs and tail, it has to commit itself

---

THE MYSTERIOUS MURRELET

In 1974, an unusual nest was discovered over 100 ft (30 m) up in a tree growing several miles inland in California's Santa Cruz Mountains. It turned out to be a unique find – the first recorded nest of the marbled murrelet (*Brachyrhamphus marmoratus*), a small sea bird that lives only in the North Pacific. The murrelet belongs to the auk family, which also contains guillemots and puffins. Most of its relatives nest among coastal rocks or in clifftop burrows, but the murrelet flies inland under the cover of darkness, to breed in coniferous forest. Fewer than a dozen nests have since been discovered in eastern Siberia and Alaska.

---

to a specific target before take-off, and must jump in exactly the right direction, without snagging any obstacles on the way. It also has to brake its glide in midair, by altering the angle of its body, so that it can land on the target tree without being smashed to pieces.

Amazingly, the flying squirrel can accomplish all this in a matter of seconds. When threatened by danger, it escapes by

GIANT COUSINS *Coast redwoods (left) have spreading leaves, small cones and relatively thin bark. Giant sequoias (right) have remarkably small leaves, but their cones are larger and their bark much thicker.*

repeatedly gliding, stowing its 'wings', climbing up from its landing point, and then gliding once more. Zigzagging vertically through the forest in this way, it provides a moving target that few predators can begin to follow.

REFUGE OF THE GIANTS

Through a remarkable biological coincidence, coast redwoods are not the only forest record-breakers in California. However, in order to encounter the others, one must journey eastwards, away from the fogbound coast and into the distant foothills of the Sierra Nevada. Here, on the sun-bathed slopes of North America's rocky spine, an ancient lineage of trees has found a final refuge in a world that has slowly turned against it.

Often known simply as 'big trees', giant sequoias (*Sequoiadendron giganteum*) are frequently confused with their lofty cousins from the coast. While both belong to the same family of conifers – the redwoods – their differences are unmistakable. The two trees have very different foliage – the giant sequoia's leaves being short and scaly, while the coast redwood's are longer and more spreading – and their bark is different in both colour and texture. However, far more striking than this is their difference in build.

Female cones

Male cones

While the coast redwood impresses with its extraordinary combination of tremendous height and sparing build, the giant sequoia astonishes with its massive and overwhelming bulk.

Giant sequoias grow in scattered open groves mixed with other trees, rather than in dense stands, so their colossal dimensions can often be taken in with a single sweep of the eye. One of the tallest of these leviathans, the General Sherman tree, is 'only' 275 ft (84 m) high, but its diameter is so great that it would take more than two dozen adults, with hands linked, to encircle it at the base. Even when it has reached a height of 100 ft (30 m), its trunk is thicker than the biggest coast redwoods, and it is still several feet across just beneath its tip, where it ends abruptly in a pyramid of tortuous branches bearing sprays of blue-green leaves. Although its wood is relatively light, its living fusion of height and breadth gives it a total weight of about 2500 tons, making it by far the heaviest single organism on Earth. By comparison, a blue whale – weighing in at just over 150 tons – seems like a mere plaything.

RISING FROM THE ASHES

When 19th-century lumber teams first came to grips with these mammoth trees, they made a curious discovery. Although it could take up to three weeks to cut through the largest trunks – using muscle power alone – the first part of the work was easy. A saw-

AFTER A FIRE *A giant redwood is scarred by fire, but has survived. Right: A redwood seedling sprouts among fallen cones and charred wood.*

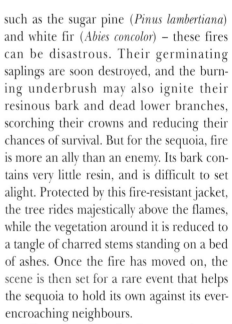

blade would sink up to 2 ft (60 cm) into the trunk with relatively little effort, only then slowing up as it bit into firmer material within.

This abrupt change marks the boundary between the sequoia's spongy red-brown bark and its living wood. As the felled giants revealed, sequoia bark is immensely thick. A young sapling is only sparingly clad, and its bark feels quite compact. But as the tree grows taller and broader, its bark quickly becomes thicker and also softer – so much so that one can punch it with only minor ill-effects to one's hand.

For most trees, bark doubles up as a moisture-retaining jacket and a barrier against animals and fungi. But for the giant sequoia, it has another and even more important function. On the slopes of the sierra, summer often brings day after day of brilliant sunshine, and the dead wood and leaves that accumulate in the groves become brittle and bone-dry. Fanned by the mountain breeze, a single lightning strike from a dry storm is enough to send fire racing across the hillside.

For the sequoia's neighbours – trees such as the sugar pine (*Pinus lambertiana*) and white fir (*Abies concolor*) – these fires can be disastrous. Their germinating saplings are soon destroyed, and the burning underbrush may also ignite their resinous bark and dead lower branches, scorching their crowns and reducing their chances of survival. But for the sequoia, fire is more an ally than an enemy. Its bark contains very little resin, and is difficult to set alight. Protected by this fire-resistant jacket, the tree rides majestically above the flames, while the vegetation around it is reduced to a tangle of charred stems standing on a bed of ashes. Once the fire has moved on, the scene is then set for a rare event that helps the sequoia to hold its own against its ever-encroaching neighbours.

Like coast redwoods, giant sequoias produce tiny seeds, each weighing just $1/5000$ oz (0.005 g). The seeds can germinate only in open ground, but all too often they fall into dense underbrush, where they eke out their tiny store of food reserves until they perish. Although a mature sequoia can produce over a million seeds a year, their mortality is so great that few – if any – survive.

When a summer fire sweeps under a sequoia, columns of searingly hot air rise

FOREST ABLAZE *In the west of America, forest fires occur naturally. Prevention can let a store of dead wood build up – with dangerous results.*

HEAVYWEIGHT CLIMBER
Despite its size, the black bear is a good climber. It grips tree-trunks with its sharp claws and keeps its head uppermost.

through its outer cone-bearing branches. The cones, some of which may have been in place for over ten years, respond as if to a starter's gun. During the following days their scales dry out and begin to open, releasing a shower of seeds that flutter onto the ground below. Arriving on a ready-cleared seedbed, complete with a layer of ash as fertiliser, they germinate in their thousands, and a new generation of sequoias is born.

The giant sequoia is one of a number of North American conifers that depend on fires to check invasive competitors. Some are simply better at surviving the flames than their rivals, but others, such as the lodgepole pine (*Pinus contorta*), shed their seeds only when their cones are exposed to intense heat.

As might be expected, most of these trees live in dry places, where natural fires are common. However, evidence from tree growth rings shows that fire acts as a natural 'weeder' even in wet areas, such as the coast

ELUSIVE HUNTER *Keen eyesight makes the mountain lion or cougar an effective nocturnal predator. Most of its kills are made at night.*

of northern California. Here, naturally occurring fires – separated by centuries rather than by decades – have helped to shape the forests that exist today.

WOODLAND WANDERERS

In the course of a year, the Sierra Nevada's big trees experience some testing extremes of climate. Little rain falls during the summer, and the sequoias rely on winter snow for their survival. The snow, when it comes, can be a mixed blessing. Although it brings much-needed moisture, branches often collapse under its weight. Giant sequoias have shallow roots, and a heavy snowfall, combined with strong winds, can sometimes bring them crashing to the ground.

For the largest mammals of the sierra, spring is a spur to leave lower ground and climb up to the level of the sequoia groves or beyond. The adaptable American black bear (*Ursus americanus*) is as much at home among the sequoias as it is in the swamps of Florida, or the forests of the far north. Males and females come together only to mate, but at other times, adult bears – which can measure up to 3 ft (91 cm) at the shoulder – are solitary animals, feeding mainly under the cover of darkness.

Female black bears usually give birth to either two or three cubs in a winter den, which she hollows out under the roots of a large tree or a fallen trunk. For such a large animal, the cubs are tiny, each weighing

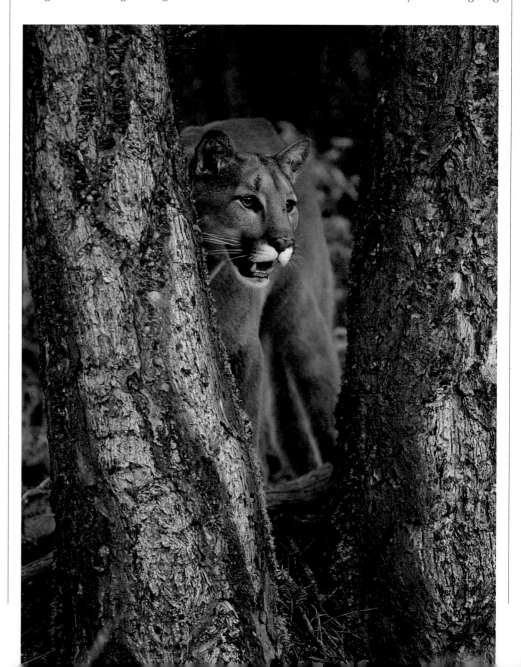

only about ¹/₁₀₀₀ as much as their mother. Initially, the cubs are blind and naked, and are capable of little more than suckling their mother's milk. But their growth is rapid. Within a month their eyes open, and within three months they are ready to take their first steps outside. Once spring is under way and the cubs are able to walk and run, the mother leads her young family uphill.

Like all bears, the American black bear is a general feeder, taking whatever it can find, from fruit and honey to young birds and small mammals. Its eyesight and hearing are unexceptional, and instead it relies mainly on smell to track down a meal. Sequoias have little to offer the bear, but the animals that live among them, which include climbing squirrels, chipmunks (*Eutamias* sp.) and tiny deer mice (*Peromyscus maniculatus*), provide it with a welcome supply of food. Using power instead of speed, the bear often tracks its prey to a burrow or nest, which it digs out or breaks open.

In the mountain forests of California, the black bear has no enemies except man. However, its position as an unchallenged predator is a relatively new one. At one time, brown bears (*Ursus arctos*) also roamed the sequoia belt, and in any meeting between the two species, there were no friendly feelings prompted by a shared ancestry. Instead, black bears were often attacked and eaten by their larger relatives. Since those times, hunters have eradicated the brown bear in this part of the world, and the black bear has taken advantage of its former enemy's disappearance to spread beyond its original range.

CATS OF THE SIERRA

While the black bear is an opportunist, ready to take anything that comes its way, another large carnivore of the sierra slopes behaves very differently. In contrast with the bear's ambling and sometimes noisy walk, with its frequent pauses and diversions, this hunter moves silently and deliberately, and focuses all its attention on tracking down large, living prey.

Despite its name, the mountain lion (*Felis concolor*) – also known as the cougar

or puma – is neither a lion nor a purely mountain animal. Even though it can measure up to 7 ft (2 m) from head to tail, and is the second largest cat in the Americas after the jaguar, the structure of its teeth and skeleton shows that its closest relatives are small cats rather than big ones. It is found only in the New World, but its range runs from Canada to Chile and Argentina, and it survives in habitats as different as tropical swamps and mountain forests.

The mountain lion will eat small animals, such as squirrels and porcupines, but it is predominantly a hunter of deer. In the Sierra Nevada, its prey is almost always the mule deer (*Odocoileus hemionus*), the only species that is widespread throughout the American west. The mule deer has a very keen sense of smell, so the mountain lion stalks its prey from downwind, eventually bursting out from cover and killing by leaping onto its victim's back and using both its teeth and claws as weapons.

A fully grown male deer can weigh twice as much as its attacker, and provides the mountain lion with far more food than it can eat at one sitting. Like many of its relatives, the mountain lion solves this problem by dragging the remains away to make a hidden food store. The cat visits the carcass over a period of several days, but abandons it once the meat begins to decompose.

The mountain lion's nocturnal habits and its justified fear of humans mean that it is rarely seen. In the same way, the smaller bobcat (*Felis rufus*) also takes great care to keep itself hidden. Unlike the mountain lion, which has spotted fur

ON THE ALERT *For the mule or blacktail deer, constant vigilance is the price of survival. Its large ears pick up sounds that could spell danger.*

only as a cub, the bobcat keeps its spots for life. It also has two distinctive features – small ear tufts and a stump-like tail – which show that it is a close relative of the lynx (*Felis lynx*) of northern forests. Bobcats feed mainly on birds and rodents, although small deer also feature in its diet. Unusually for a cat, it also shows no hesitation in eating the remains of animals that it has not killed itself.

TEMPERATE RAIN FOREST

To most people, the term rain forest provokes images of luxurious vegetation bathed in tropical heat, where brilliantly coloured birds fly over an unbroken canopy of green. While most rain forests are indeed like this, there are a few places on Earth

where rain forest of a very different kind can be found. One of them lies about 700 miles (1125 km) north-west of California's sequoia groves, on the west-facing slopes of the Olympic Peninsula.

Rising to nearly 8000 ft (2440 m), Mount Olympus stands like a jagged sentinel over the strait that divides the United States from Canada. This isolated coastal peak intercepts humid air blowing in from the Pacific, forcing it upwards and wringing out its moisture before allowing it to continue its journey inland. So efficient is this rain-making monolith that the mountain's western slopes receive over 144 in (3650 mm) of rain a year, while the low ground to the east gets as little as 18 in (460 mm).

The effect of this year-round downpour is dramatic. Nurtured by almost limitless rain, immense conifers, including western hemlocks (*Tsuga heterophylla*), Douglas firs (*Pseudotsuga menziesii*) and sitka spruces (*Picea sitchensis*) soar upwards, reaching heights of over 200 ft (60 m). Scattered among the upright trees, listing giants slump against their neighbours, while on the ground, massive logs – some shoulder-high – lie in every conceivable stage of decay. Wherever the eye settles, from the forest floor to the canopy above, the impression is one of centuries of growth, dripping water and endless green. With every available surface – bark, twigs and fallen logs – covered by a living blanket of mosses, trailing lichens and ferns, comparisons with the tropics are almost irresistible.

So how does this unique type of forest compare with its counterparts in much warmer parts of the world? As anyone who visits both will discover, the two are actually very different. A single acre (0.4 ha) of tropical rain forest may be home to over 100 species of trees that can reach canopy height, while its temperate counterpart may have as few as six, with perhaps one or two species dominating extensive areas. The

IN THE RAIN FOREST
Swathed in mosses and ferns, trees reach upwards in the Olympic Peninsula's Hoh Valley.

MOLLUSC ON THE MOVE
Slithering over the rain forest floor, a banana slug searches for food. Each slug has its own pattern of dark spots.

tropical acre will often contain dozens of species of birds, a wide variety of reptiles and amphibians, and a range of insect life that is too vast to be catalogued. Again, the temperate rain forest comes a poor second.

But what the temperate rain forest lacks in variety, it makes up for in quantity. Area for area, its biomass – a measure of its total mass of living things – is often greater than tropical rain forest, and rapid growth makes it one of the most biologically productive habitats in the world.

WILDLIFE OF THE WET FOREST

The north-western rain forest is a habitat that offers animals almost unlimited concealment at all times of the year. While the silence is often interrupted by the hammering of woodpeckers or the scolding calls of squirrels, clear views of forest wildlife come only to those armed with patience. Black bears live on the Olympic Peninsula, as does an unusually large form of the elk or wapiti (*Cervus elaphus*) – known in Europe as the red deer – but both are alert to the slightest hint of human approach.

One animal that visitors often do encounter on forest trails – with mixed feelings – is the banana slug (*Ariolimax columbianus*), a spotted yellow or green mollusc that measures up to 8 in (20 cm) in length. Using waves of muscle contraction, the slug creeps forwards on a sucker-like

foot lubricated with sticky mucus, searching out plants and fungi on the forest floor. Slugs do not have jaws, and they eat their food with the help of a tongue-like organ, called a radula, which is equipped with many rows of tiny teeth. Instead of biting, the slug rasps its way through its food.

A slug's bare skin, and its constant output of fluid, means that it can only risk venturing out from its shelter – usually under logs – in damp conditions. Slugs in many parts of the world have to hide away when the weather turns dry, but in the temperate rain forest, the banana slug is rarely troubled by this problem. On its forays over the forest floor, it finds its way with the help of two pairs of tentacles. It uses its small lower tentacles to test the ground ahead, while its upper tentacles each bear a rudimentary eye that enables the slug to tell whether it is moving towards or away from the light. A light tap with a twig triggers the slug's defences – it withdraws its tentacles and hunches up its body. If it is above ground level, it will often loosen its footing and tumble into the concealing undergrowth.

NURSERY LOGS

One of the most striking sights in the north-western rain forest is that of gigantic trees, perhaps 200 to 300 years old, straddling

fallen logs on the woodland floor. Each tree perches on its log like some outsize rider on horseback. Some sit square on, with their roots clasping their mount, but others seem to be riding sidesaddle, with a thick mass of roots reaching down one side of the log, but none on the other. Up to half a dozen trees may sit on the same fallen trunk, while in some places, trees in ruler-straight lines show where a log once existed and then rotted away.

This curious phenomenon is peculiar to this type of forest, and is the result of intense competition for light on the forest floor. When the giant conifers shed their seeds, most of them drop among the crowded mosses and ferns, where they face a formidable battle for survival. Not only is light in short supply in these conditions, but nutrients are often hard to come by, because the seeds may be trapped some distance above the ground.

When a seed flutters down onto a fallen log, it finds an environment of a subtly different kind. Here the plant layer is often

STANDING IN LINE *These young spruce and hemlock trees are growing on a nursery log. The log will decompose and eventually disappear.*

thinner and more broken, and there are no shading shrubs. The rotting log is rich in mineral nutrients, and its crumbling wood acts like a giant sponge, soaking up a vast quantity of water. The seed rapidly germinates, and within a few years sends its first fine roots down to the forest floor. It then begins the slow process of stepping off its 'nursery log' and onto the ground that lies beneath it.

Nursery logs can be immensely ancient. The ones that lie under today's giant trees are themselves the remains of trees that died many centuries ago. Beneath them, long ago dismantled by the processes of decay, are the remains of the logs that nursed them into life, stretching back not just over centuries, but millennia.

OLD GROWTH

With its seemingly chaotic mixture of giant trees, fallen trunks and open spaces, the north-western rain forest is a classic example of climax vegetation – a self-perpetuating world where, over a vast expanse of time, competing species have reached a stand-off in the struggle for survival. For the naturalist, this 'old growth' forest has an inescapable allure. The urge to explore is irresistible, because despite its simple composition, no two parts of it are ever quite the same.

At one time, old growth rain forest covered much of the Olympic Peninsula, and equally ancient forests, growing in slightly drier conditions, blanketed the whole of the Pacific north-west. However, like the redwood forests farther south, their trees have enormous value as timber, and entire mountainsides have been stripped of their original forest.

On Mount Olympus, only three specially protected valleys retain rain forest in its untouched state, and throughout the mountainous north-west, much of the original forest has been cut down and replanted. The new forests can look similar from a distance – ignoring their chequerboard outlines – and because they contain only young trees, they grow with even greater vigour. However, they are far more uniform, because all their trees are of the same age and species. Most have a planned life of

just 75 years, after which they will all be cut down, leaving the area clear to be replanted once more.

Some animals are able to live in both types of forest, although old growth usually suits them better. A few – including deer – even fare better shortly after replanting, because huge expanses of saplings are then theirs for the eating. But for other species, including bats, voles and many birds, the planted forest, with its shortage of light gaps and dead wood, is a difficult place in which to set up home. The 20 in (50 cm) spotted owl (*Strix occidentalis*) is without doubt the most famous casualty of felling and replanting.

One of the rarest of North America's owls, it lives from southern Canada to Mexico, but once had its stronghold in the north-west. The owl depends on old growth

OWL IN PERIL *The unwitting focus of a conservation debate, a spotted owl perches on a branch draped with hanging lichen.*

forest, and is unable to survive where its original habitat has been altered. It has become a symbol for conservationists wishing to protect these ancient forests, and a legal tripwire for those wishing to open them up for felling.

At present, perhaps one-fifth of North America's western forest – its cradle of giants – remains uncut, with the temperate rain forest making up a tiny but unique fraction of this whole. Its trees include some of the most majestic on the planet. With careful conservation, the new century will see them staying that way.

THE WORLD OF
BROAD-LEAVED WOODLAND

Luxuriant in summer, gaunt and bare in winter, deciduous broad-leaved trees are always in a state of change. The sudden flush of growth in spring provides opportunities for animal life, while the autumn heralds hardship to come.

On a summer's afternoon in the heart of the English countryside, a gentle breeze briefly stirs the languid air. High in the canopy of an old oakwood, two male purple emperor butterflies (*Apatura iris*), clashing for supremacy in the treetops, break off their spiralling upward flight, and drop back towards the protection of the trees. Below them, a young chiffchaff (*Phylloscopus collybita*) fleetingly pauses in its search for insects. Sensing perhaps that the weather is soon to change, it feels the first hint of an instinctive restlessness that will eventually carry it far away.

And with this slight breath of wind comes a small event laden with great significance. Among the wealth of greenery, a scattering of yellow leaves, their useful lives now past, are tugged by the breeze, and snap away to zigzag unhurriedly towards the ground. Although it is only late August, the subtle approach of autumn has begun.

LOSING LEAVES

During the height of summer, a mature English oak (*Quercus robur*) may bear over $1/4$ million leaves. Each one is a self-supporting solar panel, crafted from the minimum amount of building materials, and equipped with a battery of defences against hungry insects. Week after week, the leaves soak up the summer sunshine, using it to drive chemical processes that fashion flowers, acorns and iron-hard wood from the simplest of raw materials.

But as the summer slips away, and autumn drifts towards winter, the very features that make oak leaves so efficient threaten to become severe liabilities. Even in summer storms, a large-leaved oak is like a gigantic sailing ship straining at its moorings, with its branches like masts creaking under the strain. If the same tree were to ride out winter blizzards in full foliage, it would run the very real risk of being ripped apart.

Even if it could withstand this onslaught, another and more subtle problem

COLOURS OF AUTUMN *As the days shorten, the green pigment in leaves breaks down, and other colours are revealed before the leaves fall.*

DRIVING LIGHT *A shaft of sunlight spills through the canopy of a British beech wood and illuminates fallen leaves on the woodland floor.*

Because the Earth's continents are unevenly spread, the two temperate zones – one in each hemisphere – cover very different amounts of land. The northern temperate zone includes vast tracts of North America, Europe and Asia, but its southern counterpart covers just a small part of South America, some of southern Africa, and southernmost Australasia. This top-heavy distribution of land means that temperate forests, too, are unevenly distributed. The overwhelming bulk of temperate woodlands are found in northern latitudes, with much smaller areas in places such as Chile and New Zealand, thousands of miles away to the south.

The summer thirst of deciduous trees means that they can grow only where rainfall is reliable. Some species, such as beeches, are able to survive on drier, chalky ground, but the most impressive broad-leaved woodlands are found where the soil is deep and damp. In parts of the temperate world where summers are hot and dry, such as the Mediterranean region, broad-leaved trees can be found, but most of them are evergreen. Unlike their cousins in cooler climates, these trees – which include the stately holm oak (*Quercus ilex*) – have small, leathery leaves that are much better at withstanding the effects of the burning summer sun.

Where the climate is even more extreme, for example in mountains or on the threshold of the far north, broad-leaved trees begin to give way to conifers, which are much better at withstanding harsh conditions. The first sign that this change is taking place is the appearance of mixed forest, which contains both broad-leaved trees

lies in store. Unlike conifers, the oak is lavish in its use of water. It can soak up hundreds of gallons a day, allowing the water to evaporate continuously from its leaves. During the summer, unless conditions are exceptionally dry, the tree has little difficulty replacing this lost water. But in winter, when temperatures fall below freezing point, water is much harder to collect and the leaves risk drying out and dying. To survive this, and the effects of frost, they would need to be both smaller and far tougher.

The oak's solution to these problems is both simple and drastic. Instead of struggling to preserve its leaves through the weeks of wind, snow and frost, it simply abandons them and then grows a new set in the following spring. This ceaseless cycle of leaf loss and replacement can be seen not only in oaks, but in a myriad of other trees, such as elms (*Ulmus*), beeches (*Fagus*), maples (*Acer*), hickories (*Carya*) and hazels

(*Corylus*), which grow across the temperate world. Together these broad-leaved trees make up a unique and rich habitat – the temperate deciduous woodlands.

TREES OF THE TEMPERATE ZONE

The world's temperate zones form two wide bands, each nearly 1500 miles (2413 km) across, that girdle the Earth about halfway between the Equator and the poles. During the course of a year, these parts of the Earth's surface tilt towards the Sun and then away from it, creating a large variation in the amount of life-giving light that reaches the ground. On a clear, frosty day in midwinter, the sunlight may seem dazzling as it throws bare branches into exquisite silhouettes, but its strength is illusory. The Sun hangs low in the sky, and its daily input of energy can be as little as one-seventh of the amount in midsummer.

and conifers. Where conditions are harder still, broad-leaved trees all but disappear, leaving the hardier conifers to dominate the landscape.

HUMAN INTERVENTION

More than any other of the world's forest types, broad-leaved woodlands have been transformed by the activities of humans. In many parts of the Northern Hemisphere, trees have been felled or managed for so long that much of the original forest cover has vanished, and truly 'wild' woods – the ones that feature to such chilling effect in old nursery tales – are few and far between.

In northern Europe, this process of change started over 4000 years ago, when an expanding population sought space for farming, food for animals and timber for building. Even this far back, long before the days of the chainsaw, forests could be felled with extraordinary speed. Experiments in Denmark, using original Stone-Age axes, have shown that a pair of men could clear woodland at the rate of nearly 1800 sq ft (167 m²) an hour. Faced with attacks on this scale, the original deciduous forest, which once stretched from the British Isles eastwards to Poland and southwards to Spain, became reduced to smaller fragments, which today often resemble plump green pillows scattered across an intensively farmed landscape.

Like characters in a living history book, the trees of these surviving woodlands reveal a great deal about the past of the forest, and the way different parts of it have been managed. So, too, do the surroundings in which they stand. In some European woods, one can still see ancient overgrown banks that once marked the limits of medieval hunting grounds, where feudal nobles hunted deer and wild boar in private and jealously guarded forests. In others, two woodland curiosities can sometimes be found – majestic oaks (*Quercus*) or beeches

TREES TAMED AND WILD
Sawn through in the recent past, this pollarded willow has produced a sheaf of new branches. Right: In Utah, USA, autumn colour splashes a mixed forest.

(*Fagus sylvatica*) with unusually short but massive trunks, and hazels (*Corylus avellana*), limes (*Tilia*) or sweet chestnuts (*Castanea sativa*) that have dense sprays of branches, but apparently no trunks at all.

These strangely shaped trees are the result of two forms of woodland management that once played a vital part in rural life. The thick-trunked oaks and beeches are ancient 'pollards', or trees that were sawn through just above head height at some point during their youth. Pollarding encourages trees to produce a crop of leafy branches safely beyond the reach of browsing deer, and these were once regularly harvested for feeding animals and for use as fuel or for making charcoal.

The smaller, trunkless trees have also been sawn through, but almost at ground level. Known as coppicing, this practice also prompts the tree to grow a sheaf of straight and slender branches, which can be used for making charcoal and fenceposts. Unlike pollarding, which has largely died out in woodland management, coppicing is still widespread today.

Draconian though they may sound, these two forms of

COPPICED WOODLAND *An old coppiced hazel spreads over a carpet of bluebells. The silver-washed fritillary (below) is at home in woods like this.*

surgery seem to do little harm to a tree. Paradoxically, both can actually extend a tree's life by several centuries, by reducing the weight of branches that the trunk or roots have to support. This increased life span brings useful benefits to woodland wildlife, particularly for animals such as bats, which often roost in cavities in old pollarded trees, and also for woodpeckers and woodboring beetles, which find their food in ancient wood.

Coppicing also helps forest animals in a different way. Coppiced woodlands are usually worked on a set cycle, with different areas of woodland being cut about every 7-12 years. The result is a patchwork of trees at different stages of regrowth, with woodland flowers creating a carpet of colour before the trees close over them once more. For butterflies such as the beautiful silver-washed fritillary (*Argynnis paphia*), whose caterpillars feed on dainty woodland violets (*Viola*), coppices are among the richest of woodland habitats. And where insects thrive, their feathered enemies – which include a host of small songbirds such as warblers and nightingales (*Luscinia megarhynchos*) – are rarely far behind.

Until the arrival of European settlers early in the 17th century, almost the whole of eastern North America – with the exception of the highest mountains – was covered by a continuous forest. In the north and south, the forest contained a mixture of conifers and broad-leaved trees, but its heartland was dominated by an extraordinary diversity of deciduous species. These included towering American beeches (*Fagus grandifolia*), majestic hickories with elegantly divided leaves, fragrant-flowered basswoods or lindens (*Tilia americana*), and over 20 species of oak – many more than in northern Europe – some almost shrub-like, others over 100 ft (30 m) tall. The eastern forest was the home of deer, black bears (*Ursus americana*) and raccoons (*Procyon lotor*), and also of the passenger pigeon (*Ectopistes migratorius*), a nomadic bird whose giant flocks, sometimes over a billion strong, gorged themselves on acorns and beech nuts, and even broke branches under their combined weight.

Today, nearly 400 years later, the passenger pigeon is no more, having been wiped out during the last century by a frenzy of hunting unprecedented in its scale. However, despite an explosion in the human population, the forest that once fed these birds seems remarkably well preserved. Broad-leaved trees flank mile after mile of roads in eastern states and, from the air, open farmland still looks like an interruption in the forest, rather than the other way around.

However, as in Europe, American woodlands bear the hidden imprint of history. In

GONE FOREVER *During its heyday, the passenger pigeon was probably the world's most abundant bird. The last one died in captivity in 1914.*

less accessible areas, such as the steep ravines of the Great Smoky Mountains, broad-leaved giants such as the tulip tree (*Liriodendron tulipifera*) can reach heights of over 150 ft (46 m), punching their way through the leafy canopy with lordly magnificence. Elsewhere, particularly in the flatter land farther east, large and old trees are much less common. It is this missing element in the forest's living mosaic that provides an important clue about its past.

For almost 200 years, the great eastern forest was the scene of intense activity, as farmers cleared land around their homesteads and converted it into fields. From slow beginnings this destruction gradually accelerated, until only the most inaccessible areas of forest remained untouched. But with the invention of improved farm machinery in the mid-1800s, attention turned from the hard-won eastern fields to the wide open prairies farther west, where the ground was immensely fertile and where no trees stood in the way of the plough. Many eastern farms, so painstakingly claimed from the forest, were gradually abandoned, leaving nature silently to recover what it had lost.

Today, this naturally regenerating or 'secondary' woodland covers thousands of square miles of eastern America, and is supremely important to wildlife. Its rapidly growing trees provide a habitat for the east's original forest animals, including species such as the whitetail deer (*Odocoileus virginianus*), which browses on twigs and leaves, and the wild turkey (*Meleagris gallopavo*), an avid eater of seeds and nuts. But instead of slowly regaining ground, some woodland animals have rapidly spread throughout this new habitat, and are now common right up to its edges, where houses and asphalt back onto the trees. Foremost among them are the raccoon and a unique North American mammal, the Virginia opossum (*Didelphis marsupialis*).

RACCOONS AND OPOSSUMS

With its bandit-like eye-patches and ringed tail, the raccoon is one of North America's most easily recognised wild mammals. Although it is mainly nocturnal, it also moves

about by day, exploring woods, streams, grassy ground, and even dustbins in its search for food. Using its front paws like hands, it carefully feels for anything that might be edible, rather like a short-sighted person searching for a pair of misplaced glasses. The moment it touches anything of interest – which can range from insects and earthworms to acorns and dead birds – it picks it up and starts to feed.

Raccoons often forage near water, and

WILD TURKEY *Once endangered by agriculture, this species has staged a comeback, and is now widespread in eastern forests.*

are adept at catching small animals in the shallows. But despite old tales to the contrary, they do not wash their food before eating it. A raccoon will sometimes hold its food and give it a brief inspection before feeding, but it does not waste time on unnecessary hygiene – eating is its priority.

Raccoons have always been widespread in North and Central America, and they live in all kinds of woods and forests, and more open habitats as well. This adaptability, both in habitat and diet, has served them well in the 20th century, allowing them to move into city parks and even empty buildings. But puzzlingly, the raccoon has also managed to spread far into the coniferous forests of Canada, where the human population is low, and it is now living in places where it has never been seen before. Quite how it has managed this, scientists do not yet know.

In comparison to a raccoon, the Virginia opossum is a much smaller animal, with a cat-sized body, a long bare tail and unkempt-looking fur. While certainly less appealing, it is of great biological interest because it is the only marsupial, or pouch-bearing mammal, that is found north of Mexico.

Like other marsupials, the Virginia opossum gives birth to poorly developed

NORTHERN MARSUPIALS
Unusual, adaptable, but hardly beautiful, Virginia opossums are often highly aggressive when they meet.

young that suckle milk from within the protection of her pouch. However, few of its relatives do this on such a prodigious scale. Female opossums usually produce two litters a year, and while most give birth to about 20 young, some have as many as 50. Many of these are doomed to an early death, however, because the mother has only 13 nipples, and once each one has been taken, latecomers find no place to feed.

Before the original eastern forest was opened up for agriculture, the Virginia opossum lived only as far north as Pennsylvania. However, like the raccoon, it has now managed to push beyond the Canadian border. There is no mystery about how the opossum has achieved this – its expansion has been entirely due to its ability to live alongside people, and to its knack of making a meal of anything edible, from nuts and insects to farmyard chickens.

LIFE IN THE LEAF LITTER

During spring and summer, living leaves are the scene of intense chemical activity, as food is manufactured through photosynthesis and then shipped out to other parts of the tree. But as the days shorten and autumn approaches, these processes begin to slow down, and the leaves' food output begins to decrease. At this point, the tree begins to act like the manager of a failing factory. It cuts off the supply of water and mineral salts that keeps the leaves in operation, and at the same time removes any useful substances that can be recycled. Once this has been done, its leaves – the machinery of photosynthesis – are scrapped.

Thorough though it is, this decommissioning process can never be totally efficient. The discarded leaves still contain substantial amounts of nutrients, and their arrival on the ground is the signal for a burst of biological activity. The principal players in this are bacteria

FAMILIAR FACE *Caught out while foraging, a raccoon decides whether to run for cover. Among the trees, a whitetail deer looks on.*

LEAF LITTER *In early autumn, intact leaves cover the ground, but they are soon broken down and by spring only fragments remain.*

and fungi, sometimes joined by a select band of unusual plants, such as the rare ghost orchid (*Epipogium aphyllum*), which does not have green leaves. Collectively, these organisms are known as saprophytes or decomposers. Dead leaves provide them with the energy that they need to live and they, in turn, pass on essential raw materials to the ground, allowing trees and other plants to draw on them once more.

Although few decomposers are large enough to be visible, they exist in huge numbers, and the results of their activities are easy to see. Within a few weeks, the banks of autumn leaves are reduced to skeletons and fragments, and not long afterwards they seem to melt away, adding to a layer of organic matter that covers the ground.

So rich is this source of nourishment that every handful of leaf litter teems with life, to an extent greater than in almost any other type of forest. The upper surface is the home of millipedes and woodlice – vegetarians that live on dead plant matter – and also of carnivorous spiders and ground beetles. In the moist and dark interior of the litter, the struggle of predator against prey continues, but this time between protagonists near the threshold of human vision. The role of victim often falls to minute wingless insects called springtails, while the predators include insects called bristletails, and tiny pincered arachnids called pseudoscorpions.

Enlarged 100 times, pseudoscorpions would probably inspire revulsion in anyone but a keen biologist. But as these woodland animals rarely measure more than $1/10$ in (2.5 mm) long, they are almost universally overlooked. Distantly related to true scorpions, they do not have a sting, and they kill their prey by clamping it with their pincers, before injecting it with poison from their mouth-parts. A pseudoscorpion cannot swallow solid food, and instead liquefies its prey's soft tissues, then sucks them up as a nutritious fluid.

In the open, a springtail can easily escape the pseudoscorpion's plodding attack. It is equipped with a forked tail, called a furcula, which is normally folded forwards underneath its abdomen. At the first sign of danger, the springtail flicks its furcula downwards and backwards, catapulting itself far beyond the reach of its enemy.

THE WOODS IN WINTER

Once winter arrives, the life of many of the smallest woodland animals comes to an almost complete standstill. With the exception of some heavily 'furred' moths, which generate warmth by shivering their wing muscles, most invertebrates have few ways of building up heat and holding onto it. Deprived of heat, their body's chemistry works at such a slow pace that serious activity is impossible.

At this time of year, the accent is simply on survival. With almost no food, and little chance of reaching what there is, many butterflies soon die, but other members of the species live on in a more resilient stage of their life cycle. Cemented inconspicuously to twigs or bark, butterfly eggs sit out the coldest weather, impervious to frost, snow and icy winds. Other species spend the winter as chrysalises, protected by a hard outer skin that is almost as tough as the egg's sculpted shell.

In insects, this kind of suspended animation is called diapause. Once an insect has entered this state, it is locked into it until it has undergone a long period of cold weather. Like dormancy in many tree seeds, this locking system makes sure that the egg does not 'come to life' during an

UNDERGROUND ORCHID *The ghost orchid is pollinated by bees. This unusual plant lives beneath the leaf litter, and may flower as rarely as once a decade.*

WINTER QUARTERS
Surrounded by hibernating
snails, a European common
toad prepares for its own
winter sleep.

unusually mild spell, only to perish when temperatures drop to their normal levels.

Woodland reptiles and amphibians also rely on external warmth to remain active, and so they too are forced to shut down for the winter. Hidden under logs, in burrows, or in the water of ponds, they wait until the temperature rises once more, revitalising their sluggish bodies. However, for mammals, the picture is more complex. Mammals are warm-blooded, which means that their body chemistry generates enough heat to keep them at a steady warm temperature.

Equipped with this internal heating system, they can remain active all year round, as long as they can find enough food to act as fuel.

CONFRONTING THE COLD

For the red fox (*Vulpes vulpes*), one of the most widespread woodland predators, winter is the hardest time of year. An extra-thick coat, which develops in autumn, helps to conserve the animal's body warmth, and so does its habit of sheltering underground, in an earth or burrow. But its earth contains no food reserves, so every day – usually at dusk and in the evening – the fox must emerge to feed. Using its keen sense of smell, it specialises in catching small mammals, such as voles and mice. The fox pinpoints its prey under snow or leaves, and then drops onto them with a characteristic jump that is more like a cat's pounce than a dog's snapping rush.

That, at least, is the fox's traditional way of earning a living. But in some parts of its range – particularly the British Isles – red foxes have followed the example of the raccoon and Virginia opossum, and have taken up life in built-up areas. Here, winter food is often easier to find, particularly for an animal that is a natural scavenger. The fox's nocturnal habits mean that it is rarely seen, even though it may live within a few yards of busy streets.

Deer have none of the fox's boldness,

even though winter often forces them more into the open. In place of their summer diet of leaves and shoots, they turn to less nutritious winter fare, which includes not only buds, but also twigs and bark. Even to the inexperienced eye, evidence of this winter feeding is easy to spot. A deer will bite through the tips of young saplings, leaving a ragged stump of white wood, and it will scrape through bark with its sharp incisor teeth, biting against a hard pad on its upper jaw. Both these forms of feeding rarely kill trees outright, but they make them more liable to attack by fungi, and this can eventually prove fatal.

Sustained by this poor but adequate diet, deer remain active throughout the coldest weather. Many other mammals adopt a more cautious winter lifestyle, emerging to feed on mild days, and holing up for days or weeks when conditions turn more severe. They include the grey squirrel (*Sciurus carolinensis*), a North American species that is now firmly established in the British Isles, and also the raccoon and the

ATTACK FROM ABOVE *Snow*
keeps small mammals such as
voles warmer than they would
be in the open air, but as they
move about beneath its cover,
they can attract unwelcome
attention. Here a red fox
springs a surprise attack.

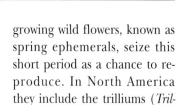

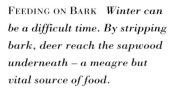

FEEDING ON BARK *Winter can be a difficult time. By stripping bark, deer reach the sapwood underneath – a meagre but vital source of food.*

Eurasian badger (*Meles meles*). Insulated from the cold in their nests or dens, they drift into an intermittent sleep, living off reserves of fat built up in easier times.

These fair-weather feeders make no special concessions to winter cold, and are easily roused from their slumbers if danger strikes. However, no amount of disturbance will wake a Eurasian common dormouse (*Muscardinus avellanus*) or a North American woodchuck (*Marmota monax*). Instead of simply sleeping, animals like these spend winter in a state of true hibernation, with their body temperature hovering just a few degrees above freezing point.

Rather than face the daily challenge of finding food, hibernators avoid it altogether. Through mechanisms that are still not fully understood, they reduce the rate of all their body processes – including heartbeat and breathing rate – until they are at the minimum level needed to preserve life, and nothing more. In some cases, they can

remain in this state for an astonishing length of time. In the relatively mild climate of western Europe, the dormouse hibernates for about five or six months, but in the woodlands of eastern Europe it may spend up to three-quarters of the year in a state of complete immobility. In Canada and the northern USA, the woodchuck – also known as the groundhog – equals this extraordinary feat.

Awakening, when it finally comes, is dramatic. Triggered by an inbuilt biological clock, the animal begins to shiver, often violently, as its muscles kick-start into life. This shivering generates heat that is carried first to its brain and other vital organs, and then to the rest of its body. Within a few hours, the hibernator is up and about, ready to explore a world that has undergone a double transformation while it was asleep.

SPRING FLOWERS

As the days lengthen between February and early April, a window of opportunity briefly opens for woodland plants. For a few weeks, the trees seem slow to respond to the advancing season, and their leafless branches allow rapidly strengthening sunlight to spill onto the woodland floor. A clutch of low-

growing wild flowers, known as spring ephemerals, seize this short period as a chance to reproduce. In North America they include the trilliums (*Trillium*), the may-apple (*Podophyllum peltatum*), and the beautiful yellow trout-lily (*Erythronium americanum*), while in Europe snowdrops (*Galanthus nivalis*), wood anemones (*Anemone nemorosa*), and – perhaps best-loved of all – the primrose (*Primula vulgaris*) are among their number. One thing that all these plants have in common, apart from their radiant colour, is an ability to begin the year in top gear.

Spring ephemerals are nearly all perennials, or plants that survive for several growing seasons. Each year, they produce a surplus of food, which they store away in bulbs, corms or specially thickened roots. As soon as spring begins, this food provides the plants with the energy they need to grow, even when the air still bears the restraining chill of winter. Their leaves rapidly open, and are soon followed by flowers. By the time the trees are leafing out above them and shutting off the light, the ephemerals have finished flowering, and are already setting seed.

The early days of spring are the time for another and much less conspicuous flowering. This is the moment when small trees, such as willows (*Salix*), alders (*Alnus*) and hazels (*Corylus*), shed millions of pollen

grains into the air, using the wind to waft them from one tree to another.

In the woods of Europe, the hazel is almost as reliable as a thermometer, flowering as soon as the temperature reaches 5°C (41°F) for more than two or three days in succession. Its catkins, which have remained tightly closed since the previous autumn, quickly expand and loosen, while its tiny female flowers develop bright red stigmas that project into the air like tiny tongues. Trees like the hazel flower early because, without leaves to stand in its way, there is a much better chance that the wind will carry their pollen far and wide.

WINGED ARRIVALS

Throughout the northern broad-leaved woodlands, spring brings an annual flood of migratory birds that have spent the winter in warmer climes. Responding to changes in day length, they leave their wintering grounds in the tropics or the Southern Hemisphere, and fly thousands of miles to an environment where food is becoming daily more abundant. The earliest migrants are often checked by fronts of cold air drifting down from the Arctic, but as warm air builds from the south, the trickle becomes a flood, and the woodland's permanent residents – which include woodpeckers, nuthatches, and tits or chickadees – suddenly find themselves surrounded by newcomers.

On both sides of the Atlantic, the vast majority of these woodland visitors are small insect-eaters collectively known as warblers. Using sharp eyesight and delicate probing beaks, they search the twigs and expanding leaves, picking off caterpillars and grubs that provide food for themselves and their nestlings. Even to an experienced birdwatcher, these energetic creatures – which number dozens of species – can look confusingly similar, particularly when they remain high in the treetops. But warblers, too, must be able to pick out their own kind from this confusing medley of bird life; and one of

the ways in which they do this is by sound.

Writing in the spring of 1768, long before the days of binoculars and tape-recorders, the distinguished English clergyman and naturalist Gilbert White was one of the first to use song to separate similar species. In a letter to a friend, he confided: 'I make no doubt but that there are three species of willow-wrens; two I know perfectly, but have not yet been able to procure the third. No two birds can differ more in their notes, and that constantly, than those two

WILLOW WARBLER *This energetic insect-eater broadcasts a stream of gently falling notes.*

that I am acquainted with; for one has a joyous, easy, laughing note, and the other a harsh loud chirp.'

Within a few months, White had identified the elusive third bird. Today, birdwatchers all over Europe are familiar with the lookalike trio – now known as the willow warbler (*Phylloscopus trochilus*), the chiffchaff (*Phylloscopus collybita*) and the wood warbler (*Phylloscopus sibilatrix*). Although practically indistinguishable at a distance, these three members of the genus *Phylloscopus*, meaning 'leaf examiner', have such contrasting songs that it is far easier to identify them by sound than by sight.

Like other songbirds, it is normally the male warbler that sings, and his song has a

SPRING VISITOR *The chiffchaff is an early arrival in northern Europe each spring.*

WOOD WARBLER *A final trill often marks the conclusion of the wood warbler's song; the singer can be hard to spot.*

twofold function. It warns rival males not to intrude in the territory that he has claimed, and at the same time it encourages prospective mates to make their approach. Unlike other forms of biological advertisement, such as bright plumage, sound carries well through the woodland environment, announcing birds not only to their own kind, but also to birdlovers on the ground below.

STRANGER IN THE NEST

Of all bird calls, one above all is supremely redolent of woodland in spring. It can be heard only in the Old World, but the bird that produces it ranges from Europe as far east as Japan. Wherever it is found, its name echoes its call: in the Netherlands it is the koekoek, in France the coucou, and in Britain the cuckoo.

The Eurasian cuckoo (*Cuculus canorus*) has one of the most remarkable life-histories of any woodland animal. Unlike the cuckoos of North America, which build their own nests, it foists its eggs on other birds, leaving the unwitting foster parents to carry out the work of raising its young. The victims of this deception are often warblers, and each pair is duped into raising an interloper that quickly grows to be several times bigger than its foster parents.

Freed from her normal responsibilities as a parent, a female cuckoo lays about a dozen eggs each year, which is many more than similar birds of her size. Her eggs are relatively small, and their colour varies between one individual and another. Each egg is laid in a different nest, with females

targeting a particular species of host – the one whose eggs most closely match her own. The process of egg-laying is extremely brief, often lasting little more than a minute, and takes place while the owners are away searching for food. Immediately after laying, the cuckoo often removes an existing egg so that the clutch seems almost unchanged.

The young cuckoo hatches after just 12 days, which usually gives it a headstart on its nest mates. From its first hour, it ruthlessly improves its chances of survival by shouldering other eggs or nestlings out of the nest. Without any competitors for food, the cuckoo then grows at a prodigious rate, fed by two parents who fail to recognise that anything is amiss.

The cuckoo's development is an example of brood parasitism – a kind of reproductive strategy seen in only 1 per cent of the world's bird species, and also in some insects. However, this is not all that makes the cuckoo unusual. Its life has a further strange twist – one that becomes evident only after it leaves the nest.

Cuckoos are migrants, spending the summer in the Northern Hemisphere, and wintering in Africa. Instead of setting off in flocks, like many migratory birds, the adult cuckoos fly alone, and they often depart a full two months before the current year's young. This means that the young cuckoos have no guides to show them the way. Somehow, they have to complete a solitary journey of several thousand miles, crossing all kinds of terrain to reach a wintering ground that they have never seen before.

Cuckoos achieve this extraordinary feat entirely by instinct. Like a program installed in a computer, instinct tells

STRANGER IN THE NEST *With its beak gaping open, a young cuckoo receives food from a hard-working reed warbler.*

them not only when to set off, but which direction to follow, which clues to use when correcting their course, and when to bring their journey to an end. Cuckoos can live for over ten years, and on each return journey they build up the expertise that makes migration easier. But in their first year, they rely entirely on their inbuilt autopilot to reach their far-off destination.

THE WOODS IN SUMMER

In early summer, deciduous trees often grow at a rate of several inches a week, briefly matching the performance of those in the hot and humid tropics. At this stage of the year, their young leaves are still soft and delicate, and the twigs that bear them are flushed with sap. For insects and other small plant-eaters, it is a time of unrivalled abundance.

The scale of this invertebrate army can sometimes be felt – quite literally – by standing beneath a tree. Once their leaves have opened, European limes and American basswoods (*Tilia*) are often plagued by huge numbers of aphids feeding on the undersides of the leaves. Using tiny syringe-like mouth-parts, the aphids drain the leaves of sugary sap. Although sap is rich in energy, it is low in other nutrients, and as a result, the aphids have to drink and excrete a large amount of fluid to survive. This surplus fluid rains down from the leaves in the form of honeydew – a fine and sticky mist that can be felt when it lands on the face.

A less uncomfortable way of investigating

GROWING FAMILY *In early spring, a female wild boar forages with her brightly striped piglets. If threatened, she will defend them fearlessly.*

brightly lit ground as a courtship arena, chasing away any rivals that intrude within. Others, such as wasps and hornets, simply pass through, and are lit up briefly as they press onwards to find their next meal.

At this time of year, walkers with luck and keen eyes sometimes stumble on the most beautiful of the woodland's inhabitants. Protected by dappled coats that almost perfectly mimic the interplay of sun and shade, young deer remain motionless in the undergrowth, waiting until their mothers return from feeding to provide them with milk. This characteristic dappling is shared by woodland deer all over the Northern Hemisphere, suggesting that it is a strong aid to survival. In most species, including the white-tailed deer (*Odocoileus virginianus*) of North America and the much smaller roe deer (*Capreolus capreolus*) of Europe, the spots disappear after three or four months. In the fallow deer (*Dama dama*), which lives in Europe and parts of Asia, they usually remain for life.

A similar kind of cryptic coloration is also shown by the young of a quite different woodland mammal, the wild boar (*Sus scrofa*). This ancestor of the domesticated pig produces litters of up to a dozen piglets, each one vividly marked with horizontal white stripes that provide them with good camouflage in dappled woodland light.

An adult wild boar, weighing up to 400 lb (180 kg) and armed with sharp upward-pointing tusks, is a formidable and impressive animal. Feeding on anything from roots and nuts to insects and small mammals, it

the animal life on trees involves surrounding a branch with an airtight bag, and then briefly filling it with a harmless gas that makes the tree-dwellers lose their grip. This kind of study shows that trees vary enormously in the amount of guests that they reluctantly host. Some trees, for example planes (*Platanus*), seem to be good at fending off attack, while others, particularly willows, elms and oaks, often yield a myriad of caterpillars, beetles and sap-sucking bugs.

One of the best studied woodland trees, the English oak, is known to support over 100 different kinds of insect, most of which live on its leaves. Faced by this onslaught, oaks have evolved an ingenious way of keeping ahead of their small but abundant adversaries. Instead of leafing out once, in spring, they do so twice, with a major leafing in spring followed by a minor one in summer. Unlike the spring leaves, the summer ones arrive too late for many leaf-eating insects, so they survive the summer relatively unscathed.

By the time high summer arrives, the woodland's short but intense burst of growth is at an end. With the leaves now fully expanded, the woodland floor is a place of deep shade, interrupted only by sporadic patches of dappled sunlight. Each patch is like a miniature theatre illuminated by a powerful spotlight, and is complete with its own cast of players. Some of these animals, such as the European speckled wood butterfly (*Pararge aegeria*), use the

THE FOREST THAT TIME PASSED BY

Straddling the border of Poland and Belarus (Belorussia), the Bialowieza Forest is the last almost untouched remnant of a great forest that once covered most of central Europe. It covers nearly 500 sq miles (1300 km²) of low-lying and often marshy ground, and has a unique history that has preserved it almost intact for hundreds of years.

During medieval times, the forest became a royal hunting ground, which effectively prevented its settlement and conversion into farmland. Over succeeding centuries, the political map of this part of Europe was redrawn time and again, but the forest managed to survive the changes, passing through the hands of Polish kings, Belorussian princes, and latterly Russian tsars. During the 1930s, the central part of the forest became a Polish national park, and today it is a World Heritage Site.

With its cold winters and warm summers, the Bialowieza Forest lies at the southern margin of Europe's mixed forest belt, in which broad-leaved trees and conifers grow side by side. It is the home of some spectacularly ancient oaks (*Quercus*), and also of red deer (*Cervus elaphus*), wild boar (*Sus scrofa*), beavers (*Castor fiber*) and over a dozen species of bats. However, the forest's most famous inhabitants are not these, but its herd of European bison (*Bison bonasus*), a species once in imminent danger of extinction.

Like its close relative, the bison or buffalo of North America, the European bison once existed in great numbers, ranging through forests and grassland across an entire continent. But deforestation and hunting both took their toll, and by the beginning of the 20th century, only two groups remained. Disaster then struck. The bison at Bialowieza were hunted to extinction in the aftermath of the First World War, and the only other population – in the Caucasus mountains – was also eliminated.

Fortunately, a few dozen animals had been kept in zoos throughout Europe, and it was from this small stock that the species was rescued. Bison were reintroduced to Bialowieza, and instead of being closely penned, were allowed to roam free in the heart of the forest.

Today, about 250 bison live in Bialowieza, and several other herds have been established in parks throughout Europe. With their shaggy forequarters and sharply hooked horns, these heavyweight browsers are a reminder of a time when wild cattle – rather than their domesticated descendants – roamed the forests.

---

lives in groups of up to 20 animals. Wild boars originally had an extraordinarily wide distribution, from Scandinavia as far as Indonesia, but in some parts of its range – for example the British Isles – hunting has since wiped them out. The wild boars of North America, which are found mainly in the south-east and in California, are probably the descendants of animals brought in by Spanish colonists in the early 1500s.

FULL CIRCLE

Throughout the northern broad-leaved woodlands, late summer and early autumn are times of fruiting, when trees conclude a process that began months or – in a few cases – over a year earlier, with the pollination of their flowers.

Some trees are exceptions to this general pattern. Species that spread with the help of the wind, such as willows and poplars, grow huge numbers of seeds, each of which is little more than a fluffy speck that rides away on the slightest breeze. These seeds – or fruits as they are more correctly known – take little energy to produce, and are ripe just a few weeks after the tree has flowered.

At the other extreme, the 2 in (5 cm) acorns of the American burr oak (*Quercus macrocarpa*), or the prickly fruits of the sweet chestnut (*Castanea sativa*), take an entire summer to form. Unlike willows, these trees stock each seed with a generous supply of food that will nourish a growing sapling. Production of this food requires the help of summer sunshine, and is a process that cannot be hurried.

Seeds of this size are far too heavy to be carried any distance by the wind. Instead, they are dispersed in another way – through the feeding habits of woodland animals. Some birds, particularly the blue jay of North America (*Cyanocitta cristata*) and its Old World counterpart the Eurasian jay (*Garrulus glandarius*), feed avidly on acorns and other nuts, as do squirrels and many smaller mammals. These seed-eaters destroy much of the crop, but they also bury surplus seeds in the ground, forming food banks or 'caches' that can be opened up in leaner times.

As the woodland year completes its cycle and the trees once more enter their winter dormancy, the time comes for the caches to be put to use. Mammals have a keen sense of smell, and use it to unearth the food that they have set aside. By contrast, most birds have a very poor sense of smell, and until the 1970s ornithologists believed that they found their caches largely by accident. However, a series of experiments has shown that birds can remember the location of cached seeds, returning months later to collect their buried stores.

Despite keen noses and good memories on the part of these creatures, some seeds escape detection. By the time spring arrives, and growth is possible once more, the pre-planted seeds are ready to germinate, and a new generation of saplings reaches upwards to the life-giving light.

NATURE'S PLANTER *A blue jay digests the acorns that it swallows, but it gives others a chance to germinate away from their parent trees.*

RICHES OF THE EAST

The Far East encompasses a vast sweep of land stretching from the Arctic to islands straddling the Equator. Its northern reaches contain some of the most remarkable temperate forests and some of the largest and rarest forest animals.

Imagine a forest where leopards (*Panthera pardus*) stalk through the trees, and lianas festoon branches and tree-trunks. A forest where giant moles tunnel through the forest floor, and where owls snatch fish from the surface of remote rivers. A forest where brilliantly coloured flycatchers flash through the foliage, and where, against almost impossible odds, some of the world's few surviving tigers (*Panthera tigris*) hold their own against the threat of extinction. If this sounds like somewhere in the tropics, think again.

Sandwiched between northern China and the Sea of Japan, the forest of Ussuriland actually lies at about the same latitude as Montreal and Paris. At one time completely closed to outsiders, this distant part of the Russian Far East marks the point where the great northern forest, with its forbidding ranks of conifers, gives way to a gentler landscape of broad-leaved trees. Here, the flora and fauna of northern Eurasia meets and mixes with the very different plants and animals of the Orient. The result is a biological treasure trove, and a perfect springboard from which to explore the unique forests of temperate Asia.

At first glance, a visitor instantly transported from the woodlands of Europe, nearly 5000 miles (8000 km) away, would find some of Ussuriland's forest wildlife reassuringly familiar. Eurasian magpies (*Pica pica*) and jays (*Garrulus glandarius*) call raucously among the trees, and Eurasian cuckoos (*Cuculus canorus*) announce the arrival of spring, just as they do in the forests of Europe. Red deer (*Cervus elaphus*) browse warily on trees and saplings, much as they do in Germany or France, and at dusk, Eurasian badgers (*Meles meles*) emerge to forage on the forest floor.

Even the Japanese mole (*Mogera robusta*), at 9 in (23 cm) long one of the biggest of its kind, would not seem too unusual, because – despite its size – its habits and appearance are very much like those of its European relative (*Talpa europaea*). Both animals are practically blind and spend nearly all their lives burrowing through the soil with their powerful front feet. Like the mole, other small mammals in this eastern forest, including voles, shrews and hedgehogs, often resemble those that live far away to the West.

Such resemblances are hardly surprising, as the two regions are directly linked, and have been for millions of years. But first impressions can be deceptive. A closer look at the trees and wild flowers shows that this forest is quite unlike any in Europe. The trees are far more varied, and include

RUSSIAN AUTUMN *Dahurian larches sport autumn colours on an Ussuriland hillside. Conifers dominate the coldest parts of the Russian Far East.*

OWL ON ICE *Thick plumage and feathered legs enable a Blakiston's fishing owl to endure winter cold, but it needs ice-free water to hunt its prey.*

many species, such as the prickly castor-oil tree (*Kalopanax picta*) and Amur cork oak (*Phellodendron amurense*), that live only in north-east Asia. The wild flowers of the forest floor often look very different from their European counterparts, and the woody-stemmed lianas that twine up tree-trunks or sag from branches have no European equivalent at all. Many of them are close relatives of the kiwi fruit (*Actinidia sinesis*), itself a plant from the temperate Far East. Over a period of decades, their flaking stems can become as thick as a man's thigh.

In summer, the mixed forest of southern Ussuriland is a blanket of green, with conifers providing a darker counterpoint to the brighter hues of broad-leaved trees. At this time of year, the mild weather and abundant food supply attracts migratory birds from as far afield as south-east Asia and Australia, bringing a hint of the tropics to this northern land. They include the beautiful Asian paradise flycatcher (*Terpsiphone paradisi*), which has two colour forms – one white, the other a rich rusty-red – and also the broad-billed roller (*Eurystomus orientalis*), an exquisite turquoise-green insect-eater that also feeds on the wing.

With the arrival of September, temperatures start to plummet, and the broad-leaved trees and lianas begin to shed their leaves. For birds used to the tropics, this formerly enticing habitat becomes a hostile one, and it is time to fly south until the following year. But not all Ussuriland's exotic-looking wildlife flees in the face of cold weather. The rare Blakiston's fishing owl (*Bubo blakistoni*) copes successfully all year round in these northern latitudes, even though most of its relatives live much farther south, and many woodpeckers and seed-eaters are also permanent residents. So, too, are the forest's largest predators – the big cats.

TOP CATS

Ussuriland's most awe-inspiring carnivore, the Siberian tiger, is the largest member of the cat family alive today. Weighing up to 800 lb (362 kg), it can measure over 10 ft (3 m) from head to tail, and its size is further emphasised by unusually long fur. While the heaviest tiger ever recorded came from India, this animal was an exception, and there is little doubt that Siberian tigers are consistently the biggest and most impressive of their kind.

The presence of this supremely effective hunter may seem surprising this far north, but this is simply a testament to the tiger's extraordinary versatility. At one time, tigers were widespread throughout southern and central Asia, showing that they could cope with the cold of northern winters just as well as the heat and humidity of tropical forests. In each part of this huge range, tigers evolved into separate subspecies, each with a body form suited to its particular habitat. Hence the Siberian tiger's shaggy coat, an adaptation that protects it from severe cold.

After a century of devastating decline, a total of perhaps five subspecies of tiger survive today. Of these five, the Siberian tiger (*Panthera tigris altaica*) is among the rarest, and also the most inappropriately named. Although Siberia has no clear-cut boundaries, it stretches across most of northern Asia, from the Urals to the Pacific Ocean. The Siberian tiger, on the other hand, is found only in the forests of the Far East. A hundred years ago, its range included large parts of northern China, Korea and Russia, but now the Chinese and Korean tigers are practically extinct. With a stable population of about 200 animals, the Ussuri forest is this tiger's final stronghold.

For thousands of years another big cat, the leopard (*Panthera pardus*), has also stalked this eastern forest. The leopard has always had a much wider distribution than the tiger, extending across Africa as well as Asia, and its habitat is also much more diverse, including deserts, mountains and all kinds of forest.

Of the two cats, the leopard has coped

COLD COMFORT *With its large body and dense fur, the Siberian tiger is well equipped to cope with the cold.*

better with the changes that it has had to face. In Africa and southern Asia, leopards are still found in some numbers, although there are far fewer than before. However, the subspecies that is found in north-east Asia, known as *Panthera pardus orientalis*, is on the critical list. In Ussuriland, zoologists estimate that fewer than 100 animals remain in the wild.

CENTRAL HEATING

Ussuriland's big cats are active all year round and depend on thick fur to survive the worst of the winter. Due east of the mainland, across the Sea of Japan, a different forest mammal has developed an astonishing way of coping with frost and snow.

THERMAL BATHS *Japanese macaques bathe in a pool of volcanically heated water. Outside, the temperature often falls below freezing.*

If humans are excluded, the Japanese macaque (*Macaca fuscata*) lives farther north than any other primate. This robust, short-tailed monkey divides its time between trees and the ground, living in groups of up to 40 individuals. Its diet is principally vegetarian, but for a plant-eating animal it displays a remarkable degree of intelligence. In a famous incident in the 1960s, a scientist studying macaques fed them with sweet potatoes, which he scattered on a sandy beach. One female macaque discovered that washing the sweet potatoes removed the sand, and soon the habit was copied by other macaques in the area.

Like the Siberian tiger, the macaque shows two important adaptations to a cold climate – it has a heavier body than most of its relatives, and its fur is long and luxuriant. But even with these characteristics, winters on Japan's largest island, Honshu, can be punishing for the macaques. In the conifer-clad mountains of the island's interior,

temperatures can fall well below freezing, and snowfall can be heavy. The ancestors of Japanese macaques came from warmer parts of the world, so for them these conditions are extreme.

However, in some places help is available from an unexpected quarter. The islands of Japan lie in an area of high volcanic activity, and some hillside forests are riddled with springs and pools that bring volcanically heated water to the surface. Here, macaques have learned to use the pools as a natural form of central heating, lazing in the water during periods of severe cold. All mammals have ways of keeping their body temperatures within strict limits, but none is more remarkable or inventive than this.

THE BAMBOO FOREST

Fifteen hundred miles (2400 km) west of Japan's southernmost islands, in the heart of central China, a range of hills rises above

FORESTS OF GRASS

What reaches a height of over 100 ft (30 m), and can grow up to 3 ft (91 cm) in 24 hours? The answer is not a tree, but *Dendrocalamus giganteus*, the world's largest species of bamboo. Found in tropical South-east Asia, it has stems up to 1 ft (30 cm) thick, and it forms dense thickets that are – quite literally – forests of grass.

Bamboos are the largest members of the grass family. There are about 1000 species, and they grow in a wide range of habitats, from snow-covered mountainsides to tropical swamps. In terms of diversity, the 'headquarters' of this group of grasses is the Far East, but wild bamboos are also found in the Americas, in Africa, and in northern Australia. Europe is unusual in having no species of its own, although several have been introduced and are now cultivated.

Grasses usually have hollow stems, interrupted at intervals by joints called nodes, where the leaves are attached. This kind of construction gives great strength for relatively little weight, and in bamboos it is stretched to its physical limits. Instead of being soft, like the stems of most grasses, bamboo stems are woody, and this enables them to reach great heights without breaking.

For animals, bamboos can be a useful source of food, but relying entirely on them carries a potentially deadly disadvantage. Bamboos spread by underground shoots, and form clumps or open thickets

containing hundreds or thousands of stems. Each plant has a precise and finite lifespan, determined by its genes. At the end of that time – which varies from ten years to over a century, according to species – the plant flowers, sets seed and dies. Wherever they are in the world, plants belonging to the same species flower together, so clumps that have existed for many decades suddenly disappear.

For the giant panda, this mass flowering is a dangerous time. Pandas feed on several types of bamboo, but they often depend principally on fountain bamboo (*Sinarundinaria nitida*), which has a life cycle of about a century. During the last flowering, in the early 1980s, at least 150 pandas died of starvation. Since then, new clumps have sprung up from seed, but their biological clocks are already ticking away, and many decades from now, they too will flower and die.

BAMBOO FOREST *On the slopes of Mount Huang Shan (left), close to China's Chang Jiang (Yangtze) River, graceful bamboo stems bear bright green foliage. Below: Some bamboos have widely spaced stems, but the largest bamboo of all grows in tight clumps. Its stems can be up to 1 ft (30 cm) across; a hollow construction gives them great strength while remaining relatively light.*

the broad floodplain of the Chang Jiang (Yangtze) River. Clothed in a deep green mantle in summer, and capped by snow in the winter, these hills contrast sharply with the well-worked farmland at their feet. Behind them, more distant ridges are faintly visible, masking even greater heights beyond. They make up an enticing prospect, beckoning the traveller with their beauty and remoteness.

The Qionlang Shan, as these mountains are known, reach altitudes of more than 15 000 ft (4570 m). Together with mountains farther north, they stand like a huge curved wall with its back to the wind, protecting this part of China from the icy winter air that would otherwise spill down from Central Asia. Thanks to the shelter provided by their taller neighbours, the lower foothills enjoy a subtropical climate, and

they support a lush mixed forest of deciduous and evergreen trees.

Tanbark oaks (*Lithocarpus*) and golden chestnuts (*Castanopsis*) form much of the canopy, while beneath them shrubs and climbers, including several kinds of clematis (*Clematis*), create a tangled understorey. Strikingly coloured birds, including brilliant lemon-yellow orioles (*Oriolus*), pluck insects from the trees, and in grassy clearings the silver pheasant (*Lophura nycthemera*) – perhaps the most elegant of over 20 species in China – forages for small animals and seeds. These plants and animals alone are more than enough to give the forest a distinctly oriental flavour. But important though each one is, the hills also harbour something of immeasurably greater value: a unique mammal, found only in this part of China, that has come to symbolise nature conservation across the globe.

THE GIANT PANDA

At one time, the giant panda (*Ailuropoda melanoleuca*) lived throughout the high ground of central and south-east China, but centuries of hunting and deforestation have taken their toll. Today, pandas are restricted to about half a dozen separate areas of forest scattered along 500 miles (800 km) of hillside, and across the whole of this range, there are probably no more than 1000 individuals.

Seeing a giant panda in the wild is an experience that few people are privileged to enjoy. Although adult pandas weigh up to 330 lb (150 kg), and are coloured in the boldest way imaginable, their rarity and largely nocturnal habits help to keep them hidden. Local people hardly ever see them, and even with the benefit of skilled trackers, they still prove elusive.

Dr George Schaller, one of the West's leading experts on pandas, spent many weeks searching the hillsides before he found pandas in the wild, and it is only thanks to

the use of radio collars, which are fitted to a small number of animals, that their movements are now becoming better known.

The Western world received the first scientific report of this highly unusual animal in 1869, when the French missionary and naturalist Père Armand David arrived in this part of China. Since then, zoologists have argued over the panda's pedigree, classifying it variously as a member of the bear family, of the raccoon family, or of a family that includes itself and nothing else. The reason for this difficulty in classification is that despite looking every inch a bear, the panda has some very unbearlike characteristics.

While most bears are happy to eat whatever they stumble across, the panda – uniquely – is almost wholly vegetarian. Pandas catch small mammals

CAREFUL PARENT *A female panda tends her young cub, born in a breeding centre at the Wolong Reserve in central China.*

DRESSED TO IMPRESS
A male silver pheasant is resplendent in its rich plumage. Pheasants feed on the ground, but most roost in trees. Right: A panda grasps one bamboo stem while it chews through another. Sharp canine teeth reveal its carnivorous ancestry.

when they can (which is not often), and are certainly attracted by meat, but their normal diet consists almost exclusively of the young shoots and roots of bamboos. In central China, these giant grasses form dense thickets at altitudes of between 6000 and 12 000 ft (1800-3650 m), where the subtropical climate of the lower ground is replaced by more temperate conditions. The pandas live in the thickets all year round, taking to the highest thickets in summer, and moving downhill in winter.

Bamboo, unlike meat, is not a highly nutritious food. To make matters worse, pandas are not very good at digesting it. In evolutionary terms, they are recent converts to vegetarianism, and their stomachs lack the special fermentation chambers found

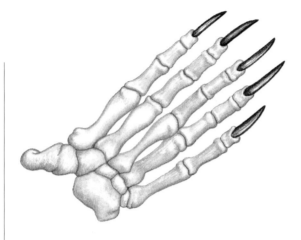

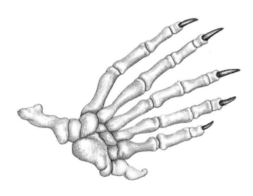

THE PANDA'S 'THUMB'
The panda's unique sixth digit – shown above in blue – is a specially extended wrist bone. Bears do not have this 'thumb'.

in cattle and many other plant-eating mammals. As a result, an adult panda has to spend up to 16 hours a day feeding, and eats up to one-tenth of its own weight every 24 hours. Instead of dining on all fours, it sits upright, snapping long stems and pushing them into its mouth like a human chewing sugar cane.

To offset these disadvantages, the panda does have some interesting adaptations that help its unique way of life. Its cheek-teeth are unusually broad, which makes them better at crushing stems than slicing flesh, and its skull has extra-large cheekbones that anchor the large muscles powering its jaws. But a more significant development can be seen in its front paws.

Bears have flat paws, and cannot grip small objects with any precision. In a bamboo thicket, a bear would be able to dig up roots or smash down stems, but it would then face an almost impossible task in getting enough food into its mouth. In the panda, evolution has solved this problem in

an ingenious way. Each of its front paws has a lengthened outer wrist bone, which acts like a static thumb. Its first and second fingers have small pads that can be pressed against the 'thumb', allowing the panda to grip the slender bamboo stems. Equipped with this special modification, it can get on with the urgent task of eating its fill.

SOUNDS OF THE EAST

For an animal that shares the same name, China's 'other' panda could hardly look more different. It, too, is an inhabitant of the bamboo thickets, and also feeds largely on plants. But unlike its much bigger relative, the lesser or red panda (*Ailurus fulgens*) is small and nimble, with a playful nature and all the curiosity of a cat. An expert climber, it uses its long, bushy tail for balance as it scampers along branches or over rough ground.

While it is hard to see any similarity between a giant panda and a raccoon (*Procyon lotor*), here the links are much more obvious. The lesser panda shares the raccoon's pointed ears and snout, and its tail has the same distinctive rings. If its rust-coloured fur were swapped for a coat of grey, the two animals would be difficult to tell apart.

In the struggle for survival, the red panda has fared better than its giant namesake, and although uncommon, it is still found in hillside forests as far west as Nepal. It is undoubtedly helped by its smaller size, which

TREETOP SLEEP *Red pandas are active mainly at dusk and after dark. During the day they sleep in the branches of a tree, usually curled up like a cat.*

means that it does not need such a large feeding range, and by its more varied diet. While giant pandas shun most plants but bamboo, red pandas also eat grass and nuts, and are not above adding eggs or insects to the menu if they get the opportunity.

When confronted by danger, the red panda's reaction is to rear up on its hind legs and hiss. In south-east China, another forest mammal has a very different reaction to danger. It starts barking. The barking is loud and deep, and it can sometimes echo through the forest for over half an hour, almost as if the hidden animal is trying to reveal its exact location. Strangely, the source of this persistent noise is not a dog, but a deer.

Although it measures just 20 in (51 cm) at the shoulder, the Chinese muntjac (*Muntiacus reevesi*) is one of the loudest animals in the forests of the East. Compared to most deer, its antlers are very small, and its only other weapons are two small, downward-pointing tusks formed by its upper canine teeth. Neither antlers nor tusks offer it

THE DISAPPEARING TIGER

At the beginning of the 20th century, there were probably 50 000 tigers in the world. Just under 100 years later, tiger numbers have fallen to about one-tenth of that number, and the decline is continuing. Without drastic conservation measures, the tiger's chances of survival in the wild look slim.

Two key problems face this biggest of the big cats. The first is hunting, which continues despite the tiger's endangered status. Tigers are sometimes hunted when they endanger people and livestock, but today a greater incentive is the demand for tiger products, which are used in traditional eastern medicine. In 1994 alone, over 100 tigers were thought to have met their end at the hands of poachers supplying the tiger-parts trade.

The tiger trade is now banned under an international agreement. But even if all illegal hunting stops, a longer-term problem still clouds the tiger's future. Like many large predators, the tiger needs a huge hunting territory. In northern India, for example, male tigers often wander through a home range of about 50 sq miles (130 km²), and in the Russian Far East, the figure is even higher because prey is more widely scattered.

Forest cover on this scale is becoming increasingly rare, so tigers are faced with a shrinking and fragmented habitat. This is particularly true of the subspecies that once lived on the densely populated islands of Indonesia. The Javan tiger (*Felis tigris sondaica*) and the Bali tiger (*Felis tigris balica*) are both thought to be extinct, but even if they could somehow be brought back to life, these species might be unable to survive in their original home.

Of all the surviving subspecies of tiger, the most numerous is the Bengal tiger (*Felis tigris tigris*), which is found in northern India, Nepal, Bangladesh and Myanmar (Burma). About 5000 animals still live here, with one of the largest single concentrations being in the Sundarbans, an area of mangrove-covered islands where the Ganges and Bramaputra rivers flow into the Bay of Bengal.

BENGAL TIGERS *This female Bengal tiger's two cubs are about one year old, and will become independent of her in another year's time.*

much protection, and its only alternative is to run. This, it seems, is where barking may help.

According to recent research, the muntjac's bark may be the mammalian equivalent of an avian alarm call. Just as a wren or blackbird scolds a cat to show that it has been spotted, the muntjac does the same to its predators – animals that include the dhole (*Cuon alpinus*), an Asian wild dog, and also the clouded leopard (*Neofelis nebulosa*), a large cat that often attacks from trees. By barking, the muntjac warns an approaching enemy that it has lost the element of surprise. Surprise is often essential for a predator's success, so if the barking continues for long enough, the predator – just like a cornered cat – may be persuaded to give up the hunt and move elsewhere.

The muntjac is the most vocal of over a dozen species of deer that live in China's forests, but it is not the only one to have tusks. The forest musk deer (*Moschus chrysogaster*), which is about the same size as a muntjac, sports tusks up to 3 in (7.5 cm) long, but has no antlers. A shy animal of the mountainous west, it gets its name from an aromatic substance produced by males and used as a territorial signpost. Unfortunately for the deer, musk is a sought-after ingredient in perfumery, so these small but hardy browsers are often the target of the hunter's gun.

TREES FROM THE ORIENT

In ancient times, the Romans regarded Africa as the source of everything that was surprising or astonishing in the natural world. In the more recent past, biologists may be forgiven for looking upon eastern Asia in the same light. For as well as producing extraordinary animals like the giant panda, the vast and varied sweep of land has achieved a similar feat with plants.

For European botanists, one of the first surprises came in the 18th century with the arrival from Japan of the ginkgo or maidenhair tree (*Ginkgo biloba*). Outwardly, the ginkgo looks very much like a broad-leaved

HUNTING PACK *The Asian wild dog, or dhole, hunts in packs of up to a dozen. Like wolves, they take prey larger than themselves.*

DEER WITH TUSKS *In a mountainside rhododendron forest, a musk deer shows off its enlarged canine teeth, which form two short tusks.*

tree, but its complete lack of flowers betrays a very different ancestry. This ancient tree, which dates back over 80 million years, is actually a relative of the conifers, although it takes an expert eye to appreciate the features that they have in common. Instead of being small and narrow, the ginkgo's leaves are broad and fan-shaped, and instead of producing cones, female ginkgoes grow seeds in a jacket of rancid-smelling flesh.

Despite extensive searches, this unique tree is unknown in the wild. For centuries, it existed only within the precincts of Chinese and Japanese temples, where it was seen by Westerners in the 18th century and where it had been preserved from almost certain extinction by its status as a sacred tree. But since its 'discovery' by Westerners, the ginkgo has taken on a new lease of life. It has proved to be exceptionally good at withstanding polluted air, and is now as much at home in the suburbs of New York as in the gardens of the Orient.

The ginkgo was an early arrival in an extensive list of trees that were collected by dedicated plant-hunters, who gathered seeds and specimens in difficult and sometimes dangerous conditions. Several years after he sent news of the giant panda, Père Armand David reported yet another

remarkable discovery, this time a tree that still grows wild in western China. Known scientifically as *Davidia involucrata*, in David's honour, it has insignificant flowers, but each cluster is flanked by a pair of large, leafy white bracts, or flaps. These hanging bracts give the tree its two common names – the handkerchief tree or dove tree. After David's time, other collectors gathered a host of ornamental species, including magnolias (*Magnolia*), Japanese maples (*Acer*), and cherries (*Prunus*), and now these beautiful trees can be appreciated far beyond their natural range.

However, the greatest surprise of all came after this main wave of discovery. In 1941, Shigeru Miki, a Japanese botanist, published a description of a fossilised redwood that was once widespread throughout the Northern Hemisphere. He called it *Metasequoia*, to distinguish it from living redwoods, and estimated that it lived up to 5 million years ago.

By complete coincidence, at almost the same time, reports began to circulate in China of a strange conifer discovered in the province of

EASTERN WONDER *Draped with white bracts when in flower, the handkerchief tree is now widely cultivated outside its native home in China.*

Hupeh, about 400 miles (640 km) to the east of the panda's home in the Qionlang Shan. At first, the story was confused. The tree had been seen by a forester, but no specimens had been collected. Three years passed before a botanist was sent to examine it, and when he did, the tree proved to be over 100 ft (30 m) high, and although apparently alive, had no leaves.

In 1948, after the disruption and turmoil of the Second World War, the American paleobotanist Ralph Chaney made the journey to central China to see the tree for himself. To his amazement, he was able to confirm an extraordinary claim – Shigeru Miki's fossil redwood was still flourishing among the terraced hillsides of this isolated part of Asia. Unlike any other redwood, the tree was deciduous, which explained why the original specimen, seen in winter, had no leaves.

Since the 1940s, the dawn redwood (*Metasequoia glyptostroboides*), as it is now known, has been successfully cultivated in many places around the world. Like the redwoods of North America, this ancient tree – once thought to be extinct – is the living legacy of forests that have long since disappeared.

FORESTS OF THE TROPICS

3

ON THE COAST *Anchored in salty mud, a mangrove survives in a demanding habitat.*

BRILLIANT COLOURS, HUMID AIR AND AN INSISTENT CHORUS PRODUCED BY BIRDS, FROGS AND INSECTS — THESE ARE SOME OF THE CHARACTERISTICS THAT SEEM TO EPITOMISE THE TROPICAL WORLD. YET THROUGHOUT THIS BROAD BAND THAT CIRCLES THE EARTH, DIFFERENCES IN CLIMATE AND GEOGRAPHY HAVE CREATED TROPICAL FORESTS OF VERY DIFFERENT KINDS. IN THE WETTEST AND WARMEST PARTS OF THE TROPICS, TREE GROWTH CONTINUES YEAR-ROUND, SUPPORTING AN INCESSANT CAVALCADE OF ANIMAL LIFE. ELSEWHERE, THE PRODIGALITY OF NATURE IS CHECKED BY PERIODIC DROUGHTS, BY THE CHILL MOUNTAIN AIR, OR BY THE EMBRACE OF THE SEA.

SIPPING SALT *Butterflies congregate on the forest floor.*

THE RAIN-FOREST REALM

Biological treasure-houses millions of years in the making, tropical rain forests contain the greatest diversity of life of any land habitat. Many animals – particularly insects – that live there still await discovery or scientific documentation.

In most parts of the world, climate acts as a brake on the growth of trees. In the far north, the unrelenting cold of winter means that trees can only grow for a few weeks a year, while in temperate regions, the growing season is much longer, but is also interrupted when summer comes to a close. Winter cold is rarely a problem in the sub-tropics, but here drought makes its mark. Trees can grow quickly if they can gather enough water, but during the dry season, many stand leafless in the shimmering heat.

In the tropics alone, the climate allows growth to continue all year long. Near the Equator, the daily average temperature may vary by as little as 2.7°C (5°F) throughout the year, and even frequent thunderstorms do little to quench the stifling air. Each day starts with an abrupt dawn as the sun climbs almost vertically up into the sky, and then closes

almost exactly 12 hours later with an equally abrupt dusk. Here, there is no such thing as a bracing spring morning or a grey winter afternoon. Instead, the climate is constant to the point of monotony, as each week of hot and humid weather succeeds the one before it.

For people who are not used to them, these hothouse-like conditions can be irksome. But for trees and other plants, they are as close to perfection as can be found on dry land. Light and water are two essential ingredients that they need for growth. When endless warmth is added to the equation, the result is an explosion of vegetation and the most luxuriant forests on Earth.

THE FOREST EDGE

To anyone exploring a lowland rain forest for the first time, this unique habitat can seem astonishing, confusing and at times unsettling. Seen from outside – for example where it overhangs a river bank – the forest edge often looks like an impenetrable wall of greenery, broken only by muddy runs made by animals coming down to the water's edge. Flowering climbers hang from the trees and trail lazily in the current, while on the river bank itself, a barricade of head-high vegetation makes landing very difficult.

Plants include wild relatives of bananas (*Musa*) and ginger (*Zingiber* and *Costus*), as well as arrowroots or marantas (*Maranta*), which are often cultivated as house plants in cooler parts of the world. But perhaps the most showy of all are the lobster-claws or heliconias (*Heliconia*), which grow in rain forests of the Americas and South-east Asia. Heliconias have giant, banana-like leaves carried on slender stems. Individually, their flowers are quite inconspicuous, but they are clasped by sharply pointed flaps or 'claws' that can be up to 8 in (20 cm) long. These claws are often brilliant orange or lurid red, and in some species they are

FINAL BLOW *Undermined by flowing water, giant dipterocarp trees lean across a river. Asian rain forests are often dominated by these trees.*

arranged in a long zigzagging stack that gradually arches over until it hangs under its own weight. The result is a structure that looks like a strangely painted carving, half-hidden in the shadows cast by the plant's formidable leaves.

The function of this striking object is to attract pollinating animals. Heliconias are often pollinated by birds, and in the course of many weeks, a heliconia in the Americas will receive hundreds or even thousands of visits from hummingbirds, which dart from one claw to another, hovering just close enough to reach the flower's rich supply of sugary nectar. As a hummingbird drinks, the flower's stamens ensure that its head becomes dabbed with pollen, and the bird carries this to the next flower it visits.

The competition for nectar is intense, and it pits hummingbirds not only against each other, but against different birds and also against insects. Despite their tiny size, some hummingbirds fearlessly defend a group of flowering heliconias against all comers. If the intruder is a bee or a butterfly, the resident hummingbird darts after it, snapping at its wings, but if it is another hummingbird, a midair skirmish often breaks out, accompanied by shrill squeaks

INSECT VISITOR *Lapping at a pool of watery nectar, a rhinoceros beetle helps to pollinate the flowers of a heliconia plant.*

and noisy twittering as the two combatants battle for supremacy. Like a security guard at a bank, the resident bird is constantly on duty and cannot afford to relax its vigilance for a minute.

WEBS AND WEB-ROBBERS

Forest edges throughout the tropics are a favourite haunt of giant orb-web spiders (*Nephila*), which produce spirals of extremely tenacious golden-coloured silk that can be more than 2 ft (61 cm) in diameter. With a leg-span of up to 4 in (10 cm), a female *Nephila* is an impressive if rather lethargic animal, and she completely dwarfs her more nimble mate. Fortunately for the male, he is so small that he does not appeal to the female as food, and this allows him to wander near his partner with impunity.

As well as sharing their webs with potential suitors, female *Nephila* spiders also entertain other guests of a less welcome kind. These are kleptoparasitic spiders, or species

UNEQUAL MATCH *Slung underneath his enormous partner, a male giant orb-web spider moves into position to mate.*

behind it lies a completely different world, where light and colour are replaced by deep and brooding shade.

THE FOREST FROM WITHIN

Arriving from the sunlit exterior, it takes several minutes to adjust to the darkness within. From here, the forest edge looks like a luminous screen beckoning to the world outside, but in the other direction, the ground seems strangely open and still. The air inside the forest is significantly cooler than it is in the open, and it carries a pervasive but not unpleasant aroma of damp decay. Rotting logs and branches are scattered over the thin carpet of dead leaves, but otherwise the only real obstacles are living trees. Some of their trunks are immensely thick, but the majority are surprisingly slender, and it is an easy matter to walk between them.

Even a short journey through the forest's interior reveals an extraordinary variety of trees – many more than can be seen in a similar area in the temperate world. In most cases, their lowest branches are well above the ground, and their leaves are too distant to be clearly visible. Their flowers – if they have any – are often far beyond reach, although in a few trees they grow directly from the trunk, creating a spectacle hardly ever seen outside this kind of forest. But even without leaves or flowers to act as clues, the tree-trunks alone hint at the immense richness of these surroundings. Some of the largest trees are

flanked by massive buttresses wide enough to stand on, or by fat cylindrical roots that snake across the ground before diving into the earth many yards from their source, but a few of the smaller trees seem to stand on stilts, their trunks no longer in direct contact with the ground.

Just as the shapes of trunks vary, so does their bark. Many of the trees have smooth bark, while others are scaly, dimpled or deeply furrowed. Their colours include sombre deep browns and shades approaching black, coppery reds, striking yellowish greens, and a hundred tints of grey. If a tree-trunk is picked at random, and its bark nicked with a sharp knife, it may yield an aromatic resin, a dribble of sticky sap or a steady trickle of poisonous milk-white latex. With so many variations in these characteristics alone, it often seems that no two trees are exactly the same.

This impression is sometimes not far from the truth. In just 2.5 acres (1 ha) of the Peruvian Amazon, for example, a team of botanists identified all the trees with trunks over 4 in (10 cm) across, and discovered that this one plot held more than 280 species – far more than occur naturally in

LIVING PROPS *Giant buttress roots support a fig tree in the rain forests of Malaysia. Roots like these are rare outside the tropics.*

that make their living by stealing food from their much larger hosts. When an insect blunders into her web, a female *Nephila* kills it with a poisonous bite and then injects digestive juices into its body, before sucking up the nutritious fluid that is produced. While she is absorbed in this lengthy task, a kleptoparasite will often sidle up to the scene of the kill and unobtrusively drain off some of the food for itself.

With its dense tangle of vegetation, this river bank world is jungle in the true meaning of the word. Jungle is found wherever daylight can reach ground level, and it springs up not only along river banks, but also along roads and around clearings. It often gives the impression of stretching back for an unfathomable distance, so that any attempt to break through it would be doomed to failure. But at the forest edge, appearances are deceptive. This living barrier is usually only a few yards deep, and

PLANT PASSENGERS

In their struggle to reach the light, rain-forest trees invest large amounts of energy in building trunks. Growing a trunk can be a slow process, particularly as it has to begin in the dim surroundings of the forest floor. Epiphytes suffer none of these problems. Instead of growing on the ground, these plants spend their lives perched on trees high above the forest floor.

Epiphytes can be found in most damp forests and even in semi-desert, but they are more abundant in tropical rain forests than anywhere else. Ferns, mosses and orchids are common epiphytes throughout the tropics, but in Central and South America epiphytes also include bromeliads, begonias, peppers and even a few kinds of cacti. Where the climate is especially wet and misty, each tree is crammed with plant passengers, turning its branches into miniature jungles.

To survive off the ground, an epiphyte has to overcome a number of obstacles. It must be able to lock itself securely to its perch, and it must have some way of collecting water. It must also be able to gather mineral nutrients – a major challenge in an environment without soil.

Most epiphytes tackle these problems with the help of special roots that wrap themselves around their host's bark instead of growing downwards in the normal way. In epiphytic orchids, the roots are often covered with a layer of dead cells that soak up water like a sponge, and the water then passes into their fleshy stems. Other epiphytes – for example bromeliads – gather water in special tanks formed by their leaves.

In the forest canopy, there are two main sources of mineral nutrients – the water that washes over trunks and branches when it rains, and the dust and debris that is constantly generated by leaves, flowers and

TREETOP FERN *A staghorn fern's upright fronds form a basket to collect nutrients; the narrow fronds gather light.*

other parts of trees. Epiphytes collect dissolved minerals when they gather water that has trickled over bark, but most also harvest falling debris, so that they can absorb the nutrients that it contains. A small orchid may collect less than a thimbleful of this mixture among its roots and leaves; but using its special basket of flaring fronds, a staghorn fern (*Platycerium*) can gather up several pounds. This organic matter forms the fern's private compost heap, supplying it with all the nutrients it needs.

TROPICAL SPLENDOUR
Clamped to a high branch, an epiphytic orchid blooms in a forest in Thailand.

To spread from tree to tree, most epiphytes rely on tiny wind-blown spores or seeds. Orchids are particularly well suited to this form of dispersal because a single orchid flower can produce over 2 million seeds. With this massive production, there is a reasonable chance that some will land on a suitable perch far above the ground.

the north-eastern states of the US, or in the whole of northern Europe. But trees are only part of the forest's plant life. There are also climbers that scramble up the trees' trunks, woody lianas which hang free from their branches, and a vast array of epiphytic plants that cling to twigs and branches high above the ground. All are engaged in an endless and silent struggle to collect light.

Seen from space, tropical rain forests form a fragmented band that seems to follow the Equator like a ragged shadow. To the north and south, this band merges with seasonal or monsoon forest, and this in turn gives way to scrub and then to desert. But within the central band itself, the rain forest is not a single homogenous unit. Instead, it varies in an almost infinite number of ways according to local conditions – some obvious, others exceedingly subtle.

One of the most important factors that shapes a forest is rainfall. True rain forest grows where the annual rainfall exceeds about 78 in (2000 mm), spread fairly evenly throughout the year. In this kind of forest, the trees are almost all evergreen, and they are densely packed, forming a continuous canopy that cuts off up to 99 per cent of the sunlight from the ground below. In a lowland evergreen rain forest, a few trees, called emergents, reach heights over 160 ft (49 m), and their umbrella-shaped crowns tower over the canopy like islands scattered in some green sea. Beneath these giants, billions of leaves form an undulating blanket, studded with points of colour where isolated trees are in flower.

This kind of forest is found throughout the lowlands of the Far East and the west of

THE WORLD'S LONGEST TREES

In rain forests, many climbing plants use trees for support. Among the most unusual are rattan palms (*Calamus* and related species) of South-east Asia, which are actually trees themselves. Rattan palms have very slender trunks armed with downward-pointing spines. During their early years most rattans are freestanding, but as they grow they gradually slump against neighbouring trees. Using their spines, they hook themselves onto trees and sprawl through the canopy. The longest recorded rattan measured 556 ft (169 m) – more than 180 ft (55 m) longer than the tallest freestanding tree alive today.

the Amazon basin, and also in a few parts of Africa. But in the eastern Amazon, most of central Africa, and also north-east Australia, the rainfall is more uneven, and in some months may drop below 4 in (100 mm). These short-lived 'dry' periods – insignificant though they may seem – have a major impact on plant life. Here, the forest is not quite as tall as its wetter counterpart, and it contains a sprinkling of deciduous species that often grow up above the rest of the canopy. Some of these deciduous trees produce a new flush of leaves within days of shedding the previous ones, but others remain leafless for several weeks.

Even in this semi-evergreen forest, rain can be so heavy that it seems extraordinary that every movable thing is not washed away. But in some parts of the tropics there are rain forests in which genuine drought – lasting just for a few days at a time – helps to create vegetation of a very different kind.

Known as *caatinga* in the Brazilian Amazon and *keranga* in South-east Asia, this type of forest grows on sandy soil, and consists of stunted trees that are often no more than 30 ft (9 m) high.

The sand beneath these 'heath forests' drains water like a sieve, and is also very acidic. It is difficult for trees to extract mineral nutrients from this kind of soil, and during the short-lived dry periods, it may also be hard for them to obtain enough moisture. Tropical biologists have yet to agree which of these two factors has the greater influence on plant growth, but the effects are startling. In place of the sumptuous and lofty canopy seen in a typical lowland rain forest, the trees in heath forest often form a dense and impenetrable thicket. Their leaves are usually small, and have a waxy or silvery surface – characteristics that help them to save water when the weather becomes dangerously dry.

LIVING PARTNERSHIPS

When flowering plants first appeared on Earth, more than 125 million years ago, animals were not slow to exploit the food that their flowers offered. Beetles and primitive flies plundered their pollen and sugary sap, and in doing so, inadvertently carried pollen from one flower to another. At first, these animals harmed flowering plants as much as they helped them, but gradually plants found ways to take advantage of their animal visitors. By providing larger amounts of food, but making sure that it was accessible only to the most effective pollen-carriers, they laid the foundations for a host of special relationships in which they and their visitors stood to benefit.

In rain forests this process of mutual adaptation has continued for longer than anywhere else on Earth, and it has produced partnerships of extraordinary diversity and intricacy. Here, some trees are still pollinated by general feeders such as beetles, but others court the attention of much more selective animals and use them as living couriers that crisscross the forest.

The South American cannonball tree (*Couroupita guaianensis*) is a spectacular example of such a plant. It has fleshy reddish-

cream flowers up to 4 in (10 cm) across, which grow from short branches sprouting directly from the trunk. At night, the flowers give off an intense musky perfume, and instead of closing, as many flowers do, they remain wide open.

As dusk falls, the heavy scent of the flowers lures nectar-eating bats in search of food. The position of the flowers – safely away from the tree's leaves – allows the bats to make a close approach, and they thrust their tongues deep into the flowers, becoming dusted with pollen as they feed. Once the blooms have been drained of their nectar, the bats move off to look for other sources of food. If other cannonball trees are flowering in the same area, the bats are likely to find them, and so the pollen from one tree is accurately ferried to its neighbours.

Compared with trees in temperate regions, those that grow in the tropics are pollinated by an extraordinarily wide variety of animals. Bat-pollinated trees are

DEPENDENT ON BATS *The fleshy petals and brush-like stamens of the cannonball tree are the hallmarks of flowers pollinated by bats.*

often easy to recognise, because their flowers are usually pale and sturdy, characteristics that make them easily visible in dim light, and more likely to survive being nudged by muzzles or knocked by flapping wings. Trees that are pollinated by birds – for example parrots – often have red brush-like flowers, opening upwards to make access easy for feathered visitors, while those that attract flying insects, such as bees and wasps, have smaller blooms, often intricately shaped to make sure that pollen is efficiently transferred as animals come and go. With so many different trees, and such a wide variety of animals, the permutations of these partnerships have infinite potential.

In nature, as in the world of business, partnerships are not always what they seem. Some rain forest plants appear to offer food to pollinators, but fail to provide it, while a number of animals eat nectar or pollen without doing anything for the plant in return. These floral burglars include heavy-bodied bees, and small South American birds called flowerpiercers (*Diglossa*). These puncture the sides of flowers to reach the nectar within, stealing a meal that is intended for other visitors.

However, this kind of cheating is unusual, and when most animals visit a tree's flowers, they work for their reward. But when something feeds on a tree's fruits, the picture is more complex. Animals that bite into seeds and digest them do not help a tree, but those that swallow seeds whole are often partners in disguise.

When a hornbill lands in a nutmeg tree (*Myristica fragrans*) and inspects its ripening fruits, the tree seems to be the loser. The hornbill looks for fruits that have partly split open, revealing the network of flesh, called an aril, that surrounds a hard black seed. The aril is bright red, making it a tempting sight to an animal equipped with good colour vision, and if the hornbill finds a ripe fruit, it pecks out the seed and its covering and swallows it whole.

But far from being the end of the seed, this is the start of a journey that may lead to successful germination. The seed lodges in the bird's crop, which is an elastic chamber that temporarily stores its food, and there it

FEATHERED COURIER
By feeding on fruit, the great Indian hornbill helps to disperse the seeds of many rain forest trees. Right: Jabbing its beak into the blooms of a fuchsia, a flowerpiercer steals nectar without pollinating the flower it is visiting.

stays while the bird moves through the canopy. Eventually the aril comes away from the seed and travels into the bird's stomach, while the seed heads in the other direction. The bird regurgitates it, and obligingly drops it onto the forest floor. For the price of a small amount of food – the arboreal equivalent of a postage stamp – the nutmeg tree ensures that its seeds are spread far and wide. Throughout the forest, many other trees have evolved their own variations on this theme. Their succulent fruits are meant to be eaten, enabling the seeds inside to be dispersed.

INSECT AWAKENING

The survival of tropical forests depends on animal life, because most trees cannot exist without their animal partners. But compared with the evident richness of their plants, rain-forest animals – at first – can seem curiously lacking. Apart from distant rustling high up in the canopy, the forest is often peculiarly quiet and still, and even the metallic screeching of cicadas stops abruptly whenever a human footfall comes too close. However, this emptiness is an illusion. The forest's animal inhabitants have keen senses, and take immediate defensive action if they detect anything unfamiliar.

The resumption of the cicadas' chorus is often the first sign that danger has passed. These large sap-sucking bugs are extremely common in rain forests, but they are so well hidden against the tree-trunks that sound alone is often the only indication that they are there. The sound is produced by the males, using a pair of drum-like membranes called tymbals, and is used to attract females. Each species has its

own characteristic song, which is often broadcast at a particular time of day. Even when several species call together, the female cicadas have no difficulty identifying suitable partners because their hearing organs are tuned in to the exact frequency of the male's call.

Cicadas fly well, but usually take to the air only after dark. During the day, the most conspicuous insects are butterflies. Compared to forest butterflies in cooler parts of the world, some of these are of a spectacular size – the brilliant blue morphos (*Morpho*) of the Americas, for example, can have a wingspan of up to 6 in (15 cm), and the birdwings (*Ornithoptera*) of South-east Asia and Australia reach a span of up to 11 in (28 cm). But although these large butterflies immediately attract attention, rain forests also contain thousands of much smaller species. In many cases their life histories are either poorly documented or completely obscure. Some of them hurry past towards unknown destinations, while others flutter nervously around leaves, tempted by odours that reveal the presence of a suitable foodplant.

FROM GROUND TO CANOPY

When it sweeps upwards from the forest floor and soars effortlessly into the canopy, a morpho or birdwing butterfly passes through a succession of very different habitats. At ground level, the forest's structure is relatively simple, and offers only a restricted range of opportunities for animal life. Like creatures of the seabed, many permanent residents of the forest floor live by eating other animals, or by processing what falls from above. A few are less fussy, and tackle almost anything edible that they find. Foremost among these general feeders are members of the pig family, which include the peccaries (*Tayassu* sp.) of the Americas and the bearded pig (*Sus barbatus*) of South-east Asia. Using their flattened

RIVERSIDE DISPLAY *These South American butterflies include the eighty-eight, a species named after the markings on its hindwings.*

snouts, they root up small animals, and also feed on fruit that has tumbled to the ground.

For every 20 ft (6 m) gain in height, the scene and its inhabitants change beyond recognition. The light becomes stronger, and the open environment of the forest floor, with its ranks of linear tree-trunks, gives way to one that is structurally far more intricate. Within the canopy, branches and leaves form a three-dimensional maze complete with its own thoroughfares and dead-ends; and on a finer scale, the surroundings are further complicated by epiphytic plants, which become increasingly abundant in the strengthening daylight. Here a butterfly or a bird has endless places in which to conceal itself, but it is exposed to a multitude of enemies, which are equally adept at hiding in the tangled vegetation.

For some animals of the canopy, the ground – while distant – is still somewhere to be visited at irregular intervals, either to feed, drink, or to breed. Toco toucans (*Rhamphastos toco*) are a typical example: although very much tree-dwelling birds, these spectacular fruit-eaters sometimes land on the forest floor and chase small animals, which they swallow on the spot or carry back up into the branches. For lizards like the common iguana (*Iguana iguana*), the need to return to the ground is occasionally a more pressing one. The female lays her eggs in a shallow hole which she excavates, and only when the eggs are safely covered up does she return to the trees.

For human beings, the rain forest canopy is one of the least accessible environments on Earth. Even with modern climbing equipment, moving about in the treetops is a slow and daunting task, and every move requires meticulous planning and an imperturbable head for heights. Quite apart from the personal danger, a single slip can send valuable equipment crashing through the leaves below, where several hours may be needed to retrieve it.

By comparison, the smallest canopy animals have no such difficulties. For worker ants and other non-flying insects, tree-trunks and branches are broad highways, and the precipitous drops beneath them are of little account. Ants are so small that they are hardly affected by the pull of gravity, and for them, climbing up a tree is almost as easy as climbing down.

Although some rain-forest ants nest in trees, others – such as the leafcutters (*Atta*) of the American tropics – are commuters to the treetop world. Leafcutters pour out from their subterranean nests shortly after first light, and troop along corridors that stretch across the forest floor towards nearby tree-trunks. The ants arrive in the treetops as little as an hour after setting off, and here each worker climbs out into the foliage and sets about the task of slicing off a small segment of leaf. When the piece of leaf is free, the ant grasps it in its jaws and

FOOD PATROL *Collared peccaries root for food in the soft mud surrounding a pool. Like other wild pigs, they have a very varied diet.*

HOLDING TIGHT *Gripping with its hands, feet and tail, a female spider monkey hangs beneath the treetops. Its single young rides on its back.*

carries it back down the tree, helping to form one of several streams of greenery that flow back to the nest. Once underground, the pieces of leaf are used to cultivate a fungus on which the ants feed.

When darkness falls, it is the turn of termites to fan out from their nests in search of food. Unlike ants, termites usually feed on dead leaves and wood, and so they rarely need to climb so high. Many species build nests in trees, using a material called carton, which they make by chewing up wood and then gluing its fibres together with saliva. These tree-nesting species commute in the opposite direction to the leafcutters, travelling inside carton tubes that meander along branches and down tree-trunks. For the travellers concealed inside, falling off the tree is a physical impossibility.

The heavier an animal, the more carefully it has to move, so while ants and termites scurry up and down trees with complete assurance, their mammalian predators have to be more cautious. The tree pangolin (*Manis tricuspis*) from Central Africa weighs 12 lb (5.4 kg) or more, and with a body of this size, has no guarantee of survival after a fall. It is protected from its enemies by a coat of overlapping scales, but its protection against the effects of gravity

are strong claws and a thick, prehensile tail. When feeding, the pangolin locks itself in position with its hind legs and tail, leaving its front claws free to break open the nests of ants and termites. It then sweeps up its food with a long, sticky tongue.

The Malayan sun bear (*Ursus malayanus*), which lives in the rain forests of South-east Asia, is one of the heaviest animals that regularly risks clambering high into the canopy. Although it is the smallest of the seven species of bears, it still measures up to 4 ft (1.2 m) in length, and can weigh 140 lb (63.5 kg). Like other bears it has no tail, so its safety high above the ground depends solely on the tight grip of four paws and their sharp claws.

Sun bears feed mainly on ants and termites, and also have a particular liking for honey. To minimise the chances of being stung while tackling its favourite food, a sun bear will climb up to a bees' nest after dark, when the occupants – which depend on sight to navigate and to locate

SKIN OF SCALES *With its covering of sharp-edged scales, an insect-eating pangolin is well protected against its enemies. Most pangolins are good climbers.*

enemies – are less well able to defend themselves. However, the process of natural selection has ensured that some bees escape these nocturnal raids. Almost as if they understand the bear's limitations, these bees nest in tualang trees (*Koompassia excelsa*), which can grow to more than 200 ft (61 m) high. As well as being immensely tall, tualangs also have unusually smooth and slippery bark, so as far as the sun bear is concerned, its bees' nests are completely out of reach.

NATURE'S ACROBATS

For a sun bear or a pangolin, the gaps between trees are unbridgeable barriers, and the only safe way to cross them is to climb down to the forest floor and back up another trunk. But during the course of evolution, many other animals have developed ways of short-circuiting this laborious process. Some of them glide, using outstretched flaps of skin, while others simply jump. Making a leap, in itself, is the easy part of the operation – landing safely is much more difficult.

In the forests of Central and South America, spider monkeys (*Ateles*) have taken this form of movement to a point that seems to approach perfection. Spider monkeys have slender legs, long fingers and toes, and a long prehensile tail with a strip of bare skin on the underside of its tip.

The tail functions as a fifth limb, and its bare patch ensures that it can be used to grip without slipping.

Even from the ground, the progress of a spider-monkey troop is easy to follow, because the forest resounds with the crash of swaying branches as the slender-bodied monkeys make their way through the trees. However, seen from within the canopy itself, it is a breathtaking and exhilarating spectacle. In the crown of a tree, the monkeys move by running on top of large branches, or by brachiating – swinging from arm to arm – beneath smaller ones. When confronted by a gap between one crown and the next, a spider monkey simply hurls itself into space, plunging perhaps 40 ft (12 m) before it breaks its fall by grabbing the flexible end of a branch. This flexibility is important because it absorbs the energy of the fall, allowing the monkey to decelerate gradually.

Despite their often casual demeanour, spider monkeys are careful to size up each jump, and they often follow well-worn trails that become thoroughly familiar to them. But even with keen eyesight and an extraordinary sense of balance, they do make mistakes. Studies of spider monkeys in Costa Rica show that older animals often have broken bones, the legacy of misjudged jumps high above the ground.

Throughout the world's rain forests, only the gibbons (*Hylobates*) of South-east Asia exceed spider monkeys in agility in the trees. Gibbons are the smallest apes, and like all their relatives, they lack tails. But even without what would seem to be a valuable asset, they swing through the branches with unparalleled expertise, hooking their hands over branches rather than tightly clasping them. In forests from China to Indonesia, their extraordinarily loud dawn choruses, consisting of long hoots broadcast in solos and duets, signal that another rain forest day is under way.

PAUSE FOR WATER *Using its hand as a scoop, a siamang takes a drink. Siamangs are the largest gibbons, found only in South-east Asia.*

LIFE AMONG THE CLOUDS

Clouds, cool air and strong winds give mountain forests a unique character. In the tropics, forests reach greater altitudes than anywhere else on Earth, and their animal life shows some remarkable adaptations to difficult conditions.

In *Alice in Wonderland*, the heroine tumbles down a rabbit hole and embarks on a series of bizarre adventures in a world of make-believe. The first occurs almost immediately, when she suddenly shrinks and then abruptly grows to several times her normal size.

In forest-clad mountains of the tropics, it is tempting to believe that some equally fantastic process has been at work. Here the scale of nature seems to have been tampered with in some way, producing a strange landscape in which trees, rather than humans, seem to change size to fit in with their surroundings. In deep ravines there are trees that would not look out of place in a lowland forest; higher up, where fingers of mist spill silently over distant ridges, the forest is very different. Here, in a realm of cool mountain air and almost perpetual cloud, gnarled

and twisted trees form a rain forest in miniature, and every available surface is blanketed by mosses, ferns and orchids. Nurtured by the soft and diffuse daylight, they thrive beneath a canopy that is sometimes less than 20 ft (6 m) high.

By definition, rain forests are wet places. But where tropical mountains stand in the path of warm and moist air blowing in from oceans, wetness can be carried to extraordinary extremes. In West Africa, for example, the giant volcanic peak of Mount Cameroun looms over the Gulf of Guinea, and its 13 000 ft (4000 m) bulk stands face-on to south-westerly air moving in from the Atlantic. As the air meets the mountain's lower slopes, it is forced upwards, cooling as it rises. Eventually the air's temperature drops so much that it can no longer hold all its water vapour, and moisture begins to condense into rain-bearing clouds. In this

humid corner of Africa, the nonstop stream of damp air generates up to 33 ft (10 m) of rain a year, making the seaward face of the mountain one of the wettest places on Earth.

Throughout the tropics, in places as far apart as New Guinea and Central America, other high mountains also squeeze water out of rising air. The moisture encourages tree growth, producing lush and often inaccessible forests in which trees seem to defy gravity by clinging to all but the steepest slopes. Like mountaineers, the trees often maintain their hold by wedging themselves into position. Their roots probe deep into the rock, seeking out the smallest cracks and crevices, and then gradually swell as they grow. As long as the rock is firm, the sideways pressure of the roots locks each tree to its precarious perch.

While trees can overcome steep gradients with surprising ease, life in mountains does bring other problems that are harder to tackle. For every 1000 ft (300 m) increase in altitude, the air temperature drops by about 2°C (3.5°F), and the air also becomes thinner, making it less well able to hold onto its warmth after dark. Even at moderate altitudes a distinctly untropical chill sets in before dawn, and in exposed places, strong winds tug against leaves and rake vulnerable branches.

FOOTHILL FORESTS

The slopes of Mount Cameroun show in a dramatic way how increasing altitude makes its mark on tropical forests and their wildlife. On two sides the mountain is flanked by some of West Africa's largest mangrove swamps, where interlocking tree roots bind together the coastal mud. The mangroves are the home of herons and egrets, which roost in the trees at night, and also of the talapoin (*Miopithecus talapoin*), the smallest monkey found outside the Americas. A little way inland, beyond

FORESTED HEIGHTS *Seen from Mount Kinabalu, the highest mountain in South-east Asia, Borneo's Crocker Range pierces a blanket of cloud.*

FOREST DWELLERS *A forest elephant browses on a low branch. In Africa, elephants range from sea level to over 15 000 ft (4572 m).*

the influence of salt water, the mangroves give way to lowland rain forest. Here the trees are much taller and far more varied, and the dense canopy casts a deeper shade.

In this part of Africa, the lowland forest zone forms an important refuge for several large primates. Among them are chimpanzees (*Pan troglodytes*) and a heavily built, ground-dwelling monkey called the drill (*Mandrillus leucophaeus*), which is closely related to the baboons. This zone is also the home of forest elephants. These elephants belong to the same species as those that live in the African savannah, but they are noticeably smaller and darker than their open-country relatives.

Forest elephants feed on leaves, fruit and bark, and do not hesitate to smash down trees to reach the upper branches. However, despite being noisy feeders, they can move surprisingly quietly, spreading

ISLANDS IN THE SKY

AUYAN TEPUI *Scattered plants cling to the eroded surface of Auyan, one of the largest tepuis. Left: A forbidding sandstone wall guards the summit of this massive plateau.*

Soaring high above the rain forest of south-east Venezuela, a cluster of flat-topped mountains form one of the strangest landscapes on our planet. Known as tepuis, the mountains are flanked by cliffs that can be up to 5000 ft (1500 m) high. The cliffs cut each mountain off from its neighbours, creating landlocked islands that are often hidden among the clouds. Venezuela's tepuis are the remains of a sandstone plateau that has been worn away by heavy rain over many millennia, widening crevices into gulleys and forming the deep valleys that can be seen today.

Because the tepuis are so inaccessible, their plants and animals have little contact with the world far below. Some lowland forest animals – for example birds and flying insects – can make the journey from valley floor to tepui top, but few do so because the conditions high up are so different from those below. Instead, the rain-shrouded summits have their own distinctive inhabitants, many being found nowhere else.

The tops of most tepuis are far too hostile and unproductive for large animals. Life on the highest tepuis centres around tenacious plants – particularly orchids and bromeliads – that provide tiny amounts of nectar for visiting insects and enough leaves to nourish a variety of small animals. These, in their turn, are often eaten by thumb-sized frogs and toads – animals that are very much at home in the permanently damp surroundings.

For tepui plants, collecting sufficient nutrients can be difficult because the heavy rain constantly flushes them away. Some sidestep this problem by trapping insects and absorbing the nutrients in their bodies. These plants include sundews (*Drosera*), and also the world's only carnivorous bromeliads, which catch their prey in pools of liquid created by rosettes of leaves. On Venezuela's islands in the sky, resourcefulness is the key to survival.

DIETARY SUPPLEMENT *This insect-eating sundew, found on Mount Roraima, survives on almost bare rock by using insects as a source of nutrients.*

their immense weight on their cushion-like feet. By contrast, a much smaller forest mammal – the rabbit-sized tree hyrax (*Dendrohyrax dorsalis*) – seems to advertise its progress deliberately by producing a series of grunts and squeals as it runs up trunks and along branches. The hyrax has small feet and stubby toes, and seems poorly equipped for climbing, but its feet have a special feature that make it very much at home in the trees. Each sole forms a sucker-like pad that is kept moist by special glands, and these give the hyrax an exceptionally good grip.

ASCENT TO THE TREELINE

Travelling farther up the mountain's shoulders, the terrain begins to rise more steeply. At about 2500 ft (760 m), the lowland rain forest starts to merge with lower montane forest, which has a slightly lower canopy. Many animals of the lowland forest venture across the invisible boundary, but this forest zone feels subtly different: the air is cooler, and, in the increasingly damp atmosphere, more plants are able to survive as epiphytes, clinging to tree-trunks or perching on branches. At first, the changes are slight, but they are harbingers of much greater ones to come.

By about 5000 ft (1500 m), the transition to mountain vegetation is unmistakable. At this altitude, the air is still warm during the day, but once the sun sets, the temperature drops sharply. The tall, large-leaved trees of the lower slopes would have difficulty coping with these conditions, and they are replaced by small-leaved species that are better at surviving in a more demanding climate. These trees often have gnarled branches, and they mark the start of the upper montane or cloud forest, a relatively open habitat that allows more light to reach the ground.

The upper montane forest lies above the cloud base and is often swathed by banks of slowly swirling mist. Even when it is not actually raining, the mist condenses wherever it comes into contact with leaves or branches, and produces an endless source of moisture that dribbles and drips its way to the ground. In this world of reliable dampness, epiphytes are everywhere, and even such delicate plants as filmy ferns, which have fronds just a single cell thick, have few problems collecting the water that they need to thrive.

With increasing altitude, clumps of mountain bamboo (*Arundinaria alpina*) start to appear, and the upper montane forest becomes ever more compact and stunted, until its trees are only head-high. This zone, known as elfin forest, is composed of

trees that are tested to their physical limits by strong winds and night-time cold. On Mount Cameroun, the upper limit of the forest zone is about 9000 ft (2740 m), and at this altitude, temperatures after dark fall close to freezing. By the time rising air reaches this height, it has shed most of its moisture, so the forest is often above the clouds. This means that the trees are frequently subjected to intense tropical sunshine and drying winds, which makes their lives even more difficult.

Beyond the elfin forest lies a subalpine world where trees cannot survive. Grass-covered slopes are crisscrossed by the black scars of old lava flows and punctuated by small cones of volcanic ash, while beyond them towers the mountain's desolate and brooding summit.

HIGH-ALTITUDE BIRDS

One of the most remarkable animal inhabitants of any mountain forest is a bird that lives in north-west South America – in the high ground that curves southwards from Venezuela to Bolivia. It spends most of its time in trees, but periodically darts out to feed on the nectar of trumpet-shaped flowers. It measures about 10 in (25 cm) from the tip of its beak to its tail, but without one important qualification this measurement is

VERDANT FOREST *In cloud forest, constant moisture turns every surface – both living and non-living – into a potential habitat for plants.*

quite misleading: the bird's body makes up only half the total length, the other half being a phenomenally long beak.

The sword-billed hummingbird (*Ensifera ensifera*) very much lives up to its name. In comparison with its body, its beak is longer than any other bird's, and it seems scarcely credible that its owner can handle such an unwieldy looking instrument with any precision at all. But the hummingbird seems to manage without any difficulty, and as well as using it to drink nectar, is even dextrous enough to snap up insects in mid-air. When resting, it holds its beak almost vertically, which helps it to reduce the strain on its neck.

There are more than 300 species of hummingbirds in the Americas, and they are at their most diverse in mountainous country. The reason for this is that mountains encourage the evolution of new species by cutting off groups of living things

TOTAL SHUTDOWN *Nocturnal hibernation allows hummingbirds to survive the cold. Above: The grey-breasted toucan is a permanent inhabitant of mountain forests.*

from their relatives. As time goes by, each group adapts to its surroundings in different ways, until they become so different that separate species are formed. It is no accident that in Africa nectar-drinking sunbirds (*Nectarinia*) show a similar pattern of evolution to hummingbirds, with particular species being confined to individual mountains or mountain ranges.

For medium-sized birds, such as South America's mountain toucans (*Andigena*), the cold nights at high altitude do not present too many problems. Their bodies have sufficient food reserves to generate plenty of heat and their feathers keep them warm. But because they are so small, hummingbirds have limited reserves, and to make matters worse they burn up their food at a much greater rate. Without some kind of special night-time protection, they risk using up all their food reserves in a few hours.

Hummingbirds that live at or above the treeline solve this problem in a drastic way. At

ADAPTABLE CAT *The margay, from the American tropics, is one of several small cats that are equally at home in lowland forest and at higher altitudes.*

dusk, they hunch up on a perch and let their body temperature drop from its normal level of about 40°C (104°F) to as little as 7°C (45°F), at which point it stabilises. At this temperature, a hummingbird is completely torpid, meaning that it is unable to move or to react to the world around it. However, because it is so cool, it loses very little heat to its surroundings. In this state, the bird burns up food gradually, allowing it to survive the night. Once dawn arrives, the bird's temperature rapidly rises, and it

is soon ready to set about the pressing task of finding food. This nocturnal equivalent of hibernation is so effective that some of these tiny birds can survive at altitudes above 13 500 ft (4100 m).

FIGHT FOR SURVIVAL

In a world in which they are relentlessly persecuted, many wild cats of the tropics find a vital refuge in remote mountain forests. In the Americas particularly, the largest of these cats – such as the jaguar (*Panthera onca*) and ocelot (*Felis pardalis*) – were once widespread in lowland rain forests, but have long been hunted, partly for their pelts, and partly because they sometimes attack livestock when farmland is opened up on the forest edge. For them, forest-covered mountainsides offer a last opportunity to avoid contact with humans.

As an evolutionary experiment, cat body design and the hunting techniques that go with it have proved extremely successful. The ocelot is a typical example: a lithe, muscular predator that uses stealth rather than force to catch a wide variety of animals, from roosting birds to young deer. The ocelot is well known to science, and is one of the most widespread predators in the mountain forests of Central and South America. But

this group of cats also contains several smaller forest species that are rarely seen. They include the elusive marbled cat (*Felis marmorata*) of South-east Asia, and the bay cat (*Felis badia*) of Borneo, both of which measure up to 3 ft (91 cm) from head to tail.

While cats can be difficult to track down, the most impressive of the world's cloud-forest animals pose very different problems for researchers and conservationists. For over thirty years, mountain gorillas have been the subject of intense study, with the surviving population of just a few hundred being carefully shielded against the worst effects of habitat destruction and hunting. But their protection has been disrupted by the civil war in Rwanda, and as a result, the gorillas now face a precarious future.

Gorillas are the world's largest apes, and are found only in the tropical forests of Africa. Despite their immense size (adult males can weigh $^1/_4$ ton/255 kg), they are placid vegetarians. As long as they do not feel threatened, they will accept the presence of human observers, and this has provided insights into the way they live.

There is a single species of gorilla, but it is divided into three distinct subspecies that live in different regions close to the Equator. One subspecies, the western lowland gorilla, lives in the tropical rain forests of West Africa, while another, the eastern lowland gorilla, lives about 600 miles (1000 km) to the east, in the forest between the Congo River and the high ground that borders Africa's Great Rift Valley. On the opposite flank of this immense natural trough lie the mist-shrouded Virunga volcanoes, which reach a height of over 14 000 ft (4250 m). The volcanoes are the only home of the mountain gorilla, a subspecies distinguished from its lowland relatives by luxuriant fur that helps to keep out the cold at high altitudes.

Because we cannot help seeing them in human terms, apes as a whole are widely misunderstood, and gorillas have fared worst of all in this regard. Despite their undeniable power and bulk, these peaceable inhabitants of Africa's forests seek only space and greenery, and they have much more to fear from our own species than we do from theirs.

ENDANGERED APE *Dwarfed by the extraordinary vegetation of Rwanda's Parc des Volcans, a female mountain gorilla cradles her young offspring.*

LANDS OF WET AND DRY

In monsoon regions, plants and animals have to withstand the twin extremes of drought and deluge each year. From the Americas to Australia, these great climatic cycles have a profound influence on forests and their wildlife.

By late October, Australia's 'Top End' is a place of oppressive expectation. After months of blowing from the south-east across the arid heart of the island continent, the wind gradually shifts around to the north-west and blows in from the Timor Sea. The thermometer begins to climb, and as it does so the atmosphere palpably changes. Gone is the dry warmth that produced the dazzlingly clear days of July and August, and which burned away pools and turned mud into dust. In its place comes air charged with tropical moisture, generating awe-inspiring thunderstorms that shed the long-awaited rain.

In this remote part of Australia, where the giant promontory of the Northern Territory bulges out towards South-east Asia, the seasons have a stark simplicity. There are only two, known locally as the Wet and the Dry. During the Wet, which lasts from October to March, more than 5 ft (1.5 m) of rain swells the region's rivers and lakes, and

WAITING FOR WATER *After months of drought, this lake bed in Australia's Top End will be cracked and dry until the arrival of the wet season.*

water pours out across low-lying ground, where it drowns the dust and laps against the trunks of thirsty trees. While the trees greedily soak up their share of the annual flood, some of the world's most flamboyant waterbirds – including the majestic jabiru or black-necked stork (*Ephippiorhynchus asiaticus*), and over half-a-dozen species of kingfishers – reap rich rewards in their ever-increasing feeding grounds.

For a time, the flood plains teem with water animals, as fish swim beneath the trees and birds roost in their branches, watching from convenient perches for signs of life below. But as March gives way to April and the wind once more changes direction, the rain is turned off like water from a tap and the floods begin to recede.

At first all is green, but as the clear and sunny days succeed each other, the spear grass (*Heteropogon*) that sprung up during the Wet starts to become baked and brown. Fish trapped in shrinking pools make easy prey for birds, but once the smaller pools have dried out, these feathered hunters must move to permanent water to find food. Around them, the landscape takes on the parched tones that herald the Dry, and the leathery leaves of the eucalypt trees hang listlessly in the intense sunlight. The land seems to be locked in silent anticipation, and it remains like this until October, when rain returns once more.

THE MONSOON WORLD

Throughout the tropics, places as far apart as India and Central America share this climate, which swings between two extremes with the predictability of a pendulum. In the monsoon zone, the rain usually follows the sun, which means that it falls during the

WET-SEASON SWAMP *In Australia's Kakadu National Park, paperbark forest is flooded by the monsoon rain.*

tropical equivalent of summer, when the sun is highest in the sky. As a result, the northern and southern tropics take turns to receive their annual rain: while northern Australia basks in the Dry, South-east Asia is soaked by its equivalent of the Wet. Six months later, the pattern is reversed.

Australia's Top End has a typical monsoon climate, divided into two roughly equal seasons. But in other places, the climatic pendulum swings to different degrees. Towards the fringes of the monsoon belt, for example in southern Brazil and southern Africa, the overall climate is more arid, and the dry season may last for seven or eight months of the year. On high ground within the tropics, particularly in southern and South-east Asia, it is the wet season that reaches stunning extremes. In Cherrapunji, a hill town in north-east India, the average monthly rainfall in December is just $^1/_2$ in (12.5 mm), but in July it averages over 96 in (2400 mm), and has occasionally topped 300 in (7600 mm). Nowhere else on Earth – not even the wettest tropical rain forest – is bombarded by so much water in such a short space of time.

This annual switch between downpour and drought makes life impossible for many of the trees that thrive in permanently

wet tropical rain forests. They have few ways of coping with water shortages, and become progressively less common where the dry season is more marked. Instead, their place is taken by a narrower range of trees that are better at coping with long periods of dry weather, and with larger daily changes in temperature. These trees are generally shorter than their rain-forest counterparts, and many of them have thicker bark, which provides protection against dry-season fires. Together, they make up tropical seasonal

EARTH'S RAINIEST PLACE *Water cascades down the hillsides of Cherrapunji in north-east India.*

forest – a more open habitat that forms a transition zone between regions that are permanently wet and ones that are permanently dry.

SURVIVING THE DROUGHT

The African baobab tree (*Adansonia digitata*) shows just how far some trees have managed to adapt in their struggle to cope with the striking contrast between the seasons. Baobabs are scattered throughout the African tropics, but they are particularly common on the edge of the seasonal forest belt, where the dry season is often long and severe. Here, most of the trees are relatively small, and many – such as the ubiquitous flat-topped acacias – are armed with sharp thorns that ward off browsing animals. The baobab, however, towers above such concerns. For it, browsing is less of a problem. Much more important is eking out precious water so that its supplies last from one rainy season to the next.

At the height of the annual drought, a mature baobab is one of the most arresting sights in the entire living world. Its smooth, battleship-grey bark looks like the skin of some giant animal, and its fat and bare branches end in tangles of spiky twigs hung

WHERE TIGERS ROAM *A sal forest in the Indian state of Madhya Pradesh at the onset of the dry season. Dead leaves already cover the ground.*

with plump oval fruit. But whenever a baobab comes into view, the eye is irresistibly drawn downwards, moving from the tree's crown to the one feature that dwarfs all others – its immense, almost monstrous trunk.

In African legends, the baobab is planted upside down, and its bizarre proportions certainly do their best to reinforce this illusion. It can reach a height of up to 80 ft (24 m) but, uniquely for such a large tree, the circumference of its trunk often matches or even exceeds its total height. This huge living pillar is made of very soft wood and acts like an immense barrel. During the rainy months, it can accumulate up to 20 000 gallons (90 000 litres) of water, which it stores during the dry months that follow. To economise on water even further, the baobab shows another adaptation seen in many seasonal forest trees: it sheds its leaves.

During droughts, a baobab's soft water-storing trunk makes a tempting target for elephants. Driven by thirst and hunger, they spear the trunks with their tusks and then wrench out shards of moist wood, which they crush between brick-sized teeth. Most baobabs can withstand a certain amount of this treatment, but if it is repeated over many years the tree dies, leaving a mass of splintered wreckage that looks like a giant carcass decomposing under the tropical sun.

LOSING LEAVES

In the seasonal forests of northern Australia, the majority of trees are either eucalypts, or their close relatives the paperbarks *(Melaleuca)*. Almost without exception, these trees keep their leaves all year round, whatever the weather brings. But in Africa and other parts of the tropics, many trees shed their leaves either just before or during the annual drought. This creates leafless landscapes

UNDER ATTACK *Using their tusks, a group of African elephants feed on the moist wood of a baobab tree.*

of gaunt trunks and naked branches, reminiscent of winter in broad-leaved woodlands much farther north.

Before human intervention, some of the largest of these forests were found in the Indian subcontinent, and even today, after centuries of clearance to create farmland, many isolated fragments still survive. These forests are the original home of one of the world's most highly prized timber trees – the fast-growing teak (*Tectona grandis*) – and also of the sal (*Shorea robusta*), an important source of fuelwood and, according to tradition, the tree under which Buddha died. Teak trees have large glossy leaves, which they seem reluctant to part with, shedding them only a few weeks before the next wet season sets in. Sal trees are quite the opposite: they often abandon their leaves as soon as the drought begins.

The sal tree belongs to an important family of tropical trees called the dipterocarps and, like several of its relatives, it has a remarkable ability to crowd out other trees, creating forests that look almost as if they have been planted with it and nothing else. During the wet season, a sal forest conceals its animal life behind a protective curtain of leaves and provides food in abundance. But when all the trees simultaneously shed their leaves, and the grass underfoot dies back, the forest's inhabitants lose their screen of greenery and often have a difficult time finding enough to eat.

For birds like the pied hornbill (*Anthraceros coronatus*), this is a time of year to stay on the move, searching out seeds and insects among the treetops. The common langur monkey (*Semnopithecus entellus*) also has to work harder to find enough to eat,

although many monkeys sidestep the problem by living in towns and villages, where they run nimbly up trees and over rooftops, snatching up anything edible that they can find. But on the floor of the forest, much larger animals do not have this option, and are forced to wander far and wide to satisfy greater appetites. For Asiatic elephants (*Elephas maximus*), the lack of shade makes it harder to keep cool, but this is often less of a problem than the lack of food.

These giant plant-eaters live in both seasonal forest and rain forest, from India to Indonesia. With a maximum weight of

IN STEP WITH THE SEASONS
Like many monsoon forest
animals, most of these
langur monkeys' young are
born in the dry season.

THE FEW *A pride of Asiatic lions in the Gir National Park. Elsewhere in India, most of the lion's former habitat has been converted to farmland.*

about 5 tons (5000 kg), they are the largest animals in Asia, and after the African elephant, the second largest land animals on Earth. In rain forests, elephants can find fresh leaves all year round and water is always close at hand. In seasonal forests, the annual drought means that they have to resort to less nutritious fare, such as dry grass, bark and bare branches, and they must always stay within a few hours' walk of the nearest standing water.

Like their African cousins, Asiatic elephants live in small groups led by an old female known as a matriarch, and each group has its own home range. Adult elephants need about 300 lb (135 kg) of food a day, and to find it during the dry season, they have to cover about three times as much ground as when the forest is green. Their path is easy to make out, because during their wanderings, the elephants uproot shrubs or pull down small trees, leaving a trail of destruction. Unfortunately, they often leave the forest and make excursions into cultivated land, transforming themselves into the world's largest agricultural pests.

As well as providing food for elephants, India's monsoon forests are also the home of much more delicate plant-eaters, such as the chital or axis deer (*Axis axis*). At one time, this beautifully spotted animal was hunted by no less than three big cats – the Asiatic lion (*Panthera leo persica*), the tiger (*Panthera tigris*) and the leopard (*Panthera pardus*), but today, all these hunters are extremely scarce in Asia. One of them, the lion, survives only in a single forest sanctuary in India's extreme north-west. Although these predators no longer pose the threat that they once did, quite different ones still take their toll.

With a body up to 20 ft (6 m) long, the Indian python (*Python molurus*) is one of the largest snakes in Asia, and its dappled brown markings provide almost

OUT IN THE OPEN *Alert for any signs of danger, female chital deer quench their thirst at an Indian water hole.*

perfect camouflage against the fallen leaves. It belongs to a family of snakes that includes the boa constrictor (*Constrictor constrictor*), and like its American relative, it is non-poisonous, killing its prey by muscle power alone.

When a python or boa attacks a small animal, a single crushing bite is often enough to kill. However, to tackle something as large as a deer, a different technique is needed. In this case, the snake lunges forwards and grasps its victim with its teeth; then momentarily pulls its victim upwards so that it can slide part of its body underneath it. It then coils around it and tightens like a clamp, preventing the animal from breathing and eventually killing it by suffocation.

THE FLOWERS OF WINTER

In broad-leaved woodlands of Europe and North America, winter temperatures often fall below freezing point and the leafless trees are completely dormant. Several thousand miles farther south, the dry season 'winter' is still warm, and although many trees lose their leaves, they are not always as

lifeless as they seem. Striking evidence of this can be seen in the seasonal forests of Costa Rica, which border the Pacific Ocean. Almost all the trees are deciduous, and the dry season transforms the forest from a sea of refreshing green into an uninviting tangle of dusty trunks and branches. Small biting flies abound in the heat, but apart from other flying insects, lizards are often the only animals that seem to be on the move.

In this part of the world, the drought is occasionally interrupted by brief rain showers, which do little more than dampen the ground. But for the spindly guayacan or Cortes tree (*Tabebuia ochracea*), these showers act like the meteorological equivalent of a starting pistol. Within less than a week, all of the guayacans in the rain's path are transformed by brilliant clusters of waxy yellow flowers. The flowers last for just three or four days and then their petals fall, leaving the trees as bare as before.

This kind of reproductive stampede is known as 'big bang' flowering. By blooming at exactly the same moment, the trees increase their chances of attracting large numbers of pollinating insects, and within hours of opening, their flowers teem with bees and beetles. These animals are guided to the flowers by their colour, and because the forest is leafless, they can easily find their way from one guayacan tree to the next.

Once the short-lived banquet comes to an end, the pollinators move on to different species. Meanwhile, heavy-bodied lizards called ctenosaurs (*Ctenosaura similis*) feast on the petals on the forest floor, ensuring that none of the floral feast is wasted. As the dry season progresses, the leafless guayacans shed small winged seeds,

ASIA'S LAST LIONS

The lion is often portrayed as an animal whose exclusive domain is the grassland of the African plains. But it is more correct to see Africa as the lion's last stronghold. Until 10 000 years ago, the lion was found in all continents except Australia and Antarctica, and even within historical times, its range stretched from Greece in the north to central India in the east. Lions were exterminated in Europe about 2000 years ago, and today the only wild lions outside Africa are a group of about 200 that live in the Gir Forest in the Indian state of Gujarat. These lions depend on strict conservation measures for their survival.

and these flutter down to the forest floor, where they wait until the rains return.

Throughout the tropics, many other trees use the dry season as a time to reproduce, although few show such precise timing as the guayacan. Their flowers transform the bleak landscape by creating splashes of intense colour, and their fruit and seeds are an important source of food for forest animals. But as the weeks of drought drag by, a more profound change begins to take place: as if responding to a secret signal, the trees start to grow leaves.

In very dry habitats, where rain is rare and unpredictable, some plants produce leaves only after the ground has been soaked by storms. But the trees of seasonal forests do not wait for water before they start to grow. Instead, they anticipate the arrival of the rainy season, so that the forest is already flushed with rapidly expanding leaves when the first thunderclouds roll overhead. It is tempting to imagine that these trees have some kind of rain-sensing system that gives them advance warning of the monsoon front while it is still far away. But the truth is rather different. Instead of sensing rain, the trees respond to the higher temperatures that come with the steadily rising sun. Primed by this sensitive trigger, they are ready for their annual burst of growth when the climatic pendulum once more swings their way.

FOREST-FLOOR FORAGER *In Central America, a primeval-looking ctenosaur searches for food among the dead leaves of a dry-season forest.*

TREES THAT TOUCH THE SEA

Changing tides, leg-grabbing mud and stifling heat make

mangrove swamps places that few people choose to visit.

But in these coastal forests, with their salt-tolerant trees,

animal life flourishes at the frontier between land and sea.

For most trees, salt water is a lethal poison. To be touched by its spray is harmful enough, but to stand in it brings danger of an even greater kind. Salt-laden water sucks the moisture out of roots, so trees that are bathed by it – like sailors cast adrift – run a real risk of dying of thirst.

In the temperate world, trees keep a respectful distance from the seashore. They are safe enough on high ground, but where the coast is low-lying they shrink away from the water's edge. Here, the salty mud is the province of a select band of plants such as sea-lavenders (*Limonium*) and glassworts (*Salicornia*), which are unusually good at tolerating saline conditions. Few of these plants are more than 3 ft (91 cm) high, and they create an open landscape of haunting beauty where sea birds look like tiny specks against an otherwise empty sky.

In the tropics, low-lying coastline looks entirely different. In place of the open mud flats, a dense evergreen forest often obscures the dividing line between land and sea. The trees march out towards the water in tightly packed battalions, and at high tide those in the advance guard are often immersed up to their necks. In a habitat that would quickly kill most trees, mangroves seem quite at home.

SURVIVING SALT WATER

Unlike many trees, such as oaks, pines or palms, mangroves do not form a single group of closely related species. Instead, they belong to several families of flowering plants, with the greatest variety being found around the shores of the Indian Ocean. Some mangroves are little more than shrubs, while others are impressive trees that reach heights of over 80 ft (24 m). But

FLOODED FOREST *Seen from the air, a mangrove swamp is a maze of meandering creeks and backwaters.*

despite their differences in size and ancestry, all are united by one key characteristic – the ability to survive in a salty and waterlogged environment.

The mud beneath most mangrove swamps is made of sediment that has been washed down by rivers and dropped where river water meets the sea. Despite its unattractive appearance, it is often rich in nutrients, which makes it potentially very fertile. But to take root and grow in this medium, mangroves have to solve a number of awkward problems. Because the mud is drowned by every tide, it is not only salty, but also very deficient in oxygen. This makes it difficult for roots to spread to any depth, because their cells – just like those in leaves – need oxygen in order to live. The mud is also unstable, because even the gentlest currents play with its surface, sweeping away one part only to build up another.

Mangroves tackle these problems in different ways. The species called *Avicennia* are the amphibians of the arboreal world,

surviving a twice-daily dip that usually floods everything but their light green crowns. They take up salt in their roots, but they concentrate it in special glands in their leaves, where it is effectively out of harm's way. During particularly high tides, the salt is washed away. To collect oxygen, *Avicennia* mangroves, and some other species, develop thin breathing roots, or pneumatophores, which grow upwards like rows of pencils protruding from the mud. At low tide, the pneumatophores rapidly take in oxygen from the air and supply it to the main roots buried just beneath the surface.

The taller species, *Rhizophora,* are better at keeping salt out of their roots, but they get rid of any that does seep in by storing it in their fleshy leaves. When the leaves are shed, the salt goes with them. *Rhizophora* mangroves can be over 40 ft (12 m) high, and have stout roots that help to stabilise the mud. Some, called prop roots, curve downwards like the legs of a giant insect, while others drop like ropes from high branches. As soon as they

TREES ON TIPTOE *Revealed by the retreating tide, the roots of Australian red mangroves arch across the shifting coastal sand. Left: Negotiating a tangle of mangrove roots, fish feed in shallow water.*

LIFE AT LOW TIDE *In South-east Asia,
low tide creates feeding opportunities
for a number of land-based animals.
Fiddler crabs (1) and mudskippers (2) provide
food for brahminy kites (3) and little egrets (4), and
also for the fishing cat (5) and crab-eating macaque (6).
The water monitor (7) – a giant lizard up to 5 ft (1.5 m)
long – has a very varied diet that includes turtle eggs,
but the unique proboscis monkey (8), which is found
only in Borneo, feeds entirely on the leathery leaves
of mangroves. It rarely strays more than a few
hundred yards from the water's edge.*

touch the mud, the roots start to divide and work their way beneath the surface. As the mud accumulates around the tangle of roots, it forms banks that dry out between the tides.

KINGDOM OF THE CRABS

As seawater floods into a mangrove swamp on the rising tide, a host of small animals greet its arrival by preparing to feed. Oysters cautiously open up their hinged shells and activate tiny hairs that draw water over their gills, while barnacles extend their feathery legs and sweep them backwards and forwards through the current. On most shorelines, these animals spend their adult lives firmly clamped to solid rock, but in mangrove swamps, tree roots serve the same purpose. For a few hours each day, these static feeders sift tiny particles of nourishment from the water, or trap small animals that drift within range.

Because most mangrove swamps shelve very gently, the change that the falling tide brings is swift, and the water only has to drop a few feet to reveal large expanses of glistening mud. Once the mudbanks start to emerge, it is the turn of a very different group of animals to feed. For fiddler crabs

COVERING UP *A heavy body-case shields this West African land crab from many of its enemies.*

(*Uca*), the surface of the mud is like a giant dining-table freshly laid with food by each tide. Using their claws, they pick over the surface layer of sediment, holding small pellets of mud up to their mouths and then scraping away anything edible. When a pellet has been processed, the crab discards it.

Just as insects dominate tropical rain forests, so crabs dominate mangrove swamps. Fiddlers are the most common species on the mud itself, but compared with many crabs, they are lightweight animals with bodies less than 1 in (2.5 cm) wide. They are dwarfed by many of their swimming relatives, and also by giant land crabs (*Cardisoma* and other species), which live just above the high-tide mark. Some of these land crabs are as big as a clenched fist, and they excavate deep burrows marked by large spoil-heaps of blue-black mud. Land crabs feed at night and, unlike

fiddlers, their eating habits are far from delicate. They quickly congregate around anything edible that is thrown up by the tide, from fallen fruit to the dead bodies of fish and of other crabs.

For most crabs, constant moisture is essential for survival. Fiddlers and swimming crabs have no difficulties staying damp, but land crabs are in more danger of drying out. They solve the problem by shaping their burrows so that they trap a pool of water, where they lounge when they are not feeding.

In mangrove swamps, a few crabs have gone much further in abandoning the world of water. Instead of digging subterranean pools or living below the tideline, they feed among the leaves of the mangrove canopy, where they eat the leaves themselves, and also small animals. These crabs are extraordinarily agile and move by scuttling over leaves and branches, and by leaping the gaps between them. They grow up in the sea, but the adult crabs only climb back down to the water to breed.

THE CRAB-CATCHERS

With their armour-plated bodies, sharp claws and lightning reactions, crabs are well able to defend themselves. When faced

LIVING PERISCOPES *Eyes on stalks enable this fiddler crab to check for danger while inching out of its burrow.*

with danger most sprint for the safety of a burrow, but if cornered they come out fighting – even if their enemy is many times their own size. But in mangrove swamps, the sheer abundance of crabs lures many predators. Scattered along the tideline, broken claws and smashed body cases show that despite their built-in protection, many crabs meet a sudden and violent end.

At low tide, some crabs fall victim to predatory birds such as the brahminy kite (*Haliastur indus*), which flies low over the ground snatching small animals in its talons. This bird of prey lives in Asia and northern Australia, and is never found far from water. In New Guinea, crabs also face another feathered adversary, the remarkable shovel-billed kingfisher (*Clytoceyx rex*). Unlike most of its relatives, this kingfisher has a short but powerful beak, which it uses to excavate crabs from the mud.

At high tide, danger more often comes in the form of long-legged waders that use the mangrove trees as night-time roosts and nesting sites. Some of these birds, including the egrets and herons, feed by stabbing into the water with spear-like beaks, and although they are more interested in fish than in crabs, they are quick to strike if the chance arises. Others, such as the beautiful scarlet ibis (*Eudocimus ruber*) of South America, have a different feeding technique. They hunt by touch rather than sight, and are adept at using the tips of their beaks to sense small crabs in muddy water. With a sudden upward flick of its neck, the ibis plucks a crab into the air and swallows it.

Because they do not have teeth, birds eat small crabs whole, and later cough up the indigestible fragments of their body cases. The mammals of mangrove swamps are better equipped for dealing with hard body cases, and they often hunt after dark when the land crabs are on the move. In South-east Asia, the fishing cat (*Felis viverrina*) scoops up crabs with its paws and

OCEAN WANDERERS

LANDFALL *A coconut sprouts on the black volcanic sand of a tropical beach. To be sure of survival, the seedling must roll beyond the high-tide mark.*

for humans, but because their shells are so hard few animals can tackle them when the fruit are fully grown. The land-dwelling robber crab (*Birgus latro*) – a fearsome-looking animal that is larger than a dinner plate – gets around this problem by clambering up trees and cutting off the nuts before they are ripe.

The Indian almond is a shorter tree than the coconut, and has spreading branches and rounded, leathery leaves. Its fruits are only about 2 in (5 cm) long, but even so, they have enough food reserves to survive a long journey across the sea. However, not all fruits actually manage to get as far as the water. They are often

attacked by parrots, such as the scarlet macaw (*Ara macao*), which bite open the fruit with their powerful beaks.

DAYLIGHT ROBBERY *With its legs clamped around a coconut palm, a robber crab clambers upwards in search of food.*

Mangroves are the only trees that live below the high-tide mark, but they are not the only ones that travel across the sea. Throughout the tropics, two widespread trees – the coconut (*Cocos nucifera*) and the Indian almond (*Terminalia catappa*) – take root behind sandy beaches when their floating fruits are cast ashore.

The coconut probably originated in the islands of Polynesia. This supremely elegant palm, which can grow up to 100 ft (30 m) high, is unusually good at tolerating salt, and can survive within a few feet of the waves. As the tree grows, it often leans outwards towards the sea, an adaptation that helps it to drop its fruits directly into the water.

A complete coconut fruit consists of a soft kernel, complete with a supply of watery 'milk', surrounded by a hard shell. The shell is encased in a thick husk, which helps the fruit to float. Once it has fallen into the sea, a coconut can remain alive for

many months, and may travel as much as 3000 miles (4800 km) before it reaches land. If it is thrown above the tideline, the nut sends up a leafy shoot, and some time later roots grow through the husk and anchor the young tree in the sand.

Coconuts are an important food

SHIFTING SHORE *This coconut is growing precariously close to the water's edge and risks being undermined and swept away.*

breaks them open with its sharp teeth be-fore extracting the meat with its tongue, while the African marsh mongoose (*Atilax paludinosus*) also crushes crabs with its teeth. The mongoose has a special tech-nique for tackling crabs that are too big to be killed with a single bite. It picks them up with its front paws, and then smashes them against tree-trunks. Once a crab has been subjected to this kind of treatment, the mongoose can feed at leisure.

In South-east Asia, crabs also have to contend with mammals that search for food by day. Crab-eating macaques (*Macaca fasci-cularis*) use their nimble fingers to scour the tideline for food, picking over the de-bris and seizing any small animals that try to run away. These medium-sized monkeys live in a wide range of forested habitats, and despite their name, they eat many dif-ferent kinds of food. But crab-eating macaques are good swimmers, and they nearly always stay close to water. If a crab tries to escape by making a dash for the sea, they will not hesitate to follow it.

For crab-eating macaques, mangrove swamps are somewhere safe to spend the night. Although the shore holds the prom-ise of food, the mangroves themselves pro-vide them with relatively little, and once dawn breaks, they often head away from the coast to the more varied forests inland.

THE SPREADING SWAMPS

With a muffled splash, a 12 in (30 cm) long spear of green falls from a *Rhizophora* tree and pierces a few inches of water to anchor itself in the mud. Below the mud's surface, the spear's plump tip quickly sprouts roots, while the opposite end develops a tuft of leaves. Within a few days, the spear is well on the way to becoming a new *Rhizophora* tree. These spear-like growths are the re-markable seedlings that help *Rhizophora* mangroves to spread.

Like all mangroves, *Rhizophora* needs to give its offspring the best chance of survival in a difficult habitat, and it makes al-lowances for the ebb and flow of the tide. If a seedling falls at low tide, it is quite likely to stick in the mud, but if the tide is high, it will be carried away from the parent tree.

ARMS AND ARMOUR *With its pincers raised, a crab tries to fend off a hungry macaque.*

The seedling can remain afloat for up to 12 months, and during this time it will begin to sprout roots, which turn it upright like a fishing float. If the seedling eventually comes into contact with mud in shallow water, it quickly attaches itself.

Other mangroves have evolved their own variations on this theme, and can sur-vive lengthy journeys along the coast or even across the open ocean. *Avicennia* man-groves have bean-sized seeds that develop roots while they are floating in the sea, and a species called *Pelliciera*, which grows in the American tropics, has heart-shaped seeds with two fleshy seed leaves, which open out like a pair of floats. With the help of these floating seedlings, mangroves have man-aged to spread all over the tropics, from continental coasts to remote islands. Wher-ever the tropical sea washes over coastal mud, these extraordinary travellers are quick to set up home.

ADAPTING TO EXTREMES

4

TENACIOUS TREES *Throughout the world, conifers are prized for their remarkable resilience.*

IN SOME PARTS OF THE PLANET, THERE ARE PLACES WHERE THE CONDITIONS ARE TOO HOSTILE FOR TREES TO SURVIVE. BUT AROUND THE MARGINS OF THESE AREAS — AT THE THRESHOLD OF ARID LANDS AND AT THE GATES OF THE POLAR REGIONS — SOME OF THE WORLD'S HARDIEST TREES MANAGE TO THRIVE.

HAVING ADAPTED TO WITHSTAND SCORCHING SUNSHINE OR INTENSE COLD, THESE TREES FORM A HABITAT FOR ANIMALS AS DIVERSE AS WOMBATS AND WOLVES, AND PROVIDE FOOD AS WELL AS WELCOME SHELTER. TREES HAVE ALSO ADAPTED TO EXTREMES OF ANOTHER KIND: THE GEOGRAPHICAL ISOLATION PROVIDED BY SOME OF THE REMOTEST ISLANDS ON EARTH.

WINTER LANDSCAPE *Spruce trees thrive in cold regions.*

SURVIVAL IN THE SUN

When strong sunshine is combined with scant rain, trees face daunting demands on their ability to survive. Some specialise in this way of life, however, creating forests that withstand fire, drought and desiccating winds.

The crunch underfoot of dry leathery leaves, the hint of aromatic oils carried on a warm breeze, and surroundings that often seem to promise shade without actually providing it – all these are features that typify sclerophyllous or 'hard-leaf' woodland. In this kind of habitat, broadleaved trees have evolved to withstand hot summer sun and drying winds. Their leaves have a hard, leathery outer layer coated with a waxy substance that prevents water loss, and are often packed with pungent chemicals that make them an unappetising meal.

Sclerophyllous woodlands are found in most of the world's continents, but their spread is very uneven. In Europe, they once flanked the northern and south-western shores of the Mediterranean, growing alongside pines to produce a richly scented forest that grew right down to the sea's edge. Most of this forest was felled long ago, but on hillsides behind the coast, scattered woodlands of deep green holm oaks (*Quercus ilex*), with their glossy leaves catching the summer sunshine, give some idea of what this forest was once like. Wild boar (*Sus scrofa*) still live in these woods, feeding on the acorns that fall in autumn, and during late spring the rocky clearings are ablaze with the flowers of rockroses (*Cistus*) and other shrubs, which bloom before the summer heat sets in.

In southern California, oaks have evolved some remarkably similar lifestyles in response to the same summer-dry climate. Just like the holm oak, California's 'live' oaks – so named because they stay green or 'alive' all year round – also have tough, leathery leaves that withstand strong sunshine. One species, the California scrub oak (*Quercus dumosa*) rarely grows more than 15 ft (4.6 m) high, and instead of being a full-blown tree, is more often a prickly leaved, straggling shrub. Thousands of miles away, a Mediterranean species called the kermes oak (*Quercus coccifera*) is much the same. Both of these shrubby trees provide nesting

WOODLAND BOUQUET *Beneath the shade of evergreen oaks, a rockrose sports its spotted flowers. The papery petals fall within hours of opening.*

sites for small insect-eating birds, and both produce food for jays, which swallow their acorns whole.

With human help, many trees – including the olive (*Olea europea*) and fig (*Ficus carica*) – have successfully made their way westwards from the Mediterranean to California. But these two regions also have some distinctive trees brought in from a very different part of the world. With hanging leaves and peeling bark, the eucalypts

SEASIDE OAKS *The kermes oak, a small Mediterranean tree with prickly leaves, produces clusters of acorns that provide food for jays.*

are the supreme exponents of survival in the sun, and in their natural home regions they form the largest sclerophyll forests in the world.

TREETOP BANQUET

With a piercing screech, the forest suddenly comes to life. It is early morning in the hill country of south-east Australia, and the rising sun is just catching the tops of the tallest trees. A spotted gum (*Eucalyptus maculata*) is in flower, and a flock of rainbow lorikeets (*Trichoglossus haematodus*), winging in from their overnight roost, are eager to start feeding.

Many birds use sound to keep in touch, but few are as noisy as parrots. Lorikeets do their best to keep up this family tradition, and their raucous calls make it possible to trace their path overhead, even when they are hidden by trees. Like other parrots, rainbow lorikeets seem to hate being alone. They normally travel in small flocks that race over the treetops on rapidly beating wings, and even stragglers often travel in pairs rather than risk flying on their own. The excited noise of the rest of the flock attracts them to their destination, and they settle in the highest branches before clambering out towards the flowers.

Eucalypts – or gum trees, as they are often known – dominate the woodlands and forests of Australia in a way that is unmatched by any group of trees in any other continent. There are about 600 species, and of these, fewer than ten are naturally found outside Australia. Even for an expert, the identification of eucalypts can be fraught with difficulties, because many species vary from place to place, and hybrids between different species are common. However, the features that link eucalypts

MEDITERRANEAN FOREST
A mosaic of woodland,
including umbrella-shaped
stone pines, covers these
hills in southern Spain.

FLORAL FEAST *Craning its neck to reach the blooms, a rainbow lorikeet feeds in the crown of a red-flowering gum, a native of western Australia.*

are easier to spot. Among the most important are their flowers, which play a central part in woodland and forest life.

When lorikeets congregate on a flowering tree, they are not attracted by sumptuously coloured petals, because eucalypt flowers do not have any. Petals are present when the flower is in bud, but they form a cap that drops away as soon as the flower opens. Once this cap has been jettisoned, a dense circle of thread-like stamens – the organs that produce pollen – unfold, turning the flower into a feathery ball. In most eucalypts the stamens are off-white, but in a few they are orange or red. Although each flower is usually less than 1 in (2.5 cm) across, they are sometimes produced in such large numbers that flowering trees look as if they have been sprayed with foam.

For lorikeets and other animals that visit eucalypt flowers, each bloom has two areas of interest. One is the circle of stamens, with their coating of nutritious pollen, and the other is an area between this

PAUSE FOR WATER *Noisy friarbirds drink at a water hole. When feeding in the treetops, they create a cacophony of staccato calls.*

circle and the centre of the flower. This inner area contains the flower's nectaries, which produce large quantities of sugar-rich fluid. When a tree is in full bloom, so much nectar is generated that the air below is often heavy with its scent.

Lorikeets not only feed at the flowers, but they are the parrot world's specialists in making use of this source of food. Most parrots have short and fleshy tongues, but a lorikeet's tongue is longer, and it has a brush-like tip. The bird uses this to lap up nectar and sweep up pollen, becoming thoroughly dusted in the process. When it travels to other trees, it takes some of this pollen with it, transferring it to the next flowers that it visits.

During the day, several other kinds of birds descend on eucalypt flowers to collect their share of the feast. In eastern Australia one of them, the noisy friarbird (*Philemon corniculatus*), rivals the lorikeets in producing a raucous cacophony in the treetops. This strange and not altogether handsome bird, which has a largely featherless head, is a member of a family of birds called the honeyeaters. There are more than 60 species in Australia and, like the lorikeets, they are important pollinators of many of the continent's trees.

NIGHT FLIGHT

At dusk, when the daytime blossom-feeders have returned to their roosts, the eucalypt flowers attract a completely different set of visitors. These are the gliding possums, a

group of engaging and often vocal marsupials that are unique to the forests of Australia and New Guinea. In a remarkable example of parallel evolution, these animals have developed the same gliding

A CASE OF SUDDEN DEATH

For male antechinuses, life is so frenetic that it is often curtailed. During the breeding season, the males of this species of small marsupial spend a great deal of energy competing with each other, and this seems to test their bodies to the point of destruction. Shortly after they have mated, the males in at least five species suddenly die in a brief but devastating bout of mass mortality. The females are unaffected, and each species survives thanks to its rapid life cycle, which produces a new wave of adult males the following year.

membranes seen in very different mammals in other forests of the world.

High up in an old forest red gum (*Eucalyptus tereticornis*), the smallest of these nocturnal fliers emerges from a leaf-lined nest hole and sets off in search of food. The tiny pygmy or feathertail glider (*Acrobates pygmaeus*) is about the size of a large mouse. It runs along the highest branches and parachutes from one tree to the next by stretching out flaps of elastic skin that run between its wrists and knees. Its flat, feather-like tail helps to buoy it up in midair, and it moves so quickly that even in the brightest torchlight it is almost impossible to follow.

Pygmy gliders feed on insects and their grubs, but are also attracted by the tempting scent of nectar. Because they weigh only $1/2$ oz (15 g), they can climb down to the tips of the thinnest flower-laden twigs to lap up food in the darkness. A pygmy glider's fingers and toes have disc-shaped pads, rather like those of a tree frog,

and its flattened tail has a prehensile tip. With these to aid its grip, not even a strong wind will dislodge it.

The yellow-bellied or fluffy glider (*Petaurus australis*) is a much more substantial animal, weighing over 40 times as much as its dainty and rather distant relative. With a body as big as a squirrel's, it has difficulty reaching the farthest flowers. For this glider, however, nectar is not the only sugar-rich food that the trees provide. By biting V-shaped notches in the bark, it stimulates the flow of kino – the viscous sap or gum that gives eucalypts their common name. Kino acts in the same way as a conifer's resin, sealing wounds in the bark by turning into a hard, solid plug. One tree in particular – the red bloodwood (*Eucalyptus gummifera*) – produces large amounts of bright red kino, and is one of the yellow-bellied glider's favourites. The glider stops the fluid solidifying by lapping it up, and often returns to feed at the same wounds for several days in succession.

Supported by its tiny 'wings', even the pygmy glider has no difficulty bridging the gaps between neighbouring trees. But of the five species of glider found in Australia's eastern woodlands and forests, the yellow-bellied glider is the expert in this method of travel. Kicking itself into the air from high up on a trunk, it can travel over 350 ft (106 m) in a single glide, steering with the help of its tail. As it becomes airborne, it often gives out a loud screech, which is followed by silence. A distant

NOCTURNAL VISITOR
Demonstrating how it gets its name, a yellow-bellied glider braces its body with its tail as it leans forward to feed.

thud then indicates that the glider has reached its target. Once it has landed, the glider's sharp claws ensure that it does not lose its grip and drop to the ground.

Small and medium-sized gliders live in large family groups, but the forest's biggest gliding mammal, the greater glider (*Petauroides volans*), is more often seen in ones or twos. Its 'wings' stretch from its elbows to its ankles, and when it leaps into the air, it tucks its forearms under its chin, producing a pale, slightly tapering shape when seen from below.

This luxuriantly furred animal can be over 3 ft (91 cm) long, and at about 3 lb (1.4 kg) in weight is much too heavy to risk clambering about among the thinnest twigs. Instead, it feeds on young leaves and

buds, climbing high up into trees to reach the fresh growth. The supply of food seems almost limitless, and it is odd that the greater glider has few competitors in its treetop world. But while pollen and nectar appeal to many animals, from birds to bats and insects, eucalypt leaves are a different matter altogether.

LIVING ON LEAVES

Even from a distance, eucalypt leaves look different from those of most other trees. Instead of spreading horizontally, they usually hang downwards, and they are also thinly scattered. As a result, most gum trees have a drooping and almost wilted look, and their open crowns let sunlight spill through onto the ground.

These characteristics have evolved to let

GUM-TREE FOREST *A forest of blackbutt trees in New South Wales. These eucalypts can reach a height of 180 ft (55 m).*

eucalypts withstand strong sunshine and prolonged droughts. The hanging leaves catch the sunlight at the beginning and end of the day, when the air is relatively cool, but around midday, when the sun is high and the air is warm, they are largely hidden from its glare. This protects the leaves, and also cuts down the amount of water that the trees lose to the outside air.

In most broad-leaved woodlands, it is an easy matter to collect leaves of all shapes and sizes. But in eucalypt woods, the same task can take much longer. Here, it is as if one design has been allocated to an entire continent. Some eucalypts have rounded leaves – particularly on young stems – but the vast majority keep to the same narrow and slightly sickle-shaped plan.

When eucalypt leaves are examined closely, two more features become apparent. The first is a waxy surface, which often gives them a distinctive dull bloom. This wax forms a waterproof barrier, and is another protection against the loss of precious moisture. The second feature is one that can be smelled rather than seen. When the leaves are crushed, they give out a powerful aroma – the characteristic odour of eucalyptus oil.

Eucalyptus oil is produced by tiny glands that can sometimes be seen when a leaf is held up to the light. To most people, it has a pleasant fragrance, but for leaf-eating animals the oil acts as a strong chemical deterrent. Its smell alone is enough to put off many leaf-eating animals, and outside their native home eucalypts are rarely troubled by any of the leaf-eating pests that afflict other trees. But in Australia itself, animals have lived alongside eucalypts for millions

of years, and during that time some have adapted to a diet of gum-tree leaves. These creatures include many insects, together with a select band of mammals. The greater glider is one of these mammals, and another is Australia's most famous tree-dweller – the koala.

According to a popular misconception, koalas (*Phascolarctos cinereus*) move slowly

LEAFY MEAL *Wedged into the fork of a tree, a koala nips off young leaves from the tips of twigs.*

because they are drugged by the food that they eat. But while a diet of eucalyptus leaves would make most mammals extremely sick, the koala's inertia has a less sinister explanation. Eucalypt leaves are low in nutrients and take a long time to digest. Like large leaf-eaters in other parts of the world, such as sloths (*Bradypus*) and howler monkeys (*Alouatta*), the koala needs to conserve energy, and it also has to set aside much of the day for breaking down its food.

Despite its superficial resemblance to a small, fluffy-eared bear, the koala is the only living member of a unique family of marsupials, and spends nearly all its life in trees. It is found only in eastern Australia, although before the last Ice Age it also lived in the eucalypt woodlands of the southwest. At one time, koalas were extremely numerous, but today they are much less so, partly because they were once hunted in their thousands for their soft grey fur.

During the day a koala sleeps with its plump grey body wedged into a convenient fork, while at night it clambers through the branches to feed, using its hands and feet like clamps. To negotiate larger tree-trunks, it uses a different climbing technique. Clasping the trunk with its front legs, it brings its feet together and digs its claws into the bark. Once in this position, it can shuffle up or down like a linesman on a telephone pole.

An adult koala consumes more than 1 lb (450 g) of eucalyptus leaves a day, and becomes so permeated with oil that its entire body – including the female's milk – develops a distinctive gum-tree aroma. Although it will eat the leaves of almost any species if it has to, given the opportunity it is as choosy as a human with a box of chocolates. It has about a dozen firm favourites, which include grey gums (*Eucalyptus punctata*) and red forest gums (*Eucalyptus tereticornis*) in the north of its range, and swamp gums (*Eucalyptus ovata*) and manna or ribbon gums (*Eucalyptus viminalis*) in the south. It grinds up each mouthful of tough leaves with its large cheek teeth, and eventually rests so that the serious business of digestion can begin.

Like all leaves, those grown by eucalypts contain large amounts of cellulose, a fibrous substance that plants use as a building material. Koalas cannot digest cellulose, but like many animals that feed on wood,

they get around this problem by enlisting the help of micro-organisms. The micro-organisms live in a koala's digestive system, in a blind-ended tube called the caecum, and here they ferment the oily leaf pulp, turning it into a form that the koala can use. In humans, the caecum is about 2¹/₂ in (6 cm) long, but in the koala it measures a colossal 8 ft (2.4 m). After the leaves have been broken down, the koala absorbs their nutrients and its liver deactivates their toxic chemicals. Once this process is complete, the koala is ready for its next meal.

Female koalas raise their young in a pouch, as all marsupials do. Given that koalas spend most of their lives crouched in an upright position, it would seem logical that the female's pouch should open upwards, like that of a kangaroo, so that the young should not fall out. But in fact, the reverse is true.

Dangerous though it may sound, this backward-opening arrangement actually has two important advantages. When a young koala is born, it is without fur, fully formed legs or eyes, and often weighs less than ¹/₅₀ oz (0.56 g). As soon as it emerges into the outside world, it hauls its tiny body

YEAR-LONG BOND *A young koala stays with its mother until it is about a year old. It will be ready to breed at the age of four or five.*

TREETOP SLUMBER *With its solitary offspring tucked safely beneath its legs, a female koala dozes high above the ground.*

through its mother's fur and makes for the pouch's entrance. Because the koala's pouch faces backwards it is a relatively short journey, and the young koala immediately makes its way inside and locks onto one of *continued on page 121*

SURVIVING FIRE

In Australia's dry sclerophyll forests, summer fires are an ever-present danger to plant and animal life. Fallen leaves and dead grass can be ignited by the smallest spark, creating a moving front of flame that burns and blackens anything in its path.

In many parts of the world, fires like this would kill many of the standing trees. But eucalypts are made of sterner stuff. They have some unusual adaptations that help them to withstand fire, and they can recover from its effects with extraordinary speed.

The first line of defence is their bark. Eucalypt bark is extremely variable in its texture and colour, but in almost all species it provides extremely good insulation against heat, so even if the bark's flaking patches or peeling strips burst into flame, the living wood beneath often escapes serious harm.

Once the fire has passed, an emergency recovery plan comes into action. Many species of eucalypt have special epicormic buds, which normally remain dormant beneath the bark. If most of a tree's leaves are burnt away, these buds immediately start to grow, and within a few weeks they produce leafy shoots that can cover the entire trunk. These shoots sustain the tree during the initial recovery period, but in time a few of them start to become dominant, forming new branches that allow the tree to regain its shape.

Some eucalypts have a final line of defence, which is used when the whole of the trunk is destroyed. This is a lignotuber – a large woody swelling that contains a store of water and food. The lignotuber forms around the base of the trunk, and can measure several feet across. It is usually half buried in the ground, where it is protected from damage. After a devastating fire or storm the lignotuber starts to sprout shoots, and these can eventually form trunks, replacing ones that have been destroyed.

BURSTING BUDS Epicormic buds sprout several weeks after a fire. Right: After seven weeks, tuft-like grass trees begin to grow new leaves. The eucalypts will take longer to come to life.

SUPERFICIAL BURNS
Paperbark trees burst into flames during a forest fire in New South Wales. These close cousins of eucalypts share the same heat-resistant bark. Right: A burnt eucalypt is surrounded by a flush of new growth.

WET AND DRY *In western Australia (above), scrubby eucalypts grow in arid surroundings. In Australia's far south-east (left), higher rainfall creates a much lusher forest with an understorey of tree ferns.*

the two nipples and begins to feed. A young koala spends about six months inside the pouch, and is held in place by its tight grip on its mother's nipple, and by the pouch's elastic neck. But as it approaches the end of its life in the pouch, its diet starts to change. As well as drinking milk, it leans forwards out of the pouch and eats partially digested leaf pulp that has passed through its mother's body. It does this for about six weeks.

When a koala is born, its intestines do not contain any of the micro-organisms that it needs to digest eucalyptus leaves, so once weaned it would quickly starve. By eating the digested leaf pulp, it inherits the exact mix of micro-organisms that it needs to survive. By the time it leaves the pouch and clambers onto its mother's back, its digestive system is fully primed and it is ready to tackle its unusual food.

LIFE ON THE FOREST FLOOR

Once a eucalypt has finished flowering, its stamens wither away and its nectar flow dwindles and then ceases. Koalas and greater gliders still have plenty of food, but for lorikeets and other flower visitors it is time to move on. Meanwhile, the flowers progress to the next stage of their development. Each one forms a dry woody capsule, or 'gum nut', that is packed with seeds. The end of the capsule is kept shut by small flaps called valves, which seal in the seeds until they are ready to be shed. Unlike eucalypt leaves, the capsules vary a great deal in shape – some look like dimpled spheres, while others are like barrels or smooth, narrow cones – and their shape and texture often provide important clues in identifying a particular tree.

During its lifetime, a large eucalypt can produce millions of seeds. This vast overproduction, which is typical of a great number of trees, helps to offset equally huge losses. From the moment they ripen, the gum nuts attract seed-eating birds such as the green and red king parrot (*Alisterus scapularis*), and the depredations increase a hundredfold once the seeds flutter to the ground.

The world that the seeds encounter when they land varies a great deal. Where there is a fair amount of winter rain, and where the soil is fertile, the ground can be crowded with trees and shrubs, leaving few open spaces. This 'wet sclerophyll' forest, which often forms on high ground, provides a habitat for tree ferns and other soft-leaved plants. It is also the home of the superb lyrebird (*Menura novaehollandiae*), which belongs to a bird family that is uniquely Australian. Named after the

male's long tail, which can be held up in a shape like a lyre, this large ground-feeder is one of the bird world's most gifted mimics. The male bird's far-carrying song often includes recognisable snatches of many other bird calls, and has also been known to include the sound of barking dogs and even passing cars.

Where rainfall is more scant and the soil thinner, a quite different type of understorey develops. In 'dry sclerophyll' forest, which is much more widespread than its wet counterpart, the eucalypts are shorter and the understorey shrubs are more scattered. With their hard and leathery leaves, these drought-resistant plants, which include hakeas (*Hakea*) and banksias (*Banksia*), mirror the adaptations of the trees above them.

In the dry forest, the eucalypt seeds land on a surface that is covered by the crisp dead leaves, and by strips of bark that have been shed by the surrounding trees. Ants eagerly seize the seeds and carry them underground, while other insects and spiders, also on the move over the parched leaf litter, search for animal prey. During the hottest part of the day, the stillness is often broken only by the screech of birds overhead, or by the pattering footfall of a lizard as it suddenly darts over the leaves, pausing to flick them aside in its search for insects. As it moves across the forest floor, halting abruptly and then running forwards once more, it has every reason to be wary, because another hunter may be watching it from the branches above.

Dry woodlands may seem an odd place to find a kingfisher, but nearly half of the world's kingfishers live away from water, and feed on animals other than fish. The largest of them all is the laughing kookaburra (*Dacelo gigas*), which measures 17 in (43 cm)

from the tip of its shovel-like beak to its short, mottled tail. Unlike its fishing relatives, which are often brilliantly coloured, it is brown and grey, a combination that pro-

THE PAST'S TALLEST TREES

The tallest trees alive today are coast redwoods, which grow in California. However, until relatively recently, these conifers were probably exceeded in height by the Australian mountain ash (*Eucalyptus regnans*), which is the world's tallest broad-leaved tree. In 1885, one mountain ash growing in the state of Victoria was estimated to be 470 ft (143 m) high, which is about 100 ft (30 m) higher than today's tallest coast redwoods. Another tree was 435 ft (132 m) high when it was measured in the 1870s, but damage to its trunk suggested that it may have been over 500 ft (152 m) high in its prime. The tallest mountain ash alive today, growing in Tasmania, measures a modest 312 ft (95 m).

vides good camouflage as it waits for its moment to attack.

The kookaburra is famous for its maniacal cry, but when hunting it is completely silent. Perched on a branch, it scans the ground below for signs of movement, keeping its body quite still until an animal gives itself away. Its reaction then is immediate. Swooping down to the ground like a bird of prey, it snatches up its victim and then returns to its perch to feed. Lizards, insects and small birds all feature in its diet, and so do small snakes. It deals with snakes by gripping them behind the head, and then either drops them from a height or batters them on a branch. It then swallows its luckless victim whole.

NIGHT ON THE GROUND

On the forest floor, life is at its busiest at night, after the kookaburras have marked sunset with a final chorus of frenzied laughter. From tree-holes, nests and deep burrows, nocturnal marsupials emerge to scour the leaf-litter for food, guided by good

NATURAL SHOW-OFF *Most male birds attract females with either loud calls or flamboyant plumage. The male lyrebird excels in both.*

SUCCESSFUL CATCH *This kookaburra has caught a short-legged, snake-like lizard. Above: The dunnart's sharp teeth will make quick work of the grasshopper's tough body-case.*

these comforting resemblances came unstuck. The sight of a tiny marsupial 'mouse', with up to half a dozen young bulging out of its pouch, is a startling one, and must have amazed many new Australians as they explored the woods and forests of their adopted land.

Despite their often rodent-like shapes, most of these small marsupials – which include dunnarts (*Sminthopsis*), tuans (*Phascogale*) and antechinuses (*Antechinus*) – only very occasionally actually eat eucalypt seeds and other plant food. Instead, they benefit from the trees indirectly, by catching insects and other small animals. All seem to live at a feverish pace, running and sometimes hopping over the forest floor, scrambling up trees, and noisily crunching into the bodies of beetles and cicadas with their sharp teeth.

In mammals, the nocturnal habit is an ancient one, and dates back to the time when the very earliest of their kind lived alongside the dinosaurs, more than 200 million years ago. Like many of today's woodland and forest marsupials, these early mammals also hunted insects under the cover of darkness, and had the same sharp teeth and keen senses. Although much has changed since those times – including the evolution of the eucalypts and all other broad-leaved trees – Australia's forest nightlife shows that the original lifestyle remains effective still.

hearing, keen eyesight, and an excellent sense of smell.

The largest of these animals is the common wombat (*Vombatus ursinus*), a bear-like animal that excavates tunnels that can be 100 ft (30 m) long. Weighing up to 75 lb (34 kg), this slow-moving vegetarian feeds on grass, which it clips with sharp incisor teeth at the front of its jaws. When fully grown it has few enemies, but its powerful legs, with their sharp claws, make effective weapons if anything gets too close.

With its low-slung, barrel-like body, the wombat is easy to identify. However, the same cannot be said of many smaller marsupials that also emerge under the cover of darkness. Given their variety, it is hardly surprising that Australia's earliest European settlers tried to see them in terms of animals that were more familiar. Many of them became labelled as marsupial 'mice', while others invited obvious comparisons with cats or rats.

However, during the breeding season,

FORESTS OF THE FAR NORTH

Subzero temperatures, ice-laden winds and the endless

winter night are just some of the problems that confront life

on the fringes of the Arctic. The trees and animals that survive

in this remote region are among the most resilient on Earth.

From the air, the scene is pregnant with drama. A line of a dozen black specks snakes its way out across the frozen surface of a lake, slowly gaining distance from the forest-clad shore. Over 400 yd (365 m) farther out, two dark smudges, larger but unequal in size, are silhouetted against the snow. They follow a less clear course, sometimes veering to the left as if making back to the shore, but then pulling back to the right and pressing onwards over the open ice. With their heavy, loping strides, they are clearly making slower progress than their pursuers, and as the minutes tick away, the gap begins to close.

Now only 300 ft (90 m) separates the hunters from the hunted. Suddenly, the pursuing line breaks up, forming a fan that consolidates into two loose groups before breaking apart once more. With a burst of speed, two of the pursuers overtake the fugitives and cut across their path. In this moment of confusion, some of the black shapes manage to work their way between the retreating figures, deftly prising them apart and then bringing them to a halt. The beleaguered pair are now clearly fighting for their lives. The larger of the two kicks out with its immense legs and successfully holds its assailants at bay, but the smaller is in difficulties. It lacks the size

SOLITARY MEAL *A female moose feeds on water plants in Alaska's Denali National Park during the summer twilight.*

and strength to fend off so many attackers, and after a short confrontation, is brought crashing down onto the ice.

Just six hours later, all that marks the spot is the remnants of a carcass and tracks that lead back to the distant shore. One set of tracks belongs to a wolf pack, sated by their kill. The other belongs to a female moose (*Alces alces*), which against all her instincts was forced to retreat onto the open ice. It was a tactical mistake, for which her single calf paid a heavy price.

HUNTERS OF THE NORTH

More than any other animal, the grey wolf (*Canis lupus*) has come to epitomise all that is dark and treacherous about the great northern forest. As far as humans are concerned, there is no doubt that it has been unjustly defamed, because wolf attacks on people are events of quite exceptional rarity. No fatal attacks have been recorded in North America, while in Europe, the attacks of earlier times may have involved hybrids between dogs and wolves, rather than

STANDING GUARD *A female moose watches over her two calves. Because she has twins, she needs to be particularly vigilant.*

pure-bred wolves themselves. Despite this evidence for the defence, the wolf has been relentlessly persecuted. Once the second most widespread land mammal after humans, it has been wiped out in many parts of the world, and its final stronghold is now the vast, thinly populated forest on the Arctic's edge.

Individually, wolves catch animals as small as mice and beetles, and are as unfussy in their eating habits as other members of the dog family, such as foxes and coyotes. But they are set apart from their solitary relatives by a unique system of co-operative hunting based around the pack. This social unit comprises a pair of adults, together with up to two dozen individuals of different ages. Working together as a team, the members of a pack can cover over 30 miles (48 km) a day, and can bring down prey that would be too big or too agile for them to tackle alone.

In the northern forest, the moose is by far the biggest prize that comes within the wolves' grasp. Known in Europe as the elk, it is the largest member of the deer family, and is the northern forest's biggest planteater. What the moose lacks in elegance, it makes up in sheer size. Its shoulders are often higher than a man, and it can weigh over $^3/_4$ ton (760 kg). Males have immense,

THE SURVIVOR *The wolf's adaptability and intelligence have helped it to succeed in the northern forests despite years of hunting by humans.*

hand-shaped antlers that can span over 6 ft (1.8 m) from tip to tip, and both sexes have a characteristically drooping upper lip that they use to grasp their food.

Compared to other deer, moose are extremely fond of water. During summer, they often wade into lake shallows to feed on water plants, and they sometimes dip their heads beneath the surface to reach those on the bottom. Buoyed up by their great bulk, they are good swimmers. In northern Lake Superior, moose are known to have reached Isle Royale – an offshore national park – by swimming across the border between the United States and Canada, which lies amid 20 miles (32 km) of open water.

A healthy adult moose has few enemies, and is rarely troubled by wolves. Moose calves, however, are more vulnerable. Female moose usually give birth to a single calf in spring, and for 12 months each mother keeps her calf by her side, using her massive body as a living shield. If a wolf pack gets wind of the calf, the mother may

feel that emergency action is needed. Shepherding her calf into shallow water, she stands between it and the pack. Wolves will not venture far into water, and in most cases they lose interest in their quarry and move off to hunt elsewhere.

But with the arrival of the winter freeze, the tables are turned. The moose calves are deprived of their refuge, and wolves can now travel where they like. Slow and weak calves may not live to see the spring, but as always in nature, the quickest and strongest survive.

NORTHERN SENTINELS

Throughout the forests of the world, nature constantly puts living things to the test. The reward for success is a chance to survive and multiply, while the penalty for failure is a decline that may eventually lead to extinction. In tropical forests, the number of species that pass this testing process runs into millions, and in temperate forests it is still many thousands. In the northern forest, conditions are far less clement and so the test is that much more severe. Only a few species have the qualities needed to succeed, but for plants in particular, their reward is a virtual monopoly on one of the Earth's most extensive habitats.

The great northern or boreal forest circles the Arctic like a giant letter C. It runs through Scandinavia, northern Russia and North America, covering immense tracts of Canada before coming to an end in the high ground of New England. Its only significant break lies to the east of this point, where the windswept coast meets the North Atlantic. Were it not for this gap, it would be possible to walk through the boreal forest right the way around the Earth.

On the southern fringes of the boreal forest, broad-leaved trees and conifers live side by side. But in the heart of the forest belt, evergreen conifers are the undisputed victors in the contest for supremacy. With their waxy and windproof leaves, spruces (*Picea*), firs (*Abies*) and pines (*Pinus*) are well equipped to withstand winter cold, and are able to begin photosynthesis the instant spring gets under way. Their conical shape is ideal for shedding snow, letting it slip away harmlessly instead of building up into a potentially lethal burden. This gives them a double advantage over broad-leaved trees, which have to produce a new set of leaves every spring, and whose spreading profile gathers snow like an outstretched hand.

SHEDDING SNOW *Like tiles on a steep roof, a conifer's sloping branches help to shed snow before it has a chance to pile up too deeply.*

Sheltered by their own endless ranks, these evergreen conifers often stand shoulder to shoulder as far as the eye can see, forming a closed forest that can seem chilling and uninviting. Writing in the 19th century about the forests in the high ground of Maine, the American poet and naturalist Henry David Thoreau captured the feelings of many when confronted by this endless

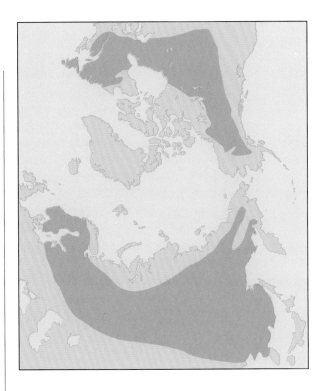

THE BOREAL FOREST ZONE
The great northern forest has a total area of about 3.7 billion acres (1.5 billion ha). In places it is over 1000 miles (1600 km) from north to south.

expanse of green. 'Except the few burnt lands, the narrow intervals on the rivers, the bare tops of the high mountains, and the lakes and streams, the forest is uninterrupted. It is even more grim and wild than you had anticipated, a damp and intricate wilderness, in the spring everywhere wet and miry. The aspect of the country, indeed, is universally stern and savage, excepting for the distant views of the forest from hills, and the lake prospects, which are mild and civilising to a degree.'

THE FOREST FROM WITHIN

To anyone used to the broad-leaved woodlands farther south, this immense and undiluted forest can indeed be a bewildering and disorienting place. In any one area, just two or three tree species predominate, giving the forest a uniformity not found anywhere else on Earth. In spruce and fir forests particularly, the dense canopy casts a deep shade, and the view ahead is blocked not only by endless trunks, but also by a filigree of interlocking branches that have died after being starved of light by those higher up. The air beneath the trees is filled with the tang of resin and the musty aroma of woodland fungi, and the pathless forest floor, cushioned by a mattress of dead needles, often gives the impression that few human feet have ever crossed it. Despite appearances, there is plenty of

wildlife in this forest, but finding it requires a keen eye and also a good sense of direction.

Towards the northern boundary of the forest, a gradual change takes place. Here, the trees thin out and become progressively more stunted, creating an open, marshy landscape splashed with brilliant green in summer by treacherously waterlogged mounds of *Sphagnum* moss. The white flower heads of cotton grass (*Eriophorum*) tremble violently in the Arctic wind, while other plants hug the ground, staying out of reach of its icy blast.

This boundary zone between the forest and the treeless tundra is often known as the taiga, although, confusingly, the same Russian word is often applied to the forest as a whole. Here, the very existence of trees hangs in the balance. A good summer allows a small amount of growth, but in winter this can easily be pruned back by intense frosts and bone-dry winds. After a century of this natural equivalent of snakes and ladders, trees are often less than 6 ft (1.8 m) high, with trunks no thicker than an adult's wrist.

Paradoxically, these Arctic outliers seem to stand logic on its head. Instead of being evergreen, like the spruces or firs, the tree-line species often include larches or tamaracks (*Larix*) – among the few deciduous conifers – and low-growing birches (*Betula*), which also shed their leaves every year. In central and eastern Siberia, where the climate is at its most severe, Dahurian larches (*Larix gmelini*) are practically the only conifers to be seen, making the winter landscape starker still.

How do these deciduous trees survive where evergreen species cannot? The answer probably lies in the fact that winters this far north are simply too cold for exposed leaves to survive. Freed of competition from the evergreens, larches and birches have the space and light that they need to survive. It is a precarious existence, but the land is theirs alone.

INSECTS OF THE NORTH

With its eight or nine-month winter, the boreal forest may seem an unlikely place to find much insect life. However, insects do live here, sometimes – in the case of mosquitoes – in overwhelming and almost unbearable numbers.

In the depths of the forest, the stillness

HOSTILE LANDSCAPE *Swampy forest with stunted trees, known as muskeg, creates difficult terrain on Mitkof Island in south-east Alaska.*

is sometimes broken by an insect of altogether larger proportions. Measuring 2 1/2 in (6 cm) from its head to the tip of its sting-like tail, the wasp-like *Rhyssa persuasoria* settles on tree-trunks and branches, tapping the wood restlessly with slender antennae before moving on. Despite its troubling appearance, *Rhyssa* poses no danger to humans, because the female's 'sting' is actually a very elongated egg-laying tube, or ovipositor, flanked by a protective sheath.

Rhyssa belongs to a group of insects called the ichneumons, and like most of her relatives, the female spends her adult life looking for a suitable place to lay her eggs.

The object of her urgent searching is not a convenient bark crevice or a cluster of newly sprouting leaves. Instead, she hunts for the caterpillar-like grubs of the wood wasp (*Urocerus gigas*), which bore their way through conifers, eating a fungus that develops on damaged wood. Having located a

grub, the female *Rhyssa* swings her ovipositor sheath upwards and out of the way, and then pierces the wood with her egg-laying tube, sliding it in with the accuracy of a surgeon making an injection. She then lays an egg next to the grub, withdraws her ovipositor and flies off. It is a slow process, lasting up to half an hour, but it seals the fate of the young wood wasp. The *Rhyssa* egg hatches into a parasitic larva, and this gradually devours the grub before emerging as an adult from the tree.

Extraordinary though it sounds, the female *Rhyssa* bores her way through over 1 in (2.5 cm) of bark and wood, using a flexible tube as thin as a hair. But more astounding still is her ability to detect her hidden victims. Wood-wasp grubs move very slowly, and make almost no detectable noise. Their feeding burrows have no connection with the surface, so to human senses at least, there is absolutely no indication that they are there.

For many years, entomologists puzzled over the uncanny accuracy shown by this parasitic insect. What are the mysterious clues that show the female *Rhyssa* where to drill? The answer to this is now known, and as is so often the case with insects, it has to do with smell. Using her antennae, the female *Rhyssa* detects the particular fungus that a wood wasp introduces when it lays its eggs, in order to provide them with a source of food. She responds by drilling downwards, helped by sensory nerve endings on the tip of her ovipositor that let her know when she has made contact with her target. Despite its somewhat gruesome consequences, her method of finding and reaching is among the most remarkable specialisations in the insect world.

ATTACK FROM OUTSIDE

For the forest's wood-boring insects, the prospect of being eaten alive by parasites is not the only hazard in daily life. Surrounded and protected by their food, they are

ON TARGET *A female* Rhyssa *drills down towards a sawfly grub hidden beneath the surface.*

usually much more secure than insects that live out in the open. However, there are times when the outside world intrudes with a sudden and shattering impact.

With a body as big as a crow's, the black woodpecker (*Dryocopus martius*) is a relentless adversary of insects that live in wood. Unlike *Rhyssa,* which carefully establishes the exact position of its prey, the woodpecker simply lands on a likely looking tree-trunk, and then starts hacking it to pieces with its chisel-like beak. Splinters of wood, some the size of a hand, cascade onto the ground beneath, while the woodpecker reaches within for its food.

The black woodpecker lives in the boreal forest throughout Europe and northern Asia, where it is the largest member of the woodpecker family. North America has a species that is as big, although the pileated woodpecker (*Dryocopus pileatus*) is rarer, and is more often found in broad-leaved woodlands than in the conifers of the north. Together with their many smaller relatives, they form an instantly recognisable group of forest birds. Not only do they have a strange way of flying – rising and falling as they flap and then fold up their wings – but they also have some unique adaptations to their unusual way of life.

Before a woodpecker can set to work on a tree, it first has to clamp itself firmly in position. It does this with the help of its large, sharply clawed feet, and also with its tail, which acts as a brace. Once it has checked its grip, it snaps its head backwards and then delivers the first blow.

When the bird's beak smashes into solid wood, the effect is rather like a car crash, with the woodpecker's skull taking the place of the car. Its skull comes to an almost instant halt, but its brain tries to keep moving under its own momentum, rather like a passenger thrown towards the windscreen. Fortunately for the woodpecker, its brain is well protected. Its skull is unusually strong, and a layer of fluid between the skull and the brain acts like a liquid airbag, cushioning the brain as it

AVIAN EXCAVATOR *A male black woodpecker clings to the entrance of its nest-hole (above), while a spruce tree (right) bears the marks of a recent woodpecker attack.*

rapidly snaps its head back, and once more its brain is thrown backwards and then forwards. A human would quickly lose consciousness under these conditions, but the woodpecker can deliver a burst of several dozen pecks without any ill effects.

Once a woodpecker has broken its way into a tree-trunk, an even more remarkable adaptation comes into play. The pecking often exposes the tunnels of woodboring insects leading up and down the trunk. Somewhere along each tunnel a grub is likely to be found, but breaking open each tunnel along its entire length would be a slow and laborious business. The woodpecker solves this by using its tongue – a sticky and spine-tipped harpoon of almost unbelievable length.

A woodpecker's tongue can often extend three or four times the length of its beak. The bird quickly flicks it out, and then probes along the tunnels, retrieving and swallowing anything that comes within its reach. Once it has finished eating, its extraordinary tongue has to be stowed away. The tongue retracts by sliding right around the outside of the woodpecker's skull, forming an almost complete loop that runs from the base of the beak to a point just beneath the nostrils.

Some woodpeckers have turned this remarkable feeding apparatus to a quite different use. Instead of probing for insects in wood, they feed mainly on the ground and use their tongues to reach into ants' nests. In North America, the yellow-shafted flicker (*Colaptes*

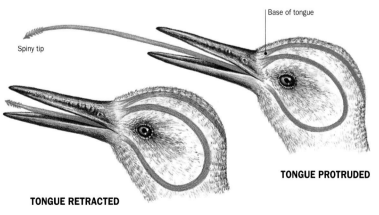

Spiny tip

Base of tongue

TONGUE PROTRUDED

TONGUE RETRACTED

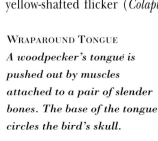

WRAPAROUND TONGUE *A woodpecker's tongue is pushed out by muscles attached to a pair of slender bones. The base of the tongue circles the bird's skull.*

auratus) devours ants throughout the northern forest, while in Eurasia, the green woodpecker (*Picus viridis*) does the same in woodlands farther south.

YEARLY BOOM AND BUST

In tropical forests, conditions are often identical from one year to the next. But in the boreal forest, the climate is far less predictable, and two years are never the same. A mild summer can lead to a bumper crop of seeds and berries, while a delayed spring followed by a cold summer has the opposite effect. Growth is slowed down, and many plants fail to set seed at all. Like ripples spreading across the surface of a pond, these changes have far-reaching effects on the forest's animal life. Some of the effects are felt almost immediately, while others may take a year or more to work their way through forest food chains.

Few animals are as sensitive to these changes as voles, pocket-sized rodents that depend on plant food. Faced by a capricious environment but endowed with a formidable ability to multiply, their population lurches up and down. During winter, vole numbers are always low, and the animals huddle together in ball-shaped nests under the snow, making forays through tunnels to find food. With the arrival of spring, reproduction on a startling scale begins.

TEMPTING TARGET
The tiny red-backed vole is on the menu of many predators in North American forests.

In exceptionally good conditions, the northern red-backed vole (*Clethrionomys rutilus*), a widespread boreal forest species, can raise up to five families a year. Each litter contains about six naked and blind young, but these grow quickly and are ready to breed themselves at the age of four months. A single female can theoretically have at least 30 young a year, but this figure is further swollen by adding her 'grandchildren', which can run into several dozen. Without some kind of check, the northern forest would soon teem with voles and little else. When it does come, that check is swift and deadly.

Voles have many enemies, but few are such efficient killers as the mustelids. This family of predatory mammals has no familiar common name, but includes a handful of omnivores, such as the Eurasian badger (*Meles meles*), and a wide range of hunters. Many of the hunters are notoriously quick-witted and aggressive, and are armed with needle-sharp teeth.

In the boreal forest, mustelids are the most numerous predatory mammals. Some of them, such as the American pine marten (*Martes americana*), are agile tree-climbers, while others, such as the fisher (*Martes penanti*), also from North America, can climb, but spend most of their time on the ground. The marten often feeds on squirrels and on roosting or nesting birds, while the fisher specialises in tackling porcupines (*Erethizon dorsatum*), dodging their sharp

CAMOUFLAGED KILLER *A stoat prepares to feed on a mouse. Like its relative, the least weasel, it is chestnut brown in summer.*

quills and then flipping them onto their backs. Once a porcupine is in this position, the fisher can attack its exposed underside, free from the threat of quills breaking off and working their way deep into its skin.

For voles, the main threat comes from ground-based hunters, including the sable (*Martes zibellina*) – long prized for its sumptuously soft fur – and the tiny least weasel (*Mustela nivalis*). With a slender body measuring just 8 in (20 cm) from its nose to the base of its tail, this tiny mammalian carnivore – the world's smallest – is able to slip along vole runs, pursuing them into their nests. It dispatches them with a stabbing bite to the back of the neck, and does not hesitate to sink its teeth into human fingers if it is caught and picked up. Even if sables or weasels do not find them, voles are still not free from mustelid attack. The lumbering wolverine (*Gulo gulo*), which looks like a small bushy-tailed bear, tracks them down with its acute sense of smell, and tears the nests open with its powerful paws.

Owing to the depredations of mustelids and other hunters, the expanding vole population eventually reaches a plateau. Once breeding halts in autumn and food becomes harder to find, numbers start to dive.

AGGRESSION PAYS *Although less than 4 ft (1.2 m) from head to tail, the wolverine is very strong and often drives other predators from their kills.*

Voles usually store winter food in their nests, but by early spring, these supplies are often exhausted. Many animals that have successfully avoided being eaten and have pulled through the coldest months fail this final test as the 'hunger gap' of early spring takes its toll.

When midsummer comes to the boreal forest, it brings some strange consequences. North of the Arctic Circle, daylight is uninterrupted, while to the south, the fading dusk leads seamlessly into the brightening dawn. For a few weeks of the year, nocturnal predators are deprived of the cloak of night, while diurnal animals lose the protection that darkness normally brings. During this season of the ascendant sun, the symphony of life – normally divided into two contrasting movements – becomes merged into one.

Of all forest animals, owls are most affected by this unusual state of affairs. Throughout the north, the boreal owl (*Aegolius funereus*) – also known as Tengmalm's owl – is forced to abandon its nocturnal habits, and hunts rodents and small birds in the bright summer evenings. It is an agile flier, twisting and turning through the trees on rapidly beating wings, before dropping suddenly onto its prey. Like all owls, its approach is almost silent, due to a special modification of its flight feathers. Their leading edges have soft fringes, and these muffle the sound of the parting airstream, allowing the

---

THE SNOWSHOE HARE'S TEN-YEAR CYCLE

Like shares on the stock market, northern forest animals have their good years, and they also have their bad ones. For most species, good years are difficult to predict, and depend largely on the vagaries of the weather. However, for one animal – the North American snowshoe hare (*Lepus americanus*) – success seems to follow failure with the regularity of a ticking clock.

In Canada, trappers' records extending back over two centuries provide a detailed record of the hare's changing fortunes. They show that its numbers peak about once every ten or eleven years, reaching up to 100 times their normal levels. Then, quite abruptly, the numbers plunge, and another decade passes before the next boom arrives. This population explosion takes place at almost exactly the same time across the whole North American forest. It affects not only the hares, but also many of their predators, such as the lynx (*Felis lynx*), the American pine marten (*Martes americana*) and the red fox (*Vulpes vulpes*).

CLOSING-IN *A lynx lunges with a fur-clad paw at a retreating hare. With the lynx this close, the hare is unlikely to escape.*

When biologists first investigated these figures, they concluded that the cycle was generated by the simple effect of predators on their prey. Hares can reproduce rapidly, and their expanding population provides easy food for their enemies. Their enemies take longer to multiply, but when they do, the hares fall victim in huge numbers. The predators – the argument goes – provide the push that drives hare numbers downwards. But like investors trapped in a falling market, the predators, too, begin to suffer, and it is the fall in their numbers that eventually enables the hares to take off once again.

More recently, evidence has come to light that refutes this idea. On Anticosti Island, in the mouth of the St Lawrence River, snowshoe hares live without any large mammalian predators. However, their numbers still rise and fall every ten years, just as they do almost everywhere else. Clearly, something other than predators triggers each catastrophic decline, and what is true of this large island is probably true of the rest of the northern forest.

Many biologists now believe that predators play only a secondary role in this natural cycle. In a boom year, the hares ransack the forest's reserves of winter food, and soon start to go hungry. Underfed young hares are less likely to survive the winter, and those that do produce fewer young. As a result, the population begins to fall, and it keeps falling for several years until the fertility of the hares starts to rise once more. It therefore seems that the hares' ultimate enemies are not their predators, but themselves.

AERIAL ATTACK *With talons outstretched, a great horned owl swoops in for the kill. This impressive bird is found from the treeline to the tropics.*

owl to strike before its victim is even aware of its approach.

With a body measuring about 10 in (25 cm) long, the boreal owl is a relative lightweight in the forest line-up. Far more formidable is the great grey owl (*Strix nebulosa*), a superbly camouflaged hunter that is found in both the Old and New Worlds. Instead of quartering the ground in search of food, the great grey remains seemingly aloof, surveying its surroundings with staring yellow eyes set in a curiously flattened face. Its face acts like a sound-recordist's collecting dish, channelling the faintest noises to its ears, which are beneath a thin layer of feathers. When the owl pinpoints the movement of a rodent or bird, it drops from its perch and snatches up its target with thickly feathered toes.

The great grey is one of the largest boreal forest owls, and has a wingspan of about 5 ft (1.5 m). However, it is not the heaviest, because much of its bulk consists of a thick layer of feathery insulation. The Eurasian eagle owl, which tips the scales at 6 lb (2.7 kg), weighs twice as much and is able to tackle much larger prey. Hares and foxes frequently feature in its diet, as do birds up

to the size of grouse and ducks. Like its close relative, the great horned owl (*Bubo virginianus*) of North America, it hunts perfectly successfully by day, refuting the popular belief that owls are blinded by daylight.

For birds of prey, midsummer is a time of unrivalled opportunity. Most owls use their eyes and ears to find food, but these feathered hunters rely entirely on vision, and the long Arctic days work very much to their advantage. The dense forest is not an easy habitat for birds that spot their prey by soaring high up, so this is not a place to see buzzards and their relatives (*Buteo* spp.). But for a different group of predatory birds, the sparrowhawks or accipiters (*Accipiter* spp.), the maze of trees and branches makes a perfect hunting ground.

AIRBORNE HUNTER *A male goshawk launches itself from a tree. Female goshawks are brown rather than grey, and are larger than the males.*

Unlike buzzards, these lightly built predators have short, rounded wings, and they move with a swift, scudding flight, skilfully swerving around any obstacle in their path. The North American sharp-shinned hawk (*Accipiter striatus*) and Eurasian sparrowhawk (*Accipiter nisus*) are both found in the far north, but throughout both Old and New Worlds, the species most at home among the endless conifers is the northern goshawk (*Accipiter gentilis*). This rare and secretive bird, once prized for use in falconry, is a master of the aerial ambush.

Instead of swooping from above, the goshawk hunts horizontally, bursting through forest glades with the explosiveness of a low-flying fighter plane. Its targets are often other birds, and it takes just a split second to lock onto its victim, bringing it down after a brief high-speed chase. The instant of the goshawk's arrival brings palpable panic among forest birds, and also among hares, squirrels and other small mammals, for these, too, feature in the hunter's menu. But as soon as the goshawk has moved on, life immediately returns to

normal. It is as if the prospective victims instinctively understand their enemy's hunting technique – if the goshawk fails in its surprise attack, it does not waste time staging a second attempt.

FAMILY STYLES

Returning to its nest after a successful hunt, a breeding owl or goshawk is likely to be greeted by the plaintive calls of its chicks, urgently demanding food. Young owls can swallow small animals whole, but goshawk chicks must wait until their parents tear the food into strips, and then offer it to the nearest hungry mouth.

When mammals raise a family, their young are born in quick succession. In a few forest species – for example, the Virginia opossum – some of the young soon die, but in nearly all cases, the siblings that do survive have equal access to their mother's milk, and so grow up in step. The same is true of family life in most birds. In the boreal forest, ground-feeders such as the spruce grouse (*Bonasa umbellus*) and the turkey-sized capercaillie (*Tetrao urogallus*) usually

FLIGHT FROM THE NORTH

In the boreal forest, an unpredictable food supply often triggers sudden bird migrations, known as irruptions, which bring northern species flooding south – sometimes over 2500 miles (4000 km) beyond their normal range. Unlike ordinary migrants, birds that irrupt do not navigate their way to any particular destination. Instead, they stop once they have encountered better conditions. In both North America and Eurasia, the species most often involved in irruptions are small seed and berry-eaters. Among the most important are waxwings (*Bombycilla*), grosbeaks (*Pinicola*) and crossbills (*Loxia*). Crossbills are highly specialised finches that use their unique cross-tipped beaks to prise seeds from cones.

lay about a dozen eggs, over a period of a week or more. Nevertheless, all the eggs hatch within a few hours of each other, and because the chicks are the same size, they

stand a roughly equal chance of success in the struggle to find food.

In an owl or goshawk's nest, however, inequality is the keynote of family life. The female bird lays about three or four eggs, and unlike a female grouse – who waits until her clutch is complete – she starts incubating the moment the first egg appears. As a result, the eggs hatch in a staggered sequence, the oldest chick having a head start on those that follow. The chicks are graded like a set of Russian dolls, and because the oldest is always the biggest and strongest, it gets more than its share of the food.

To a human observer, it is tempting to attach emotive labels to this situation. The oldest chick seems like the spoilt bully of the family, while the younger chicks are the innocent victims of its greed. The parents appear incapable of confronting the bully's bad behaviour, and by giving in to its demands for food, they often allow the youngest chicks to starve to death.

It seems extraordinary that parents can go to such lengths to produce young, only to let them perish. But an animal's behaviour, just as much as its body, is the product of evolution and comes about through the stringent testing process of natural selection. Parent birds have no understanding of fairness or favouritism, but act simply through instinct. That instinct must confer some advantage on their species – the question is, what?

It takes one of the northern forest's

JUMPING THE QUEUE When a great grey owl returns to the nest with food, the oldest chick is often first in line for a meal.

cold years to provide the answer. When conditions become severe and food is hard to find, similarly sized siblings have to share an increasingly meagre supply. If they start to starve, they do so together, and there is a very real danger that the entire family will perish. But for owls and goshawks, the unequal family comes into its own, because it shrinks to fit the changing conditions. In an exceptionally good year, all the chicks survive, while in a bad one the oldest, at least, is likely to pull through. To us it may seem a harsh system, but it has one key advantage – it works.

THE FOREST IN WINTER

Six months after the race to reproduce reaches its height, the forest world looks very different. The endless daylight is a distant memory, and the far north is a place of dark and crystalline harshness, where exposed skin freezes and warm breath condenses into clouds of vapour. Even on the southern fringes of the forest, temperatures plunge far below zero, while in north-east Siberia – the coldest part of the forest zone – they can drop to a numbing –60°C (–76°F).

It seems logical that the colder it is, the more snow there must be. The reverse is, in fact, the case. For much of the year, the far north is dominated by large masses of high-pressure air that holds little moisture. Near the northern treeline, the annual precipitation is often less than 16 in (400 mm), while in parts of Siberia it sometimes struggles to reach 10 in (250 mm). Despite its stunted

THE WORLD'S MOST NORTHERLY TREES

A group of stunted Dahurian larches (*Larix gmelini*), growing in Siberia at latitude 72°N, probably forms the most northerly outpost of the great boreal forest. Here, close to the icy Laptev Sea, the annual growing season is less than six weeks long. Although no trees grow farther north than these, other woody plants do survive on the open tundra. These include dwarf willows (*Salix*), mat-like shrubs that produce a blaze of yellow catkins in June and July. Some dwarf willows creep over the ground, while others spread horizontally beneath the surface. Unlike most willows of warmer climes, they have small coin-shaped leaves.

trees, this area is technically a desert.

Snow – or the lack of it – plays an important part in the life of the forest's animals. Although it is cold, snow is a good insulator, and where it is deep enough, warm-blooded animals often use it to protect themselves from the much colder air outside. In Scandinavia and western Russia, the hazel grouse (*Bonasa bonasia*) tunnels its way deep into snowdrifts to sit out the coldest weather, and throughout the forest,

many mammals also retreat beneath the snow's cover. Some of them, including voles, remain active throughout the winter. Others doze, while a few fall into the much deeper sleep of hibernation.

Contrary to popular belief, the boreal forest's biggest and most dangerous predator is a dozer, rather than a true hibernator. From about October to April, the massive brown or grizzly bear (*Ursus arctos*) spends its time in a heavy slumber, hidden away in a den excavated beneath a large boulder, or under the roots of hill-slope trees. From the outside, all that can be seen of the den is a small hole, which allows the sleeping bear to breathe. It may look like a tempting retreat for anything seeking shelter, but any animal that ignores the strong scent and ventures within does so at its own peril. Unlike a true hibernator, a sleeping brown bear can wake within a few minutes, and its enormous body is then ready for action.

Brown bears live throughout the boreal forest zone, and also in mountainous regions as far south as Mexico and the Balkans. Across this huge range, they show a great amount of variation in size and colour, with bears in Alaska weighing as much as 1650 lb (750 kg) – making them the largest terrestrial meat-eaters – while those in Russia and northern Europe are sometimes just one-third of this size. This great diversity has produced much scientific debate about exactly how many types of brown bear there are. According to some experts, North America has two species, the Alaskan brown bear and the grizzly, while Eurasia has one. To other scientists – the 'lumpers' rather than the 'splitters' – all these bears belong to the same species and are simply different local forms.

FORMIDABLE FIVE-YEAR-OLD
This young grizzly is at the threshold of adult life, and may live to the age of 25. Right: Intense frost, rather than snow, is the chief adversary of these isolated black spruces, which mark the edge of the forest in Alaska.

What is not in dispute is this animal's adaptability, and its unchallenged supremacy in its natural habitat. Brown bears have immense strength and stamina, and wander over home ranges that can cover up to 200 sq miles (500 km²), crossing all types of

ground from closed forest to open mountainsides. Rivers are no obstacle to them as they swim well, and although they normally walk quite slowly, they can run very rapidly over short distances.

Over the centuries, many animals have earned a largely unjustified reputation for being dangerous to humans. In the case of the brown bear – unlike the wolf – this reputation is based firmly on fact. Although they live mainly on plant food, brown bears – particularly the large North American subspecies – can kill animals as large as a horse, and in a few areas they live entirely by hunting. Brown bears normally avoid humans, but if a bear unexpectedly comes into contact with solitary hikers or hunters, it may attack – with fatal results.

ISLAND WORLDS

Hundreds or thousands of miles from the nearest landmasses, remote islands are the living laboratories of evolution. In these oceanic retreats, nature has crafted forests that contain plants and animals found nowhere else on Earth.

According to legends from long ago, they were the fruit of an undersea tree that grew at the navel of the Earth. Floating up to the surface from unknown depths, they would travel the Indian Ocean until eventually the interplay of tides and currents brought them to land. Here, cast up on beaches or trapped among rocks, they awaited the moment of discovery. Their size alone made them easy to spot,

because even after being eroded by the sea, they could still measure around 1 ft (30 cm) in diameter. However, much more astonishing than this was their form. Once the outer husk had been removed, the inner shell bore the unmistakable and sensuous

outline of the female pelvic region.

For centuries, the coco de mer or double coconut (*Lodoicea maldivica*) was an object of mystery and veneration, and commanded extraordinary prices. Its shell was often hollowed out and decorated with silver and precious stones to produce an ornamental object, ownership of which was a sign of distinction and great wealth. Traders who dealt in this fantastic fruit were naturally at

FABLED FRUITS *A clutch of coco de mer fruits hang from a female tree. Each contains a single nut surrounded by a green husk. Below: A tree flaunts its enormous leaves.*

pains to speak of its supreme rarity, and to describe in the most vivid terms its remarkable odyssey from beneath the sea.

But the legend overlooked a crucial fact. Instead of floating, a ripe coco de mer fruit sinks like a stone. It cannot drift a few feet, let alone thousands of miles, and is quickly killed by seawater. Far from being a fruit of the sea, the coco de mer is not produced by an ocean plant at all, but by a tree that lives in one of the world's most extraordinary island forests. It is, in fact, the husks and shells that are found floating in the ocean after the kernels have rotted away.

THE SECRET FOREST

The Vallée de Mai, on the island of Praslin in the Seychelles, is a deep ravine set in hills of eroded granite. Here, on a speck of rock 1000 miles (1600 km) east of the African coastline, the world's only coco de mer forest flourishes in the tropical warmth. It is a place of restful stillness, tempered only by the sharp calls of birds and by the clacking of giant leaves as they shift in the gentle breeze. Within this valley, time seems to have moved elsewhere, allowing millions of years of steady growth.

Over half the trees in the valley are palms, and of these the coco de mer, with its huge fan-like leaves, is the dominant species. There are about 5000 trees altogether, and each one is either male or female. The two kinds of tree are markedly different in size, with male trees reaching a maximum height of about 100 ft (30 m), and females about 80 ft (24 m). The leaves, carried on long stalks, are some of the largest in the plant world, and cast a deep shade on the forest floor.

It seems remarkable that such huge fruits, which each contain the biggest seed of any plant – can be carried by such a slender trunk, but the female coco de mer shoulders its extraordinary burden without any apparent difficulty. However, growing these immense seeds does take time. Trees do not begin fruiting until they are about 25 years old, and each fruit needs about seven years to develop from the moment a female flower is fertilised to the time when the enormous nut is mature. Once it is

ISLAND RARITY *The magpie robin, found only in the forests of the Seychelles archipelago, is one of the world's rarest species.*

ripe, the 40 lb (18 kg) fruit crashes to the ground.

When a coconut (*Cocos nucifera*) drops from its tree, it is wise not to be standing underneath. This is even more true of the coco de mer, whose nuts are many times heavier. But while coconuts are well suited to dispersal by the sea, the nuts of the coco de mer are not. They usually remain where they land, or roll just a few feet, where they begin the two-year process of germination. Compared to many tree seeds, their journey is one of trifling proportions.

The existence of the coco de mer palm came to light – to European science at least – in 1768, when a French expedition reached the hidden valley. Since that time, much of the Seychelles' original forest cover has been destroyed, but the areas that are left still harbour many other endemic species, or forms of life that are found nowhere else in the world. They include five more species of palms, several spiny-leaved plants called screw-pines (*Pandanus*), and the exceedingly rare jellyfish tree (*Medusagyne oppositifolia*), which is found only on one area of granite hillside. This tree gets its name from the shape of its flowers, and is one of the most isolated and endangered plants in the world.

The forest's animal life also has its share of unique species. The islands are the only home of the Seychelles paradise flycatcher (*Terpsiphone corvina*), which hunts insects from the woodland edge, the magpie robin (*Copsychus sechellarum*), a ground-feeding member of the thrush family, and of the

ANCIENT REPTILE *A giant tortoise feeds on the beach on Curieuse, an island in the Seychelles.*

Seychelles kestrel (*Falco araea*), one of the world's rarest birds of prey. Giant tortoises (*Geochelone gigantea*), too, are found on some of the islands. Once used as a source of fresh meat by passing sailors and carried away in thousands, to the point where they were on the brink of extinction, they have now been successfully reintroduced in places.

LIFE CAST ADRIFT

On other remote islands throughout the world, equally strange plants and animals can be found. Due north of the Seychelles, for example, the arid island of Socotra is

the only home of the cucumber tree (*Dendrosicyos socotrana*), whose swollen trunk is topped by a cluster of short and fleshy branches, and also of the dragon's blood tree (*Dracaena cinnabari*), which produces a resin once used as a medicine. About the same distance to the south, the island of Mauritius has a large number of unusual trees, and was formerly the home of one of the world's most celebrated birds, the dodo (*Raphus cucullatus*). This giant and flightless relative of today's pigeons, which became extinct in about 1680, measured nearly 4 ft (1.2 m) from head to tail, and once wandered the island's hillside forests, feeding on leaves and fallen fruit. Two similar birds, the Réunion and Rodriguez solitaires (*Raphus solitarius* and *Pezophaps solitaria*), lived on neighbouring islands and died out in the 18th century.

LAST SURVIVOR *Historical illustrations show the dodo as a portly bird, but this plumpness may only have developed when it was kept in captivity.*

In times gone by, the crews of passing ships running short of food gratefully seized on animals such as the dodo, and probably spent little time wondering how such peculiar creatures had actually come

about. But in more recent years, oceanic islands have been the focus of an immense amount of study. Today, the combined work of geologists and biologists explains how islands come into being and why their wildlife is often so unusual.

In the case of the Seychelles, the story began over 125 million years ago, when a giant slab of the Earth's crust began to break up, tearing apart the huge landmass that had once dominated the Southern Hemisphere. During this process, Madagascar split away from Africa, and India – which had been joined to Madagascar – broke lose in turn. But as India travelled north-eastwards, the space it left behind was not simply a vacant expanse of open water. Scattered in its wake was a cluster of islands perched on an undersea plateau. These islands were once part of the original landmass, but they had become abandoned in the vastness of an expanding ocean.

Like lifeboats cast adrift, the Seychelles inherited a unique mix of passengers. Some of these – for example, sea birds – could easily make the passage from the islands back to the mainland. Others, including many forest trees, were completely cut off in their new home, because they had no way of spreading across the sea. As their isolation continued, the passengers found new ways of making use of each other, and of adapting to their changed circumstances. Eventually, some changed so much that new species were born.

The coco de mer, and the other unique palms of the Seychelles, are the results of that process, and are the living descendants of those original passengers long ago.

PRIMEVAL PRIMATES

On small oceanic islands, the variety of forest life is necessarily limited, because there is simply not enough room for a large number of species to make a living. But when a much larger area of land is cut loose, the richness of forest life is far greater. Cocooned in their own private world, plants and animals evolve in partnership with each other to produce forms that range from the mildly eccentric to the wholly bizarre.

In the forests and mangrove swamps of

Madagascar, dusk brings to life one of the rarest and most extraordinary of these products of island evolution. Emerging from a leafy nest, it moves slowly among the trees, forming a squirrel-like silhouette that alternately crawls and scampers in the fading twilight. It measures about 3 ft (91 cm) from its nose to the tip of its long, bushy tail, and its head bears a pair of spoon-shaped ears, held outwards rather than upwards. Every few seconds it halts, and the

THE STRUGGLE TO SET UP HOME

When new islands appear, would-be colonists not only have to find them in the first place, but they also have to survive ashore. Studies of plants in the Hawaiian Island chain show that this process can be surprisingly difficult. The main islands in the Hawaiian group date back over 5 million years, but have only about 1600 native species of higher plants, which have evolved from perhaps as few as 400 original ancestors. This means that plant colonists have successfully established themselves at a rate of less than one species every 100 centuries. This average rate probably disguises important changes as each island has aged. To begin with, the physical environment would have been hostile, but settlers would have faced little competition from other plants. Later on, after fertile soil had developed, the environment would have been less harsh. However, the early colonists would by now be well entrenched, making it harder for later arrivals to establish a toehold.

faint sound of tapping can be heard. Sometimes the tapping is followed by silence, but at other times there is the unmistakable crunch of teeth against bark or decaying wood. After another pause, the dark shape moves on.

Throughout the world's forests, many animals feed on insect grubs in living or dead wood, but no other animal approaches the task in the same way as the aye-aye (*Daubentonia madagascariensis*). This aye-aye is a primate – a member of the group of

LAST REFUGE *Rain forest flanks the Namorona River in western Madagascar. Forest cover like this is fast disappearing from the island.*

mammals that includes monkeys, apes and ourselves – and like its relatives, it has long fingers that enable it to climb. Compared to human fingers, however, the aye-aye's look gaunt and skeletal, and the third digit on each hand carries this to an extreme degree. It is even more slender than the rest, and looks almost dangerously fragile. This third finger, however, provides the aye-aye with its main way of getting at food.

The characteristic tapping produced by a foraging aye-aye is the sound of a skinny finger being lightly struck against wood. Like someone tapping a wall, the aye-aye listens for signs of hollowness, which might indicate the presence of insect grubs within. When it finds a likely spot, it sometimes bites away the bark, or, if there are any open crevices, inserts its long finger and probes inside. The finger's sharp claw hooks anything edible, and the aye-aye extracts it from the wood and quickly eats its prize. Aye-ayes also feed on eggs, sap and insects, and they sometimes gnaw holes in coconuts and use their long third finger to scrape out the nutritious flesh.

At first sight, it is hard to see how this peculiar animal, with its wizened face, protruding eyes and pointed snout can possibly be a relative of the monkeys and apes. The

CAUGHT IN THE LIGHT
An aye-aye searches for food after dark. Its immensely long fingers are clearly visible.

relationship is actually an ancient one, because the aye-aye belongs to a group of primitive primates called the prosimians, rather than to the more advanced anthropoids, which include monkeys, apes and ourselves. The prosimians appeared before the anthropoids and became widespread throughout North America, Eurasia and Africa. But with the evolution of the anthropoids, many prosimians began to lose out in the competition for survival. A few

species, such as the bush babies of Africa and the tarsiers of South-east Asia, still manage to carry on the original line, but almost everywhere else, anthropoids have gained the upper hand.

In Madagascar, however, evolution followed a quite different course. Anthropoid primates never gained a firm foothold on this giant island, so prosimians were able to flourish without having to struggle against their bigger-brained and often brasher relatives. Some of these species, such as the aye-aye, kept to the old prosimian habit of being active at night, but many others ventured into the light of day.

MADAGASCAR'S MONKEY LOOKALIKES

In the forests of Madagascar, it can sometimes seem as though monkeys have indeed arrived from the African mainland, across 250 miles (400 km) of open sea. The trees overhead resound with barks and song-like calls, and branches dip and sway as animals run along them, or leap from one tree to the next. This method of moving about needs a quick brain and keen eyesight, and Madagascar's lemurs have both.

Lemurs form a confusingly varied collection of 29 different species of primates, found only in the forests and scrub of this one island. At one end of the size scale are the tiny mouse lemurs (*Microcebus*), which weigh as little as 2 oz (60 g) and feed after dark. Their bodies look uncannily like those of small rodents, except for their forward-facing eyes and flat-tipped fingers and toes. Even on dark, moonless nights, mouse lemurs scuttle nimbly along branches in search of food, leaping across gaps and using their long, slender tails to stay balanced.

At the other extreme are the day-living lemurs, which often move about in noisy family groups. Although Madagascar has no monkeys of its own, these animals mirror their lifestyles almost exactly, running and jumping through the forest in search of leaves, shoots and fruit. From a distance, the illusion is almost complete, but a closer look reveals some clear differences between

JAUNTY WALKERS *A band of ring-tailed lemurs, a species that spends much time on the ground, display their long tails as they move along a track.*

lemurs and the animals they seem to imitate. Lemurs have sharply pointed muzzles, rather than flat faces, and although they normally use their hands to feed, they lack the manual dexterity of many of their monkey relatives.

The largest of the diurnal lemurs is a handsome black-and-grey animal called the indri (*Indri indri*). This is the biggest prosimian in the world, with a body up to

TREETOP SIESTA *Two sifakas lounge in a tree during the heat of the day. On the ground, sifakas often walk upright, using their arms for balance.*

3 ft (91 cm) long. It clings to tree-trunks in an upright position, and hurls itself between branches in vertical leaps. Unusually for a lemur, the indri has only a short,

ON THE LOOKOUT   A black-and-white ruffed lemur gazes intently from a fork in a tree. Active mainly at dusk, it lives chiefly on fruit. Right: Hanging on with one hand, an indri pulls at a leafy branch. Although a slow climber, it can make athletic leaps.

For millions of years, Madagascar has provided lemurs with a safe haven from the outside world. Within this 900 mile (1450 km) long island, they have adapted to woodlands of all kinds, from the rain forest of the eastern highlands to the open scrub of the far west. But with the arrival of humans, probably about two millennia ago, their world has undergone a transformation. Today, only one-tenth of the island's original forest cover is left, so the lemurs and aye-ayes are confined to tiny fragments of their original range.

As conservationists battle to protect these unique animals, surprises and disappointments seem to come in almost equal measure. One species, the hairy-eared dwarf lemur (*Allocebus trichotis*), was not seen for over 20 years, and was thought to be extinct until it was rediscovered in the late 1980s. A much larger species, the golden-crowned sifaka (*Propithecus tattersalli*), also from the east, was only discovered in 1987. This beautiful, silky-furred animal immediately earned itself a place on the endangered list, and like many of its kind it faces an uncertain future.

MAMMALS MISS OUT

Scientists are not entirely sure when Madagascar's prosimians took to their island lifeboat. They may have been present before it broke away from Africa, or they may have clambered aboard after it departed, via smaller islands that have since disappeared. But while mammals as a group managed to reach Madagascar, they failed to occupy another group of islands that was created in the Southern Hemisphere. Instead of becoming dominated by mammals, its forests became dominated by giant flightless birds.

It is difficult to imagine what it would feel like to be confronted by a bird weighing 500 lb (227 kg) and standing up to 12 ft (3.7 m) high. But for the first human inhabitants of New Zealand, who arrived on

JUDGING A JUMP   Like other primates, the red-bellied lemur uses its large, forward-facing eyes to judge distances in the trees.

stumpy tail. All other species have long tails, often covered with luxuriant fur, which they use both to balance and to signal to their companions. When walking on the ground, they often hold their tails upright in a shape like a letter S, making each animal look as if it is equipped with a furry handle.

MINIATURE CLIMBER   At only 10 in (25 cm) long, the mouse lemur from eastern Madagascar is among the smallest primates in the world.

these remote southern islands over 1000 years ago, this moment would have been one of tremendous opportunity, mixed with considerable danger. With legs as high as a man, New Zealand's great flightless birds were of incalculable value. Their bodies contained a massive supply of meat. They provided skins for making clothes and bones that could be fashioned into implements as varied as clasps and fish-hooks. A single one of their enormous eggs could feed several people, and if broken open with care, could also be used for carrying water. The birds were huge but slow-witted, and for their hunters the main problem was to get close enough to throw a spear without risking a fatal kick from an enormous claw-tipped foot.

NEW ZEALAND'S WALKING BAT

It is often said that New Zealand had no land mammals of its own. However, this statement overlooks two animals that existed in New Zealand's forests long before the first humans stepped ashore. Both these mammals are bats. One species, the long-tailed bat (*Chalinolobus tuberculatus*), belongs to a group of bats that is widespread throughout Australasia. Like all its relatives, it emerges at dusk to hunt flying insects, and uses high-pitched pulses of sound to track down its prey.

The second species, the New Zealand short-tailed bat (*Mystacina tuberculata*) is a creature of quite different habits. It spends some of its time catching insects on the wing, but it is also very adept at moving about on the ground. It scuttles over the forest floor, and can climb up sloping trees. During these terrestrial expeditions, it pounces on resting insects, and also feeds on fallen fruit.

The short-tailed bat is able to do this thanks to its unusual anatomy, seen in no other bat species. When it closes its wings, the thin wing membranes roll up under the thicker margins, which protect them from damage. The thumb on each wing has a large claw, and so do all the toes on the bat's short and powerful feet. Equipped with these, the bat can scramble its way up steep slopes and cling onto tree-trunks. Its fur is also extremely thick, and this probably helps it to stay active during mild winter weather, when the long-tailed bat hibernates.

HUNTING ON A LOG *With its wings folded, a short-tailed bat searches for food.*

ISLAND GIANT *Compared to ostriches, most moas were thickset and slow-moving birds. The largest were much taller than a man, while the smallest were about the size of a turkey.*

These immense plant-eaters belonged to a species called *Dinornis maximus*, and were the tallest birds ever to have existed on Earth. They were the largest of over 20 species once found in New Zealand, living either along forest edges and in open grassland, or within the forest itself. Known collectively as moas, they fed on leaves, seeds and fallen fruit, and without any mammals to compete against they had a virtual monopoly on their island home.

Moas were birds of an ancient pedigree, and relatives of similar birds that lived in Madagascar. In New Zealand they became well adapted to their new home and managed to survive the last Ice Age, which brought testing times this far south. Deep piles of moa bones, fractured and disorganised by the passage of time, have been found in swamps and sand dunes throughout New Zealand, showing that these birds were once extremely successful and widespread.

In some places, moa skeletons are accompanied by collections of stones that throw a revealing light on the way they lived. Like chickens swallowing grit, moas swallowed stones to help them digest their food. The stones lodged in a moa's gizzard, and here they ground up leaves and seeds as they passed through the bird's body. A chicken's crop contains less than 1 oz (30 g) of grit, in pieces that are rarely bigger than a pea. By contrast, the remains found in New Zealand sometimes reveal up to 5 lb (2.3 kg) of stones, many bigger than a golf ball. Equipped with these, large moas could process the toughest of foods.

Despite their success, moas had few defences against human hunters. The largest species were wiped out first, leaving the smaller ones clinging on in remote and inaccessible areas of forest. By about 1800, these too had disappeared. However, although the moas failed to adapt when their world suddenly changed, not all New Zealand's flightless birds suffered the same fate. In the depths of the island forests, their closest relatives still survive today.

Most birds have good eyesight but a feeble sense of smell. The world they perceive is primarily one of light and sound, with vision and hearing conveying all they need to know to find food, to escape their enemies and to interact with their own kind. For New Zealand's most famous living bird, the kiwi (*Apteryx*), however, vision plays little part in daily life. Emerging from its burrow as the day comes to an end, this solidly built creature, with its humped back and strangely hair-like plumage, often finds food by smell and touch alone.

There are three species of kiwi and – uniquely in the bird world – all of them have nostrils at the far end of their long and curved beaks. As a kiwi lumbers forward, shifting its weight ponderously from one thickset leg to the other, it sniffs the forest floor for signs of insect grubs, slugs and earthworms.

Although kiwis can see little of their surroundings once

SMELLING THE WAY A kiwi makes it way over the forest floor. Its streamlined shape helps it to push through dense undergrowth.

night has fallen, they seem to have no difficulty finding their way along paths and through undergrowth. One feature that helps them is the ruff of bristle-like feathers that sprouts from the base of the beak. These feathers are thought to act like a mammal's whiskers, enabling kiwis to feel their way through the darkness.

In an interesting convergence of evolution, a similar adaptation is also shown by another of New Zealand's band of nocturnal flightless birds, the extremely rare kakapo, or owl parrot (*Strigops habroptilus*), which is now perilously close to extinction. Weighing up to 7 lb (3.2 kg), this is not only the heaviest parrot in the world, but also the only one that has lost the ability to fly. The kakapo is a vegetarian, and it probably uses its 'whiskers' to help it locate edible leaves and fallen berries in its forest home.

A kiwi's wings are only 2 in (5 cm) long, and are completely hidden by its plumage. When kiwis sleep, they often tuck their heads under one wing, but apart from this, the wings seem to have few uses. By contrast, a kakapo's wings are much larger and more robust, and have fully formed flight feathers patterned with the same beautiful, brown, yellow and emerald-green camouflage that covers the rest of its body. Kakapos are good climbers, and after they have clambered up roots or low branches, they often launch themselves into a short glide

CLIMBING PARROT The kakapo uses its claws and beak to good effect when clambering up trees.

rather than climbing back down. This ability to glide, which has completely vanished in kiwis, shows that kakapos are relative newcomers to the ground-based way of life.

THE OUTSIDERS

Before humans arrived in New Zealand, over three-quarters of the country was forested. These forests had existed since the islands first broke away from the southern super continent, and they consisted of trees that were unique to the Southern Hemisphere. In the northernmost tip of North Island, immense and bulky conifers called kauris (*Agathis australis*) grew to heights of over 140 ft (42 m), while farther south, another group of conifers – the podocarps – formed extensive forests that also contained many evergreen broadleaved trees. In the south, particularly among the mountains, southern beeches (*Nothofagus*) were among the most widespread trees. With their small evergreen leaves, they managed to thrive in the cool, wet weather that often drenches the mountains and the lower slopes facing the coast.

During the last 1000 years, this remote island world, complete in itself for so long,

GIANT CONIFER *An ancient kauri soars upwards in New Zealand's North Island. Below: moss-based southern beeches arch over a river near the west coast of South Island.*

NATURAL ELEGANCE
A podocarp catches the low light of the sinking sun. Podocarps are found mainly in the Southern Hemisphere.

has undergone the greatest change since it first split away from the ancient southern landmass. Much of the original forest has been cut down and replaced by fields or by plantations of 'foreign' trees, such as fast-growing conifers from the Northern Hemisphere. But far more damaging than this has been the long list of animal arrivals from distant parts of the world. Released either accidentally or deliberately into the wild, these have upset a natural balance that lasted for millions of years.

In a land that, until the arrival of humans, had only two species of terrestrial mammal – both insect-eating bats – the introduction of others triggered off the greatest and most far-reaching changes. Cats, rats (*Rattus*) and stoats (*Mustela erminea*) all attacked the eggs and chicks of ground-nesting birds, and wild pigs and deer tore up the undergrowth or browsed on the trees. For birds like kiwis and the kakapo, it was a terrible and inescapable onslaught.

Kiwis continue to survive in some

numbers, although one of the three species – the little spotted kiwi (*Apteryx owenii*) – is seriously endangered. For the kakapo, the outlook is much less certain. Its only protection is its camouflage, a form of defence that is of little value against predators with keen ears and noses. Kakapos have died out entirely on New Zealand's two main islands, and are now found only on three offshore islands in the far south – one where they lived originally, and two where they have been introduced, in the hope of protecting them from their enemies.

ISLANDS FROM THE SEA

Less than a million years ago, when New Zealand had practically completed its journey to its present position, a momentous event was taking place in a distant part of

ALIEN INVADERS *Neat ranks of introduced conifers envelop a New Zealand hillside. Good for timber, they are poor for native wildlife.*

the Pacific Ocean. A submarine volcano, which had built its way up through 18 000 ft (5480 m) of water over many millennia, at last burst through the surface. Raked by hissing breakers and masked by clouds of steam and acrid gas, a new island was born.

Unlike islands formed from ancient continents, Hawaii had no living inheritance when it came into being. The intense heat of its lava was lethal to all forms of life, and anything that flew nearby risked being asphyxiated by sulphurous fumes. But as the new island continued to grow, its oldest lava flows started to cool, and the sterile landscape became fractionally less hostile. From that moment, the race to colonise this new land began.

During the island's infancy, living things arrived on its shores from all the corners of the Pacific. Some made their way from older islands in the Hawaiian chain, while others – travelling either by their own efforts, or with the help of wind and waves – reached it after immense journeys over the open sea. Sea birds, seals and flying insects would have been among the first animal arrivals, along with small spiders, which can travel for huge distances by 'ballooning' on long threads of silk. But if the new island was to sustain land-based

life, plants were needed as well.

For the seeds of flowering plants, and the spores of ferns, the chances of survival were slim. Any that settled on the iron-hard lava plains were almost certain to die, but those that dropped into cracks were sometimes more fortunate. Sheltered from the wind and sun, their roots penetrated shallow pockets of fertile volcanic ash, seeking out the moisture that gathered there after rain. From these tenuous beginnings, a lush living carpet crept slowly over the volcanic rock, eventually covering all but the steepest cliffs and the highest slopes. In time, the carpet became a forest, filled with flowers, leaves and edible fruit. For animals it was a place of immense opportunity – if they were able to reach it.

At some point in Hawaii's past, a small

A BIRD WITH TWO BEAKS

The huia (*Heteralocha acutirostris*), which once lived in the forests of New Zealand, is the only known bird in which the sexes had different shaped beaks. Male huias had straight beaks, and used them to chisel their way into wood to extract insect grubs. Females had slender and strongly curved beaks, which they used like forceps, extracting their food by probing rather than by digging into wood. Huias needed dead wood to supply them with grubs, and declined swiftly when New Zealand's original forests were cleared or replanted. The last living huia was reported in 1907, and today this remarkable species is almost certainly extinct.

flock of finch-like birds was blown off course and swept out over the Pacific Ocean. No one knows where these birds came from – Central America is a strong possibility – but they pressed on beyond sight of land towards the featureless horizon, unable to stop and perhaps unwilling to turn back. In ordinary circumstances, the birds would

PLANTS APART: THE TREES OF MADAGASCAR

With its enormous vertical fan of gigantic leaves, the traveller's tree (*Ravenala madagascariensis*) is one of the most striking sights in the whole of the tropics. In its wild state, this unique plant is found only in Madagascar, and is one of the many trees that make this island a botanist's paradise.

The traveller's tree looks like a palm, but is actually a relative of the bird-of-paradise flower (*Strelitzia*). Its leaves grow one at a time, and each one starts life in the centre of the fan. As a leaf ages, it is pushed aside by younger ones; it gradually works its way to the right or left until it forms the edge of the fan. Eventually its base snaps, and the leaf falls off.

Palm leaves grow in a similar way, but spread in all directions. A recent expedition to Madagascar discovered that the island has at least 170 species of palms, which is nearly three times as many as in the whole of Africa. Among them are the raffia palm (*Raphia farinifera*), whose leaf blades, measuring over 60 ft (18 m) in length, are the largest in the plant world. At the other end of the scale are tiny dwarf palms, such as *Dypsis tenuissima*, which has a 'trunk' much thinner than a pencil, and grows to about 1 ft (30 cm) high. One newly discovered rain forest palm, belonging to the genus *Satranala*,

PLANT-WORLD EXOTICA
The cluster of overlapping leaf stems on the traveller's tree creates a strange, fan-shaped structure.

produces nuts that may originally have been dispersed by elephant birds (*Aepyornis*). These flightless giants, weighing up to 1000 lb (450 kg), once roamed Madagascar's forests, but became extinct some 700 years ago.

In the dry south-west of the island, plants belonging to the Didiereaceae family – which is found only in Madagascar – have evolved bizarre shapes to cope with drought. Most of them are spiny bushes with tiny leaves, but one, *Alluaudia procera*, looks like a tortuous tree-trunk that has been stripped of all its branches. Remarkably, it closely echoes the shape of the cirio or boojum tree (*Idria columnaris*), a quite unrelated plant that grows in the deserts of north-west Mexico.

IN THE SPINY FOREST *The octopus tree is one of the most bizarre inhabitants of Madagascar's unique dry forests. Its short, fleshy leaves grow in long rows, alternating with short, sharp spines.*

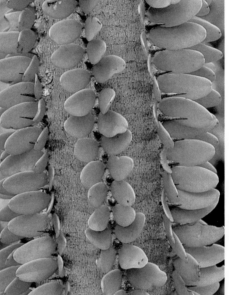

have been condemned to a watery death, but in this case luck was on their side. A far-off island came into view, and a new and remarkable group of colonists headed towards its distant shores.

When they arrived in Hawaii, the birds found an extraordinarily varied environment where there were very few competitors for food. There were no reptiles, amphibians or land mammals in its forests, but some plants and insects had already arrived, and existed in abundance. In an explosion of evolution, the original birds began to specialise in different ways of life. The result, many millennia later, is a group of about two-dozen species that are found

Ou

Akiapolaau

Iiwi

HAWAIIAN HONEYCREEPERS
In Hawaii, a single flock of birds that arrived long ago has given rise to at least 20 distinct species. Many are now very rare.

only in Hawaii and other islands in the Hawaiian chain.

Hawaiian honeycreepers, as they are now known, have kept their finch-like shape, but their beaks have changed to suit the lifestyles that they now follow. The akiapolaau (*Hemignathus munroi*), for example, has a slender, down-curved beak that is over

2 in (5 cm) long – an ideal shape for probing into moss and rotting wood for insect grubs. The ou (*Psittirostra psittacea*) has a short, powerful beak for crushing seeds, while the iiwi (*Vestiaria coccinea*) has a sickle-shaped bill that it uses for drinking nectar from flowers. Like the famous finches of the Galapagos Islands – which prompted Charles Darwin's insights into evolution – these birds show how natural selection can make much from a single original design.

The honeycreepers were fortunate, because many forms of life that arrive on remote islands fail to colonise their new home. However, once established, early arrivals to volcanic islands have a unique opportunity to make their mark. In the Hawaiian Islands, a form of evolutionary overdrive has produced more than 1000 unique species of land snails, a quarter of the world's species of fruit flies, and dozens of species of lobelias. Some of the islands'

trees, such as the beautiful red-flowered ohia (*Metrosideros polymorpha*), are found in other parts of the Pacific, but many more are unique to the Hawaiian chain, and some are restricted to a handful of valleys.

Today, many of the products of Hawaii's short but extraordinary history are threatened by a wave of new arrivals, brought in with human help. The Hawaiian Island chain is now home to at least 70 species of introduced birds – a world record – and hundreds of introduced plants. But where the original forest still survives, on high ground and in remote valleys, the descendants of those early arrivals persist in their remote and once inviolate island home.

ISLAND ABUNDANCE *In a steep valley on Hawaii, a lush forest grows on fertile volcanic soil. Some of the trees are unique to the island, others introduced.*

FORESTS AND THE FUTURE

More than any other natural habitat, forests have been transformed by human activity. After millennia of clearance, efforts are under way to safeguard those that remain and preserve the animals that depend on them for survival.

In the 3rd century BC the Chinese philosopher Meng-Tse or Mencius wrote: 'The Bull Mountain was covered by beautiful trees. But it is near the capital of a great state, and people came with their axes and cut the woods down, so the mountain lost its beauty. But even so, the air came to it day and night, and the rain and dew moistened it until fresh shoots began to grow. But soon cattle and sheep grazed on them, and in the end the mountain became gaunt and bare. Seeing it thus, people imagine that it was always so.'

This sequence of events is as familiar today as it was more than 2000 years ago. Ever since humans discovered that by growing crops and raising animals they could provide food more reliably than by hunting or gathering from the wild, the Earth's natural vegetation has been transformed by the thirst for land. Today, about 10 000 years after agriculture began, that thirst still shows no signs of being quenched.

By about 5000 years ago, during the time of the ancient Egyptians, an international timber trade had already become well established. One of the most striking pieces of evidence for this is the funerary boat of the Pharaoh Khufu or Cheops, who created the Great Pyramid at Giza. Unearthed in the 1950s from the desert sand close to the pyramid, the remains of this mysterious vessel were more than 130 ft (40 m) long, and made almost entirely of cedar wood. Because Egypt was too dry for most trees apart from palms, this wood had to be imported from the mountains of Lebanon, more than 600 miles (960 km) away.

Since those times, the demand for timber and timber products has mushroomed, along with the demand for land. It was the Chinese who devised a process that used wood for paper-making. In the age of electronic communication, paper is still one of the most important products in everyday use, and it is manufactured on a massive scale. Wood is also used to produce a range of other products, including chipboard and charcoal, and also cellulose, a raw material that is an ingredient of plastics, fibres and explosives. Altogether, about 65 billion cu yd (50 billion m³) of paper are traded internationally every year, along with five times that amount of timber.

The effect that this has had on the world's forests is difficult to exaggerate. Many areas of forest have been completely destroyed, while others have been changed beyond recognition. Even if this process continues unchecked, forests as a whole are unlikely to disappear altogether. But truly natural forests – of the kind that are described throughout much of this book – may well become a thing of the past.

When tropical rain forest is felled and burned to make way for fields, blackened

CLINGING ON *On Crete, some trees have been spared by inaccessibility from the destruction of the original forest. Right: An oriental plane, a species once widespread in the eastern Mediterranean area, clings to barren ground.*

tree-trunks and billowing smoke make it very evident that a change of great significance is taking place. Dramatic though it is, this kind of onslaught has so far accounted for a small percentage of the world's forest loss. In the world's temperate regions – chiefly that of the Northern Hemisphere – deforestation has already happened on an even greater scale, but so long ago that its after-effects are often mistaken for natural features of the landscape.

In the eastern Mediterranean, the islands of the Aegean Sea give some idea of what can happen when deforestation runs

CEDARS OF LEBANON *Stranded on a bare hillside, this fragment of woodland is almost all that remains of the cedar forests of Biblical times.*

unchecked. In early classical times – roughly at the time that Meng-Tse bemoaned the fate of Bull Mountain – many of these islands were clothed in forest that came close to the shore. The trees included conifers such as pines and junipers, several kinds of evergreen oak, and the oriental plane (*Platanus orientalis*), a stately deciduous tree that often lives to a great age. The trees shielded the ground from the full heat of the summer sunshine, and also helped to create soil as they shed their leaves.

However, centuries of deforestation have left their mark, and in the Aegean today it is hard to believe that trees could ever have existed in such unpromising surroundings. Many of the smaller islands consist of little more than bare rock, because without tree roots to bind it together the soil has disappeared, and rainwater quickly runs away. On the larger islands, gnarled olives and dark green carob trees (*Ceratonia siliqua*) offer some shade, but otherwise the vegetation consists mostly of phrygana – a Greek word for low-growing bushes scattered over open ground. In winter and spring the phrygana is pleasantly green, but by midsummer it is scorched and laden with dust, and even goats have difficulty finding enough to eat.

The forest that once shaded the ground and stored up rainwater is beyond even the most distant memories, and the wild animals that lived in it are long gone.

THE NEW FORESTS

In the last 10 000 years, nearly one-third of the world's original temperate forest has been destroyed. In some places, including the Aegean islands and much of the Middle East, the forest has been almost entirely eradicated, although tiny remnants still survive in ravines and on inaccessible hillsides. In the plains of north-east China deforestation has been even more drastic, and here botanists have no clear idea how the landscape looked before tree-felling began. The picture in central Europe and North America is not quite so catastrophic. Large fragments of woodland have managed to survive, although scarcely any have escaped some kind of human interference.

Given this history, and the continuing growth of roads and cities throughout the developed world, it might seem obvious that temperate forests are still shrinking. But throughout the Northern Hemisphere, the exact opposite is true. Across North America, Europe and Russia, trees have become an important crop, and by planting them in huge numbers, deforestation has been halted or even reversed.

In the Highlands of Scotland, the results of this planting boom are easy to see. Until about 3000 years ago, this part of northern Britain was covered by the great Caledonian forest, with Scots pine (*Pinus sylvestris*) being the most important tree. The forest was home to many animals once widespread in northern forests, such as wolves and beavers, and it was – and still is – the only home of the Scottish crossbill (*Loxia scotica*), a seed-eating bird with a cross-tipped beak. But over many centuries, standing trees have been cut down and saplings nibbled to the ground by sheep and deer, and today the forest teeters on the brink of extinction. A few valleys have their native pines, but

CONIFER CLADDING In the Scottish Highlands ranks of conifers flank open moorland. These trees are bred to ensure that they are almost identical.

beyond them lies a treeless landscape cloaked in heather-clad peat.

In these desolate but strangely beautiful surroundings, the silence is sometimes broken by the sound of tractors lumbering slowly over the ground. Each tractor pulls a plough consisting of a single giant blade, and this gouges out a deep furrow, turning up a parallel ribbon of peat that looks like an immense brown worm. The furrow acts as a drainage channel, while the peat alongside it provides conditions that are dry enough for young trees to survive. Within a few days, teams of planters arrive with thousands of saplings, and the moorland takes the first step to becoming forest.

For the first few years, little can be seen of the trees, but as time goes by, their growth accelerates, and dark green blocks begin to emerge from the surrounding heather. In many plantations, the young trees are not Scots pines, but Sitka spruces (*Picea sitchensis*) from western North America. Packed together in close ranks, these alien evergreens grow remarkably well far from their native home, and within 25 years they are often ready to be harvested for wood pulp. The ground is then replanted and the cycle begins again.

For many people, the rectangular blocks of trees are eyesores that intrude on one of Europe's few remaining areas of wilderness. But while views differ on their appearance, it cannot be denied that conifers are the natural vegetation for this northern landscape. However, on one subject there can be no argument: there is a world of difference between these planted forests, with their regimented rows of identical trees, and the original Caledonian forest, which had a rich mixture of trees of all ages. Natural forests provide animals with a multi-layered habitat and many kinds of food, from young shoots and leaves to seeds and dead wood. Planted forests provide shelter, and often very little else.

FORESTS FOR WILDLIFE

Wherever they are grown, plantations like these pose problems for wildlife. They often consist of trees that have been introduced from distant parts of the world, and

STRANGERS FROM AFAR
An area of native forest in central Africa has been cleared to make way for a plantation of Australian eucalypts.

the more 'foreign' the tree, the more difficulty animals have in making use of it. Of all the trees widely planted today, few highlight these problems more clearly than Australian gum trees, or eucalypts.

During the 19th century, eucalypts were planted in southern Europe to help drain marshy ground, where malaria-carrying mosquitoes could breed. These fast-growing trees proved remarkably successful at this task, and they also became a useful source of wood. Today, eucalypts are grown for timber in many parts of the world with mild winters, and they can be seen in countries as far apart as Spain and Argentina.

In their native Australia, eucalypts have lived alongside marsupials, birds and insects for millions of years, and the local animals have evolved many ways of exploiting them. Some of these animals are harmful to the trees, but others – particularly those that pollinate their flowers – are distinctly beneficial. When the same trees are planted in a country like Spain, however, they are like intruders from another world. Here, very few animals can make use of them. This is good news for timber growers, but it can be very damaging for anything that

depends on native trees for its survival.

Planted forests do bring some benefits for the environment, because they are a source of timber that can be harvested in a completely sustainable way, if the fuel that is needed for felling and replanting is ignored. But for natural forest wildlife to survive, native forests have to be encouraged as well.

From Scotland to New Zealand, the value of these native forests is now more widely recognised, and efforts are being made to safeguard their future. Scotland's pines will never win back all the ground they have lost, but with careful protection, they and their wildlife will at least keep a toehold on survival.

CRISIS IN THE TROPICS

In recent years, few areas of biology have generated so many disturbing statistics as the study of tropical rain forests. More than 60 000 sq miles (155 000 km²) of rain forest are lost every year, an area slightly larger than Greece, or as big as the American state of Georgia. Costa Rica's rain-forest cover fell by three-quarters in just four decades, a degree of deforestation that took many centuries to accomplish in northern Europe. The rate of rain-forest loss in Nigeria is running at about 4 per cent a year, and this country – once famous as a source of some of Africa's most highly prized timber – now has to import timber itself.

Outside the tropics, the destruction of rain forests has risen to the top of the environmental agenda. Rain-forest animals like the toco toucan have become as well known as the blue whale or giant panda, and for many people rain forests are now a symbol in the fight to save the natural world. But in

tropical countries themselves, where rain forests actually grow, not everybody sees them in the same protective light.

For cattle farmers in Brazil, which has the largest remaining area of tropical rain forest, the forest is an unproductive wilderness that stands in the way of progress. Just like European or North American farmers before them, they see forested land as waste ground waiting to be put to better use. In West Africa and South-east Asia, many governments regard untouched forest as an industrial resource, to be exploited and managed. The developed countries of the Northern Hemisphere have already swept away most of their original forest cover and

---

THE DANGERS OF DISEASE

Virulent tree diseases are one of the prices that are paid for increased trade and contact between distant countries. One of the worst examples began in 1904, when a species of fungus called *Endothia parasitica* was accidentally introduced from the Far East into the area around New York city. In the Far East, the fungus attacks chestnut trees, but usually does them little harm. However, American chestnuts (*Castanea dentata*) had no resistance to the fungus, and within 20 years most chestnut trees had been infected and many had died. Dutch elm disease has had a similar effect on elm trees (*Ulmus*) in Europe and North America.

---

many of the animals that once lived in it. So why, many would argue, should developing countries not follow suit?

There is no single answer to this question but a clutch of them, each with the power to persuade. Some relate to the localised effects of deforestation, but others concern dramatic implications that forest felling may have for the whole of our planet.

DIMINISHING RETURNS

With their tails swishing to ward off biting flies, a herd of brahma cattle graze on knee-high grass in a rain-soaked field. Around them, cattle egrets (*Bubulcus ibis*) keep

TOURISTS TO THE RESCUE?

The Central American republic of Costa Rica highlights many of the problems involved in rain-forest conservation, and a possible solution. Despite being smaller than Tasmania or West Virginia, its wildlife is staggeringly varied: it has more than 1000 species of trees, 200 kinds of mammals, and about 800 species of birds. However, many of these rely on rain forest for their survival, and since the 1940s Costa Rica's rain forests have been disappearing at one of the fastest rates the world has ever seen.

During the 1960s, the Costa Rican government realised that without action, nearly all of the country's original forest cover was doomed to disappear. It initiated an ambitious conservation programme that created 20 national parks and many forest reserves and wildlife refuges. Nearly one-quarter of the country is now partly or fully protected from development.

Several decades later, the results of this programme are easy to see. The protected forests remain almost pristine, and their wildlife has survived largely intact. In unprotected

AFLOAT IN THE FOREST *A memorable experience for holidaymakers in Costa Rica is provided by watching monkeys from a boat.*

INTO THE CANOPY *Aerial tramways and walkways allow tourists to visit the rain forest canopy – a habitat that is normally hidden from the ground.*

areas, however, nearly all the original rain forest has been replaced, largely by banana and coffee plantations or by cattle pasture.

To pay for this conservation effort Costa Rica relies heavily on tourism. The money generated helps to maintain the reserves, and provides employment for local people. This is vital for the survival of the protected areas as it gives Costa Ricans an incentive for supporting conservation.

Costa Rica is undoubtedly a special case, because of its small size, varied geography and immensely rich wildlife. But it is proof that rain forest conservation can be made to pay its way. In many parts

of the world, tourists spoil the very things that they seek to enjoy, but in Costa Rica – at present – they play an active part in preserving them.

PAYING GUESTS *A nature trail in Costa Rica's Monteverde Cloud Forest reserve. Visitors help fund the reserve's upkeep.*

watch for any small animals disturbed by the grazers, while from time to time, small bands of parakeets fly overhead, screeching noisily. This pastoral scene, which could be almost anywhere in the American tropics, lies at the battle front of deforestation. The cattle and their feathered attendants are a sign that – in this area at least – the latest engagement is over and the forest has been forced into a retreat.

Looking at this newly won farmland, even the most ardent forest-lover must sympathise with the people who rely on these cattle for their survival. Many of them live in simple huts draped with plastic to keep out the driving rain, and the animals are often their most valuable possessions. Life is not easy, but at least they have land they can call their own.

However, more often than not, the immense work that goes into clearing this land brings short-lived results. Where the original forest grows on volcanic soil, for example throughout much of Central America, the ground contains a good supply of minerals and can be very fertile. However, in the lowlands of Brazil, as in many other parts of the tropics, the soil is often poor and is easily eroded. Initially, the pasture is productive, but the first flush of useful grass is quickly replaced by tick-infested weeds and its usefulness plummets.

The returns are equally fleeting when rain forests are cut for timber. To begin with, logging in an area of untouched forest can be very profitable, and it also produces a boom in local employment. But in

DISAPPEARING LANDSCAPE
After rapid deforestation, rain has gouged out deep gullies in Madagascar's central plateau.

GLOBAL HARVEST Throughout the world, timber is treated as an extractive resource: it is removed, like coal or oil, even though it has limitless potential if carefully harvested. Areas of forest are cleared while the logs are processed and exported in an international trade that is focused on ever smaller areas of natural forest.

roads open it up to agriculture and the familiar spiral of decline sets in.

For the planet as a whole, tropical deforestation has less immediate effects, but the impact may eventually be more serious. Unlike deforestation in temperate regions, where wildlife is less diverse, deforestation in the tropics threatens to destroy plant and animal species at an unprecedented rate. In a world in which all living things are interlinked, no one knows what long-term consequences this may have. Also, by unlocking the carbon in trees and releasing it as carbon dioxide, tropical deforestation threatens to increase the Earth's temperature. Ultimately this may change its climate in ways that no one can confidently predict at the present time.

Given these threats, petitions and appeals for conservation are not enough. Practical ways are needed to preserve these unique forests before they finally disappear.

PROTECTING TROPICAL FORESTS

In south-west Costa Rica, a torchbeam flashes over the sand of a remote beach. On the left, the Pacific surf crashes onto the volcanic sand, while on the right, a dark wall of forest seems to press against the shore, blotting out part of the night sky. For a while,

the beam wanders aimlessly between the beach and the trees, but then suddenly it fixes on a point just behind the forest edge, as if staring at something that is just beyond view. Without warning, another light cuts through the darkness, revealing two figures retreating into the trees. Above the noise of the breakers comes the sound of shouting, as park guards set off in pursuit of their quarry.

Across the world, effective forest preservation often requires hard decisions to be made, but few places highlight the difficulties as sharply as Costa Rica's Corcovado National Park. Set in one of the last parts of the Central American lowlands that still retain their original rain-forest cover, Corcovado is a place of extraordinary natural beauty. Flocks of scarlet macaws (*Ara macao*) are a common sight on the forest's edge, where they feed on the fruit of sea almond trees (*Terminalia catappa*), and tapirs can occasionally be seen trotting along the beach.

From the beach, the forest's deep green hinterland stretches away across the low coastal hills, with every appearance of being untouched by humans. Until recently, however, the very existence of this forest, with its estimated 350 species of birds and nearly 150 species of mammals, rested on a knife-edge, with conflicting interests threatening to destroy its natural wealth for ever. These threats included local hunters, settlers in search of land, international timber companies, and also gold-panners, who invaded the forest after gold was discovered in the 1930s. Faced with this kind of pressure, the forest seemed to have little chance of survival.

Fortunately for the region's wildlife, Costa Rica's government has shown a remarkable commitment to conservation, despite the country's extraordinarily rapid deforestation. In 1975, enough money was found to buy out Corcovado's logging interests, to relocate the settlers, and to set up a national park. Hunters and gold-panners were moved out, although not with so much success. Many still find their way into the forest, and it takes constant vigilance by the park's guards to keep them under control.

For places such as Corcovado, round-the-clock protection conserves a unique

the tropics, only about 1 per cent of logging is conducted on a sustainable basis. Instead of treating the forest as a capital asset and harvesting the income that it generates, most logging operations attack the asset itself. Once the forest has been stripped of its most valuable trees, logging

habitat. However, this kind of operation is expensive, and it can only save relatively small areas of forest that are of particular environmental or scenic interest. In the vast expanses of the Amazon, or in the islands of South-east Asia, some other driving force is needed to prevent forests being destroyed. Many environmentalists believe that the future of these forests is best guaranteed not by putting them out of bounds, but by making them pay their way.

For thousands of years, the indigenous peoples of tropical rain forests have harvested products such as medicinal herbs, fruits and nuts. Some of these products – for example the Brazil nut – have never been cultivated successfully, and even today they are still gathered from the forest by hand.

In the late 1980s, there was a flurry of interest in the idea that this natural harvest could be expanded and used to keep forests intact. However, the enthusiasm proved short-lived. These rain-forest products have only ever supported relatively small numbers of people, and few of them are in worldwide demand. For rain forests to survive, a much more powerful incentive is needed to leave them intact.

Today, it seems more possible that a different kind of harvest might be able to save rain forests from complete destruction. If trees are selectively logged, with care being taken to minimise any damage to other trees, a forest's most valuable resource can be exploited without destroying the forest in the process. This kind of sustainable forestry can provide much-needed employment, and it gives local people a strong motive for protecting forests, rather than clearing them out of the way.

So far, very few rain forests are worked in this way, but projects in Ecuador and New Guinea, using small, portable sawmills, have shown promising results. While the idea of exploiting rain forests may seem to fly in the face of conservation, it may be the last and best chance of saving some of the most important forests on Earth. On its own, the threat of extinction that hovers over beautiful and fascinating animals, such as toucans or orang utans, will not prevent forests being destroyed. History shows that deforestation stops only when people have a powerful reason to prevent it.

PROTECTED *Towering rain forest meets the Pacific Ocean in Corcovado National Park. Once threatened by development, the forest's future is now more secure.*

PICTURE CREDITS

T = top; B = bottom; C = centre;
L = left; R = right.

3 Planet Earth Pictures/Anup & Manoj Shah, C. **6** Auscape International/J. Plaza Van Roon, BC. **7** Auscape International/Wayne Lawler, TR; DRK Photo/Michael Fogden, BC. **8** DRK Photo/Fred Bruemmer, TL; DRK Photo/Larry Ulrich, B. **9** OSF/Stan Osolinski, BR. **10** DRK Photo/Michael Fogden, T; The Wildlife Collection/John Giustina, BL. **11** Bruce Coleman Ltd/Kim Taylor, TL; Bruce Coleman Ltd/Jeremy Grayson, BR. **12** Woodfall Wild Images/Nigel Hicks, BL; Siena Artworks Ltd, London/Ron Hayward, BR. **13** NHPA/G. I. Bernard, TC; Siena Artworks Ltd, London/Catherine Moss, BR. **14** Bruce Coleman Ltd/John Cancalosi, TR; NHPA/John Shaw, BL. **15** Auscape International/J. Plaza Van Roon, B. **16** Tom Stack & Associates/Doug Sokell, TL, T. **17** NHPA/David Middleton, BL; NHPA/Morten Strange, CR. **18** NHPA/John Buckingham, TL; Premaphotos Wildlife/K.G. Preston-Mafham, TR; OSF/Waina Cheng, BR; NHPA/Laurie Campbell, BC; Planet Earth Pictures/W.B. Irwin, BL. **19** DRK Photo/Stanley Breeden, TR. **20** Siena Artworks Ltd, London/Ron Hayward, TR; DRK Photo/Stephen J. Krasemann, BR; OSF/Breck P. Kent, BL. **21** FLPA/M. Walker, BR. **22** DRK Photo/Kennan Ward, BL; Michael & Patricia Fogden, CR. **23** FLPA/Roger Wilmshurst, T; Bruce Coleman Ltd/P. Clement, BR. **24** DRK Photo/Larry Ulrich, TR; DRK Photo/S. Nielsen, BC; Jacana/Claude Nardin, BL. **25** Bruce Coleman Ltd/George McCarthy, BR; Bios/Dominique Delfino, BL. **26** NHPA/Morten Strange, TL; Bruce Coleman Ltd/Dick Klees, CR. **27** Heather Angel, TR; DRK Photo/John Gerlach, BR; DRK Photo/Jeff Foott, BL. **28** Auscape International/Jean-Paul Ferrero. **29** Windrush Photos/Richard Revels, TC; NHPA/Stephen Dalton, BR. **30-31** Siena Artworks Ltd, London/Ron Hayward. **32** Siena Artworks Ltd, London/Jeremy Simmonds, TR; Bruce Coleman Ltd/Kim Taylor, BC. **33** Windrush Photos/Richard Revels, CL, BR. **34** Ellis Nature Photography/Gerry Ellis, TR; Siena Artworks Ltd, London/Jeremy Simmonds, B. **35** FLPA/Chris Mattison, BL. **36** OSF/Richard Packwood, BL. **37** Planet Earth Pictures/Scott McKinley, TR; Bios/Klein & Hubert, BR. **38** Planet Earth Pictures/Martin King, TR; Siena Artworks Ltd, London/Catherine Moss, B. **39** Aquila Photographics/R. Glover, TC; Planet Earth Pictures/Dr. Peter Gasson, BR. **40** Auscape International/John Cancalosi, TR; Siena Artworks Ltd, London/Ron Hayward, BL. **41** Science Photo Library/David Scharf, CL, CR. **42** Bruce Coleman Ltd/Jan Taylor, TL; Planet Earth Pictures/Wendy Dennis, BL. **43** Windrush Photos/David Tipling, TL; DRK Photo/Steve Kaufman, BR. **44** DRK Photo/Tom Bean, BC. **45** DRK Photo/Larry Ulrich. **46** Planet Earth Pictures/Ken Lucas, TR; Colin Woodman, BL. **47** OSF/Tui De Roy, BR. **48** Siena Artworks Ltd, London/Ron Hayward, B. **49** NHPA/Stephen Dalton, TL; Bruce Coleman Ltd/Jeff Foott, R. **50** Siena Artworks Ltd, London/Sharon McCausland, B. **51** Tom Stack & Associates/John Gerlach, TC; NHPA/David Middleton, TR; Bruce Coleman Ltd/Erwin & Peggy Bauer, BL. **52** NHPA/Rich Kirchner, TL; Tom Stack & Associates/Dominique Braud, BR. **53** Bruce Coleman Ltd/Erwin & Peggy Bauer, BR. **54-55** Bruce Coleman Ltd/Jules Cowan. **56** OSF/Michael Fogden, TL; DRK Photo/T.A. Wiewandt, BR. **57** Tom Stack & Associates/Greg Vaughn, TR. **58** Bruce Coleman Ltd/Hans Reinhard, BL. **59** FLPA/Roger Wilmshurst, TL. **60** FLPA/Tony Wharton, TC; OSF/Terry Button, BR; Planet Earth Pictures/Steve Hopkin, BL. **61** DRK Photo/Larry Ulrich. **62** DRK Photo/Larry Ulrich, TL; Siena Artworks Ltd, London/Sharon McCausland, BR. **63** Planet Earth Pictures/David E. Rowley, TR. **64** OSF/Tom Ulrich, TR; DRK Photo/Stephen J. Krasemann, BL. **65** Tom Stack & Associates/Doug Sokell, TL; Bruce Coleman Ltd/Gordon Langsbury, BR. **66** Bruce Coleman Ltd/Jane Burton, TL; DRK Photo/Stephen J. Krasemann, BR, BC, BL. **67** DRK Photo/Stephen J. Krasemann, TL; Bruce Coleman Ltd/Adrian Davies, TR. **68** DRK Photo/Bob Gurr, TL; OSF/Mark Hamblin, CR; OSF/Tony Tilford, BC. **69** Bruce Coleman Ltd/Konrad Wothe, TL; FLPA/Martin Withers, BR. **70** Bruce Coleman Ltd/Hans Reinhard, TL. **71** FLPA/S. Maslowski, BR. **72** Planet Earth Pictures/Yuri Shibnev, TR. **73** DRK Photo/Steve Kaufman, TL; DRK Photo/Tom & Pat Leeson, BR. **74** DRK Photo/Steve Kaufman, B. **75** A-Z Botanical Collection, TC; Auscape International/Jean-Paul Ferrero, CR. **76** Bios/Roland Seitre, TR; Bruce Coleman Ltd/Dr. John Mackinnon, BL. **77** Ardea London Ltd/ Jean-Paul Ferrero. **78** Siena Artworks Ltd, London/Sharon McCausland, TL; Bios/Michel Gunther, BR. **79** DRK Photo/Belinda Wright, TC; Bruce Coleman Ltd/Rod Williams, BR. **80** Ardea London Ltd/Joanna Van Gruisen, TL; OSF/Deni Bown, BR. **81** NHPA/A.N.T., TL; DRK Photo/Michael Fogden, BR. **82** Gerald Cubitt, B. **83** Planet Earth Pictures/Philip Chapman, TR. **84** Premaphotos Wildlife/K.G. Preston-Mafham, TL; Gerald Cubitt, BR. **85** Gerald Cubitt, TR, CL. **86** Bruce Coleman Ltd/Marie Read, BR. **87** Bios/Cyril Ruoso, TR; Vireo/Doug Wechsler, CR. **88** Bruce Coleman Ltd/Gunter Ziesler, T. **89** Natural Science Photos/Carol Farneti Foster, B. **90** Auscape International/François Gohier, TR; FLPA/M. Gore, BL. **91** Bios/Roland Seitre, R. **92-93** Ellis Nature Photography/Gerry Ellis. **93** Bios/M. & C. Denis-Huot, TR. **94** The Wildlife Collection/Jack Swenson, TL; Bruce Coleman Ltd/Brian Henderson, TR; Bruce Coleman Ltd/Luiz Claudio Marigo, BC. **95** Bruce Coleman Ltd/Gunter Ziesler, TR; DRK Photo/D. Milner, BL. **96** Natural Science Photos/Carol Farneti Foster, TL; Vireo/R.S. Ridgely, TC; Natural Science Photos/Carol Farneti Foster, BR. **97** Ellis Nature Photography/Gerry Ellis, B. **98** Auscape International/Jean-Paul Ferrero, B. **99** Auscape International/Jean-Paul Ferrero, TR; DRK Photo/Stanley Breeden, BR. **100** Bruce Coleman Ltd/Gerald Cubitt, TR; NHPA/Steve Robinson, BL. **101** Bruce Coleman Ltd/Gunter Ziesler, B. **102** Gerald Cubitt, TL; The Wildlife Collection/Martin Harvey, BR. **103** Ellis Nature Photography/Gerry Ellis, B. **104-105** Auscape International/Jean-Paul Ferrero. **105** Auscape International/Jean-Paul Ferrero, TR; Planet Earth Pictures/Gary Bell, BC. **106** Siena Artworks Ltd, London/Sharon McCausland. **107** OSF/Colin Milkins, TR; Planet Earth Pictures/David Maitland, BL. **108** Ellis Nature Photography/Konrad Wothe, L. **109** Ellis Nature Photography/Gerry Ellis, TL; Auscape International/Jean-Paul Ferrero, CR; Bios/Yves Lefevre, BR. **110** Bios/Roland Seitre, T. **111** Hedgehog House New Zealand/Peter Harper, TL; DRK Photo/J. Eastcott & Y. Momatiuk, BR. **112** NHPA/Pierre Petit, CR; Bios/Michel Gunther, BL. **113** BBC Natural History Unit/Bengt Lundberg, B. **114** Auscape International/D. Parer & E. Parer-Cook, TL; Bruce Coleman Ltd/Frithfoto, BR. **115** NHPA/A.N.T., TL; Auscape International/Jean-Paul Ferrero, BR. **116** OSF/Steve Turner, TR. **117** Auscape International/Jean-Paul Ferrero, TR; Planet Earth Pictures/Gary Bell, BR. **118** Auscape International/Jean-Paul Ferrero, TR; Auscape International/Reg Morrison, BR; Bruce Coleman Ltd/Alan Root, CL. **118-119** Auscape International/Jean-Paul Ferrero. **120-121** Auscape International/J. Plaza Van Roon. **121** Premaphotos Wildlife/K.G. Preston-Mafham, TR. **122** Auscape International/Hans & Judy Beste, BL. **123** Bruce Coleman Ltd/John Cancalosi, TL; Bruce Coleman Ltd/Jan Taylor, TR. **124** Bruce Coleman Ltd/Johnny Johnson, B. **125** Tom Stack & Associates/Joe McDonald, T; DRK Photo/Johnny Johnson, BL. **126** DRK Photo/Darrell Gulin, TR. **127** Colin Woodman, TL; OSF/Duncan Murrell, BR. **128** Premaphotos Wildlife/K.G. Preston-Mafham, BL. **129** Bruce Coleman Ltd/Janos Jurka, TC; FLPA/Fritz Polking, TR; Siena Artworks Ltd, London/Sharon McCausland, BC. **130** DRK Photo/Wayne Laniken, TR; DRK Photo/Wayne Lynch, BL. **131** Bruce Coleman Ltd/Erwin & Peggy Bauer, TL; DRK Photo/Tom Brakefield, C. **132** DRK Photo/S. Nielsen, TR; BBC Natural History Unit/Seppo Valjakka, BL. **133** OSF/Daniel J. Cox, TR. **134** Tom Stack & Associates/Thomas Kitchin, BL. **134-135** DRK Photo/Kim Heacox. **136** Bruce Coleman Ltd/Jeff Foott, BR; Planet Earth Pictures/Richard Coomber, BL. **137** OSF/Stan Osolinski, TR; Planet Earth Pictures/Pete Oxford, BR. **138** Siena Artworks Ltd, London/Jeremy Simmonds, BL. **139** Ellis Nature Photography/Gerry Ellis, TL; Premaphotos Wildlife/K.G. Preston-Mafham, BR. **140** Premaphotos Wildlife/K.G. Preston-Mafham, TR, BL. **141** Planet Earth Pictures/Nick Garbutt, TL; The Wildlife Collection/John Giustina, TR; Ellis Nature Photography/Gerry Ellis, BR; Premaphotos Wildlife/K.G. Preston-Mafham, BL. **142** FLPA/Geoff Moon, TR; Siena Artworks Ltd, London/Ron Hayward, BL. **143** Bruce Coleman Ltd/Gerald Cubitt, TR; FLPA/Geoff Moon, BC. **144** NHPA/John Shaw, TL; Hedgehog House New Zealand/Pat Barrett, TC. **144-145** Hedgehog House New Zealand/Rob Brown. **145** Hedgehog House New Zealand/Lynda Harper, TC. **146** Bios/Michel Gunther, TR; Biofotos/Brian Rogers, C; OSF/Mark Pidgeon, BC; Premaphotos Wildlife/K.G. Preston-Mafham, BL. **147** DRK Photo/Larry Ulrich, BR; Siena Artworks Ltd, London/Ron Hayward, CL. **148** Woodfall Wild Images/David Woodfall, B. **149** Robert Harding Picture Library/Fred Friberg, TR; Woodfall Wild Images/David Woodfall, BC. **150** Tom Stack & Associates/J. Lotter, BC; NHPA/Laurie Campbell, BL. **151** Bios/Michel Gunther, TR. **152** DRK Photo/Steve Kaufman, TC, BR; Tom Stack & Associates/Inga Spence, TR; The Wildlife Collection/Jack Swenson, BL. **153** Bruce Coleman Ltd/Konrad Wothe, B. **154** Planet Earth Pictures/Richard Matthews, TL; Bios/J.F. Noblet, CLT; Bios/Michel Gunther, CLB; Tom Stack & Associates/Milton Rand, BL. **155** Ellis Nature Photography/Gerry Ellis, B.

FRONT COVER: Hedgehog House New Zealand/Peter Harper; Bruce Coleman Ltd/Erwin & Peggy Bauer, C.

BACK COVER: Gerald Cubitt.